PREACHING
Character

PREACHING
Character

*Reclaiming Wisdom's Paradigmatic
Imagination for Transformation*

Dave Bland and David Fleer, Editors

Abilene Christian University Press
Abilene, Texas

PREACHING CHARACTER:

Reclaiming Wisdom's Paradigmatic Imagination for Transformation

ACU
PRESS

Copyright 2010 by Dave Bland and David Fleer

ISBN 978-0-89112-544-0
LCCN 2010033251

Printed in the United States of America

LIBRARY OF CONGRESS CATALOGING-IN-PUBLICATION DATA
Preaching character : reclaiming wisdom's paradigmatic imagination for transformation / Dave Bland and David Fleer, editors.
     p. cm.
Includes bibliographical references.
ISBN 978-0-89112-544-0
1. Preaching. 2. Wisdom--Biblical teaching. 3. Character--Biblical teaching. 4. Wisdom--Biblical teaching--Sermons. 5. Character--Biblical teaching--Sermons. 6. Sermons, American--21st century. I. Bland, Dave. II. Fleer, David.
BV4211.3.P728 2010
241--dc22

2010033251

Cover design by Jennette Munger
Interior text design by Sandy Armstrong

For information contact:
Abilene Christian University Press
1626 Campus Court
Abilene, Texas 79601

1-877-816-4455 toll free
www.abilenechristianuniversitypress.com

10 11 12 13 14 15 / 7 6 5 4 3 2 1

*To Nancy for her faithful partnership in ministry
with me for thirty-four years.*

*Nancy and I would also like to offer a special tribute to Bobbie Fry
who has supported, encouraged, and inspired
our family for many years.*

*For Mae whose love, tender mercies,
and wisdom in all matters of import have sustained my life.*

*Thank you to Sean Webb,
a student at Harding University Graduate School of Religion,
for his careful reading and valuable
editorial assistance on this project.*

CONTENTS

CONTRIBUTORS

Dave Bland is Professor of Preaching at Harding University Graduate School of Religion in Memphis, Tennessee, where he has taught for seventeen years and directs the Doctor of Ministry program. He has written a commentary on *Proverbs, Ecclesiastes, Song of Solomon,* in the College Press NIV Commentary Series. Dave complements his teaching activity with preaching responsibilities at the Church of Christ at White Station in Memphis where he has served as one of the preaching ministers for the past fourteen years. Dave and his wife, Nancy, have been married thirty-four years. They have three sons who are all married and two grandchildren.

Sally A. Brown is Elizabeth M. Engle Associate Professor of Preaching and Worship at Princeton Theological Seminary. Before beginning her teaching career, she spent twenty-two years in parish and non-parish ministries, combining the care and formation of persons in crisis with preaching and teaching. Her interest in biblical wisdom literature is anchored in those years and continues in a course on Christian formation through preaching and worship. Her publications include *Lament: Reclaiming Practices in Pulpit, Pew, and Public Square* (Westminster John Knox Press), co-edited with Patrick Miller, and *Cross Talk: Preaching Redemption Here and Now* (Westminster John Knox Press).

Callie Plunket-Brewton is an independent scholar of Hebrew Bible affiliated with the University of North Alabama where she teaches courses in Old Testament, Ancient Near Eastern History, and the Prophets. Born in New Zealand, Callie has a B.A. in Latin from Texas Tech and a Master's and Ph.D. from Princeton Theological Seminary. Her interests include biblical Hebrew poetry and the prophetic books. Her research explores figurative patterns of national identity in the exilic and post-exilic periods. Callie is a postulant for ordination in the Episcopal Church. For five years she has served as campus chaplain at UNA. Callie is married and has two children.

Ken Durham holds the Batsell Barrett Baxter Chair of Preaching at Lipscomb University in Nashville, Tennessee. After thirty years of preaching for Churches of Christ in Stamford, Connecticut, Springfield, Missouri, Falls Church, Virginia, and Malibu, California, he is now dedicating much of his energy to the training of ministers as a member of the faculty of Lipscomb's College of Bible and Ministry and the Hazelip Graduate School of Theology. He has authored or co-authored four books, including *Speaking from the Heart: Richer Relationships through Communication*.

David Fleer is Professor of Bible and Communication and Special Assistant to the President at Lipscomb University and advisory board chair for the Christian Scholars' Conference. Fleer's teaching focus is homiletics and for twelve years he has directed the Sermon Seminar in Rochester, Michigan and Lipscomb's Conference on Preaching. He preaches and teaches in congregations across the country and has published articles in peer reviewed and popular journals. David and Mae have been married thirty-six years and three sons grace their lives: Josh, Luke, and Nate. They are proud grandparents of Levi and Lyle.

Jennifer Green is an adjunct instructor of Old Testament at Candler School of Theology at Emory University and Columbia Theological Seminary. Her research and teaching interests focus largely on wisdom literature. She wrote "Proverbs" in *The Transforming Word: A One-Volume Commentary on the Bible* (ACU Press) as well as entries in *The Lectionary Commentary: The Psalms and Hymn Responses for Worship and Preaching* (Eerdmans). She enjoys gardening and hiking, especially with her three young children who seem particularly enthralled with all of the dirt involved in those activities.

Stephen Johnson is Associate Professor of Preaching and Ministry in the Graduate School of Theology at Abilene Christian University where he also serves as the Director of Contextual Education. He is a member of the Academy of Homiletics and serves as the editor of its website (*homiletics.org*). Stephen has served churches in Texas and Ontario over the last twenty years and preaches regularly for the Buffalo Gap Church of Christ.

Jim Kitchens is interim pastor of Calvary Presbyterian Church in San Francisco, California, and a minister in the Presbyterian Church (USA). Jim has a deep interest in the ways social media are changing the boundary between the private and the public in American's lives, especially for young adults. This interest leads him to experiment with how the sermon form can still speak to younger Christians whose attention spans are shaped by 140-character Tweets. Jim considers sermon preparation his primary spiritual discipline. He is the author of *The Postmodern Parish: New Ministry for a New Age* (Alban).

Paul E. Koptak is the Paul and Bernice Brandel Professor of Communication and Biblical Interpretation and Associate Academic Dean at North Park Theological Seminary, Chicago and an ordained minister of the Evangelical Covenant Church. He is the author of *Proverbs* (New International Version Application Commentary), editor of the *Covenant Quarterly*, and a member of North Park's gospel bluegrass band, The Lonesome Theologians. Some have said the name is redundant.

Thomas G. Long, a minister in the Presbyterian Church (USA), is the Bandy Professor of Preaching at Emory University's Candler School of Theology in Atlanta. He has a long-standing interest in literary and rhetorical biblical criticism and its impact on preaching, a topic he first explored in his book *Preaching and the Literary Forms of the Bible* (Fortress). His primary textbook in preaching, *The Witness of Preaching* (Westminster John Knox), is used in classrooms around the world and has been translated into French, Korean, and German. His latest book, *Accompany Them with Singing: The Christian Funeral*, is the fruit of over a decade of research on American death practices, including brief service on the staff of a funeral home.

Tremper Longman is the Robert H. Gundry Professor of Biblical Studies at Westmont College, Santa Barbara, California. He teaches often on the wisdom literature of the Bible and has authored books and commentaries on Proverbs and Ecclesiastes. In addition, he was the senior translator in charge of Psalms and wisdom books for the New Living Translation. Tremper and Alice have three sons and two granddaughters. For fun and exercise, Tremper plays squash.

Alyce McKenzie, a United Methodist elder, is Professor of Homiletics at Perkins School of Theology, Southern Methodist University. She has written several books on preaching the genres and themes of biblical wisdom in contemporary society. A common thread among all of them is her admiration for the biblical sages' habit of close attention to the details of daily life. Her most recent book, *Novel Preaching*, offers advice from fiction writers to preachers on observing life and crafting enthralling tales. She enjoys leading workshops with both clergy and laity around the country. She and her husband Murry have three grown children, Melissa, Rebecca and Matthew. Her hobbies are Yoga, reading mystery novels, travel, and, last but not least, baking.

Scot McKnight is the Karl A. Olsson Professor in Religious Studies at North Park University, Chicago, Illinois, active in the Society of Biblical Literature and academic meetings, the author of more than thirty books, and a licensed minister. Primarily a scholar in Jesus studies, Scot has published popular level books on spiritual formation and biblical interpretation. Scot was a high jumper in high school and played college basketball, and does what he can to maintain a single-digit handicap in golf. His most recent book is *The Epistle of James* (NICNT; Eerdmans).

Karl McLarty has worked in Tennessee, Mississippi, West Virginia, and Arkansas in a variety of ministry areas over the last twenty-five years. Karl's work has cycled from youth ministry to preaching to missions to campus ministry and back to preaching. He has enjoyed listening to the challenges facing each age group, and exploring age appropriate methods to share the treasures of wisdom. Karl enjoys dialoguing on wisdom in the woods, on the lake, and waist deep in a cold, trout stream. For the last four years he has preached for the Cloverdale Church of Christ in Searcy, Arkansas.

Glenn Pemberton teaches classes on the Old Testament and Hebrew at Abilene Christian University, including a popular undergraduate course each semester on Israel's wisdom and devotional literature. As preacher among churches for over twenty years and a student curious about the behavior of bass and basset hounds, Glenn looks for the connections between God's created order and a life lived by faith. He has published various essays on Proverbs and one book, *When God Calls* (21st Century Christian, 2007).

Micki Pulleyking is a senior instructor in philosophy of religion at Missouri State University and has served as the preaching minister of the Billings Christian Church (Disciples of Christ) near Springfield, Missouri, for the past nineteen years. She grew up in the Churches of Christ and was the co-minister of the Brookline Church of Christ while completing her M.Div. at Harvard and Ph.D. at Boston University. At Harvard she received the "excellence in preaching" award for the class of '88. She and her husband Joey love life with their children, Spenser and Quinlan.

Chris Smith has served as the pulpit minister for the Harpeth Hills Church of Christ in Brentwood, Tennessee for the past thirteen years and has previously served churches in Tennessee, Kentucky, and Texas. He received his B.A. from Lipscomb University, the M.Th. from Harding Graduate School of Religion, and the D.Min. from Abilene Christian University. The major influence on Chris and his preaching is his spiritual mentor, Jimmy Moffett.

Jonathan Storment serves as the preaching minister for the Highland Church of Christ in Abilene, Texas. Jonathan earned a B.A. from Harding University and is currently completing graduate work at Abilene Christian University. Jonathan is passionate for preaching Scripture in fresh and creative ways and understands the goal of preaching as opening up the Bible in a way that allows God's story to become the church's story. Storment is a popular speaker who travels all over the U.S. But his favorite places to preach are his home congregation and the local jail where he serves as chaplain.

Jerry Taylor is Associate Professor of Bible and Ministry at Abilene Christian University. Taylor is one of the principal founders of the New Wineskins Ministers Retreat and the School of the Prophets. His gifted and powerful oratory, which reconstitutes the world Scripture imagines, has made him a frequent speaker at college and church conferences, and a popular lecturer at conventions, retreats, and gospel meetings. He and Pat have been married for eighteen years and have two children, Alisha (15) and Jeremiah (11). The Taylors live in Abilene, Texas, and attend the Highland Church of Christ.

Kevin Youngblood is Associate Professor of Bible at Harding University where he teaches OT Wisdom Literature and preaching. He has taught at Freed Hardeman and Ohio Valley Universities as well. He lives with his wife, Becky, and their children Karissa (13) and Khyle (5 months) in Searcy, Arkansas. When Kevin is not in the classroom or the pulpit, he enjoys practicing martial arts and going fishing with his family.

Introduction

WISDOM'S JOURNEY OF TRANSFORMING CHARACTER

DAVE BLAND AND DAVID FLEER

The most climbed mountain in the Western Hemisphere is Oregon's Mount Hood, located about forty miles east of Portland. Part of the reason for its popularity is that from the base of the mountain the climb looks deceptively easy. The two of us with our families lived in the Portland area during the 1980s and early 1990s and were blessed every clear sunny morning to step out of our front doors and see this magnificent mountain rising from near sea level to 11,200 feet.

On May 12, 1986, thirteen high school students from Oregon Episcopal School, a small private institution in Portland, set out to climb to its majestic peak. It was an annual rite-of-passage for those who had completed their sophomore year. The traditional way to climb Mount Hood is to begin at 2:00 A.M., reach the summit to see the sunrise, and then hike back to the base camp at Timberline by noon. The teenagers approached the climb with little thought, little sleep the night before, and no preparation. They wore casual dress and shoes and light coats. They took along no special climbing gear. As they trekked along, a sudden change of weather rolled in. Trapped in a snowstorm, a whiteout, the hikers dug a snow cave for protection. Four days later help finally arrived, but it was too late. Nine hikers were dead in one of the worst climbing accidents in this nation's history.[1]

The group was young, inexperienced, and ill prepared for the climb. Yet not just the inexperienced are vulnerable to Mt. Hood's treachery. Even the most experienced climbers have lost their lives to its unpredictable weather patterns, hidden crevasses, and unexpected drop offs. During a December weekend in 2009, three well-trained and well-equipped climbers were killed as they attempted to scale its summit. What makes experienced climbers vulnerable is that they tend to be overly confident in their skills, equipment, and physical abilities.

Shortly after the 1986 disaster, technology was put in place that made signal transmitters available to hikers at Timberline Lodge, at the mountain's base. The three climbers who perished in 2009 refused to carry the tracking devices, which is not uncommon for mountaineers because for them such technology removes the freedom of the climb, spoils the experience, and detracts from the authenticity of the challenge. It intrudes on mountaineers' self-reliance. While the downfall of inexperienced hikers is their naïveté, the downfall of experienced climbers is their pride. Both are vulnerable.

The way hikers approach Mount Hood serves as analogy for the way we face life. Life is an exciting journey, an adventure with unknown challenges stretching before us. For those venturing into adulthood, it can appear deceptively easy to manage. But life often throws unexpected twists and turns along the way. While it presents wonderful opportunities and joys, hidden perils abound. It's an exciting adventure that involves perilous risks and difficult decisions. In different ways both the novice and the experienced must remain constantly vigilant. Our world does not well prepare individuals for this journey, regardless of the level of experience.

It is at this point that wisdom speaks a profound word into our experience. Wisdom capably negotiates the complexities of life. The wise person is one who develops expertise in living responsibly.[2] Wisdom seeks to discover God's order in life and then proceeds to successfully fit into that order, always acknowledging human limitations.[3] Divine order demands moral behavior and wisdom's ultimate goal is the formation of moral character.[4] This quality of character is the thicker, richer meaning of wisdom[5] and as Michael

Fox succinctly states, "Moral character . . . is at all times the greatest goal of education."[6] Character is one of the primary products wisdom produces. At the same time, as one's character matures so does wisdom. A dialectic exists between the two. It is wisdom, however, that initiates the process. This book is about wisdom and how wisdom creates and matures character.

Our culture and churches desperately need wisdom. We live in technologically advanced but character challenged times. We have gone from fighting with swords during WWI to fighting wars with the most sophisticated technology, destroying the enemy at great distances without ever setting foot on the ground. Yet we observe little if any progress made in the way humans treat one another. Thanks to technological advancements, our culture does better at providing skills appropriate for a successful career or comfortable home than it does in making life more meaningful.

Sadly, the church has contributed to this moral bankruptcy by transitioning from a *moral* to a *therapeutic* community. Instead of looking to the church to tell us what choices to make, we expect the church to affirm the choices we have already made. Popular Christianity no longer offers guidance in making daily moral decisions about Christian conduct. Instead, it helps individuals relieve anxieties and frustrations.

This is why wisdom, and in particular biblical wisdom, must play a vital role in the instruction and worship of the church. This volume explores biblical wisdom's power to equip individuals to manage life's complexities and contribute to a healthy community. Wisdom is a journey (Prov. 1:15; 2:20; 3:6, 17, 23; 4:11, 14, 18, 26; 6:21),[7] a destination, not a direction. One never arrives (Prov. 1:5; 9:8-9).

A person is not born with wisdom; it is a learned quality. It is not a spur of the moment decision to *try* to be a wise person. It is a process of *training*. An individual might pick up a violin and *try* to play it but won't get very far. Even a gifted musician is limited to mediocrity without practice. An individual has to *train* to play it through instruction, regular and disciplined practice, listening to experienced violinists, going to concerts, and living within a music culture. There is a big difference between *trying* to play the violin and *training* to play it.

In the same way, wisdom is the training process that develops character. It's not something that we spontaneously decide, "Okay, today I'm going to display strong character." Instead, through humility, openness to instruction, learning from mistakes, observing those who are wise, making good choices in the little daily decisions that arise, and deepening one's relationship with God, character takes shape and matures.

Popular culture insists that spontaneous actions are the main mark of genuine humanness. Any action that requires repetitive training and practice is inauthentic. But these impressions are *false*. In fact, when a person chooses, for example, to practice honesty over and over again, eventually it becomes easier and eventually part of that individual's character. That is how personal traits are developed. The traits that we choose to repeatedly practice, as difficult as they initially may be, eventually become second nature.

This process of character formation might sound like a throwback to a kind of works righteousness scenario and may appear as a list of rules to follow. Proverbs, James, and the Sermon on the Mount have all been accused of promoting a works oriented lifestyle. We as a church have discovered grace—praise God! Salvation is a gift; we do not earn it. True. Yet grace that accepts us where we are is not satisfied to leave us as we are.[8]

The training involved in the formation of character occurs in the *faith community*. For instance, Job's character is refined by the fire of a community of friends who appear genuine in their faith but who hold to faulty theology. Job must reach into the depths of his soul to discover his true character and whether or not he will hold fast to his integrity or curse God and die. In the end, Job is provided a mature community that continues to foster his growth (Job 42:10-17). For Ecclesiastes, the answer to the despair and disappointment life brings is the fellowship of community (Eccles. 2:24-26; 9:7-10). The wisdom poem in Proverbs 2:1-9 describes a collaborative effort at work between sage, youth, and God to develop character. Wisdom's goal is to assimilate a community into the worldview that demonstrates the fear of the Lord. Out of that worldview individuals manifest particular ways of speaking and acting.

For moral development to take root in the lives of individuals, communities must approach character formation holistically. Individuals learn values through receiving instruction and seeing virtues modeled and practiced. Individuals learn values through accountability to authority figures who take an active role in their lives. They learn values as a part of a larger, supportive environment.

The cumulative image that unfolds in wisdom literature is of a community working toward a common goal. Character is not generated in a vacuum but flows out of a vision of the nature of God, in the context of a community, and in the presence of a goal greater than the self. James Davison Hunter describes well the context in which character manifests itself: "In such settings people will not merely acquire techniques of moral improvement but rather find themselves encompassed within a story that defines their own purposes within a shared destiny, one that points toward aims that are higher and greater than themselves."[9]

It takes the collaborative effort of a faith community to train and transform women and men into the people of God. This educational process, however, is not primarily intellectual. Its goal is not to raise up intellectual giants who possess a wealth of information in their field of expertise. Rather, the educational process is primarily relational. Through entering into relationship with Yahweh and parents, spouse, or neighbors (Prov. 5:15-19; 12:4; 27:5-6; 31:10-31), the open-minded gain wisdom and learn to live responsibly. The process culminates in a people whose lives manifest the most fundamental character qualities: "righteousness and justice and equity" (Prov. 1:3; 2:9).

We are part of the larger story of a God who created the world, who worked through Abraham, Isaac, and Jacob. We are part of the story about a God who sent an only Son to reconcile sinners. In that context, moral values assume a whole new meaning. We realize then that this task of moral development is not about "me." Developing character is about initiating God's kingdom into the world.

And so, this volume takes up our challenge and moves in a deliberate fashion, with each chapter setting the course for the three sermons that follow.[10] As you would hope, three chapters feature essays written by leading homileticians whose expertise revolves around biblical genres and wisdom literature. Two other lead essays are crafted by biblical scholars whose career efforts focus on wisdom literature. The remaining chapter is led by a "renaissance man," Scot McKnight, whose scholarship in the book of James is enhanced by his leadership in the Emerging Church.

In a foundational survey of wisdom in the Bible, Tremper Longman's opening essay, "Wisdom as Paradigmatic Literature in Scripture," provides a keen appreciation for wisdom's rich witness to God while illustrating the life resources wisdom tradition offers.

In the second chapter, Glenn Pemberton investigates the persuasive qualities of the primary genres of Proverbs to reveal that the sages' work is to solicit an authentic hearing, speak the truth about the path of wisdom, convince the audience that the difficult trail is the way to life, and never stop teaching the way of wisdom and engaging culture with effective techniques.

The third chapter begins with Tom Long's call to move away from the delightful season of narrative preaching to a different genre: *phronesis,* with a focus on what he terms "Christian *savoir faire.*" Long encourages us to hold in tension Ecclesiastes' voice of the disillusioned along with its tacit positive theology because we eagerly seek practical wisdom and need a counter-wisdom to keep preaching honest before those caught up in life's ambiguities.

In the fourth chapter, Alyce Mackenzie proposes that our sermon's answer to the congregation's question, "How will we live today?" might focus on folly, the "flipside of wisdom." Why? To accent in high definition folly's shallow and destructive face. In her proposal, our "attention to shadow" creates appreciation for light.

Dave Bland's essay launches the fifth chapter as he traces the process of character formation in the book of Proverbs, from the scandalous self-centered gang introduced at the beginning to the valorous God-centered woman described at the end. The process from the gang to the woman is arduous. The sages, however, provide the necessary resources for those who choose this path and who possess the passion to pursue wisdom.

In the final chapter Scot McKnight charts our understanding of wisdom in the Letter of James' as wisdom from one who had acquired *receptive reverence,* whose heart, mind, soul and body *absorbed* the wisdom of Jesus, intending to *incarnate* that wisdom in addressing the messianic community.

The sermons in each chapter help us digest these essays' instructive and provocative insights and open us to their wide-ranging implications. Each sermon, working with one particular pericope, interacts with the lead essay. From a diversity of perspectives (women and men, African American and white, young and more seasoned, and a variety of Christian traditions), sermons integrate the essays and thus create models that inspire best practices.

This volume grows from Lipscomb University's 2009 Conference on Preaching and continues that exciting adventure where scholars and practitioners, professors and preachers, biblical scholars and homileticians gather to consider the claims biblical wisdom makes on our lives and preaching. Representing Churches of Christ, the Christian Church (Disciples of Christ), the Church of God-in-Christ, the United Church of Christ, Episcopalian, Southern Baptists, Canadian Baptists, AME, UMC, PCUSA, all denominations and non-denominational, we join in the common purpose of doing what we most love: to prepare to live and preach the world Scripture envisions.

One identifying mark unites us all. We are the Reforming Center of Christianity, united beyond denominational boundaries, beyond the *two parties*: Evangelical *or* Mainline; conservative *or* liberal. We are part of a growing center of Christianity, united in a common desire to pursue the world imagined in Scripture, a vibrant resurgence of the early vision of the ideal, "the unity of all believers in the pursuit of Scripture." We desire to model a kind of scholarship and practice that enables the text and our preaching to "come alive" through an immersion into the realities pictured in Scripture.

Throughout Scripture, wisdom material provides vital resources necessary for a community to train its members for character formation and transformation. As you engage this volume, you will be introduced to the diversity and complexity of life that wisdom reflects. No simple solutions here. That is not the way in which character is formed. Instead, we preachers will be on a journey, exploring the breadth of the wisdom paradigm and the rich resources it offers a church striving to be the people of God.

In this final installment in our series of volumes on preaching, we thank you for exploring with us wisdom's paradigmatic voice for preaching, allowing the wisdom envisioned in the quintessential biblical texts to dramatically shape our preaching and lives.

Chapter
ONE

WISDOM AS PARADIGMATIC IN SCRIPTURE

TREMPER LONGMAN

I n order to preach wisdom, we must first understand its meaning, scope, and shape in the Bible. The purpose of this chapter is to provide an introduction to wisdom and thus lay a foundation for the following chapters that address more specific topics in wisdom. The chapter is organized around four questions:

- What is wisdom?
- Where does one get wisdom?
- Where is wisdom found in Scripture?
- How does wisdom relate to the broader canon?

What Is Wisdom?

The main Hebrew word for wisdom is *hokma*.[1] Rather than beginning with a short definition, we will work toward an understanding of wisdom through several steps.

First, wisdom is the skill of living; it is not the same as intelligence. An IQ test cannot measure it. Wisdom is not, in the first place, a mastery of information or facts about the world but rather a skill of living. A wise person knows *how* to live in the world, *how* to navigate life in a way that maximizes success and minimizes pitfalls. If one does run into trouble in life, the wise person knows the best way out of the problem.

That wisdom is skill is illustrated in the life of Bezalel, the chief craftsperson of the tabernacle. His ability to "devise artistic designs, to work in gold, silver, and bronze, in cutting stones for setting, and in carving wood, in every kind of craft" originates in his divinely-given "ability" (*hokma*; Exod. 31:3). Furthermore, the ant, which can hardly be said to have intelligence, is a paragon of wisdom and an example of such for lazy people:

> Go to the ant, you lazy people!
>   See its path and grow wise.
> That one has no military commander,
>   officer, or ruler;
> it gets its food in summer,
>   gathers its provisions at harvest. (Prov. 6:6-8)[2]

Biblical wisdom involves knowing how to live, and knowing how to live involves a sense of timing. For instance, a wise person says the right thing at the right time and does the right action at the right time:

> It is a joy to a person to give an answer!
>   How good a word at the right time! (Prov. 15:23)

One of the more humorous proverbs points out that it is problematic to say otherwise welcome things at the wrong time:

> Those who bless their neighbors with a loud voice in the early morning—
>   it will be considered a curse to them. (Prov. 27:14)

In this regard, biblical wisdom is similar to what is today called "emotional intelligence." Dan Goleman, a pioneer in the study of emotional intelligence, defines it as "abilities such as being able to motivate oneself, and persist in the face of frustration; to control impulse and delay gratification; to regulate one's moods and keep distress from swamping the ability to think; to empathize and to hope."[3] The most fascinating aspect of Goleman's research is the connection between emotional intelligence and success in life. People with a high degree of emotional intelligence have a much better chance of getting a good job and keeping it and having meaningful relationships with other people. This correlation is not true for those who have a high IQ.[4]

Second, wisdom leads to skillful living because people who are wise live in harmony with the world as God created it. The connection between wisdom and creation is well known and is captured by a passage like Proverbs 3:19-20:

> Yahweh laid the foundations of the earth with Wisdom,
>> establishing the heavens with competence.
> With knowledge the deeps burst open,
>> and the skies drop dew.

If the creation was formed with wisdom (as we will see later in Prov. 8:22-32), then to know wisdom is to know how the world works. Later we will see that the connection between wisdom and creation provides the theological foundation for gaining wisdom through experience and observation.

Third, biblical wisdom is much more than skill of living. Indeed, according to Proverbs 1:7, "Fear of the Lord is the beginning of knowledge."[5] Wisdom, thus, is primarily relational. One must have a relationship with God characterized by fear. Of course, this fear is not the type that makes one run away; it is not horror. However, the emotion represented by the Hebrew term (*yir'a*) is more than respect. Perhaps the best English term to represent the idea is "awe" or "reverence." One who has such "fear" understands that they are not the center of the universe. God is. Those who do not understand this most basic truth about the universe are indeed foolish. Such a relationship is the "beginning" of wisdom. Here "beginning" (*re'shit*) is to be understood in two ways. First, in its temporal sense, wisdom does not start until one experiences this fear. Second, fear is the foundation on which wisdom is built.

Proverbs further discloses the relational nature of wisdom in the figure of Woman Wisdom. The book of Proverbs has two major parts. The second part of the book (chapters 10-31) presents proverbs per se: pithy observations, admonitions, and prohibitions. Chapters 1-9 contain discourses, the largest number of which are speeches of a father to his son, but in these chapters we also hear from Woman Wisdom who speaks to all the young men who come into her presence (1:20-33; 8:1-9:6).

But who is Woman Wisdom? In 9:1-6, her large (seven columned) house is situated on "the pinnacle of the heights of the city" (9:3). From this location, she sends out her maidservants to invite all the young men to come dine with her. In the ancient Near East, the invitation to dine is an invitation to relationship. She wants the young men to know her and make her an integral part of their life.

Chapter 8 provides the background to the invitation of chapter 9. Her description is too rich and complex to fully unpack in this short chapter, but she is full of knowledge (v. 12), speaks truth (vv. 7-9), has wealth to share (vv. 18-19), and guides rulers (v. 16). Most intriguing is her connection with creation (vv. 22-31). While debate surrounds the details of this passage, it is clear that Wisdom was involved with creation, perhaps as a participant, but certainly at least an observer. The underlying message is that if you want to know how the world works, then this is a woman worth knowing.

But who is this woman? The key is the location of her house. Only one building would occupy the highest point of the city, the temple. Woman Wisdom represents God's wisdom and indeed God himself.

In chapter 9 there is another woman who also lives "at the heights of the city" (9:14), Woman Folly. She too invites the men over for a meal, but her meal is deadly. Those who respond to her invitation end up in the "depths of Sheol" (9:18). The location of her house also indicates that she represents the divine, but in her case, she stands for all the false gods and goddesses that try to lure Israel away from their true God.

The figure of Woman Wisdom, thus, indicates that the biblical idea of wisdom is more than skill of living. Wisdom is relational and theological. One must have a relationship with Yahweh to be wise, and to form a relationship with another deity makes one a fool. The call for a decision between Wisdom (Yahweh) and Folly (other gods) takes place at the transition point of the book before the proverbs (chapters 10-31) and the theological understanding of wisdom and folly applies to those proverbs.

Where Does One Get Wisdom?

In the light of this understanding of the nature of wisdom in the Bible, where does one get it?

It is common to hear that there is a universal quality to wisdom. Listen to this description of Solomon's wisdom: God gave Solomon very great wisdom and understanding, and knowledge as vast as the sands of the seashore. In fact, his wisdom exceeded that of all the wise men of the East and the wise men of Egypt. He was wiser than anyone else, including Ethan the Ezrahite and the sons of Mahol—Heman, Calcol, and Darda. His fame spread throughout all the surrounding nations (1 Kings 4:29-31).

Notice that this compliment to Solomon implies that foreign sages were extremely wise. One could not imagine a comparable statement concerning a prophet, say that Jeremiah was a better prophet than a prophet of Baal. A prophet of Baal was a false prophet who deserved to die (Deut. 13:1-5), but foreign sages were respected. This helps explain why the book of Proverbs contains many statements that are related to Sumerian, Aramaic, and especially Egyptian sources.[6]

What are we to make of this? We have already observed that there is a connection between wisdom and creation. Other ancient Near Eastern peoples could observe the world and how it works and encapsulate their insights into pithy statements that the Israelite sages could appreciate.

This leads us to consider the sources of wisdom for the sages. There are four main sources.

First, wisdom comes from watching the world and observing how it works. A wise person lives reflectively. Provided a person is self-aware, one should grow in wisdom as one ages.

Above we quoted Proverbs 6:6-8 where the sage instructs his disciple concerning laziness to observe the industrious nature of the ant. From this experience, the teacher feels confident that the hearer will draw the lesson that follows in the text:

How long, you lazy person, will you lie down;
    when will you rise from your sleep?
"A little sleep, a little slumber,
    a little folding of the arms to lie down"—
and your poverty will come on you like a prowler
    and your deprivation like a person with a shield. (6:9-11)

Since experience and observation lead to wisdom, the Old Testament assumes that older people have more wisdom than young people.

Second, wisdom based on tradition can be taught apart from the student's experience. Experience and observation lead to insight. Those insights can be passed on to others who have not had these experiences. In this way they become traditions that can also be passed down from generation to generation. Proverbs 4:1-4 introduces the father's instruction that is based on a tradition that he received from his father:

> Hear, sons, fatherly discipline,
>> and pay attention to the knowledge of understanding.
> For I will give you good teaching;
>> don't forsake my instruction.
> For I was a son to my father,
>> tender and the only one of my mother.
> He taught me and said to me:
>> "Let your heart hold on to my words;
>> guard my commands and live."

Here is where we should situate the wisdom inherited from the broader Ancient Near East that has influenced biblical wisdom that we described above. Israel's wisdom teachers depended not only on native Israelite tradition, but also on wisdom that originated in Egypt and Mesopotamia.

Third, wisdom may be acquired from one's mistakes. Proverbs drives this point home hard by stressing the importance of humility and condemning pride. The humble person will listen to correction offered by others. Rather than avoiding criticism, the wise person will attend closely to it:

> Those who love discipline love knowledge,
>> and those who hate correction are dullards. (12:1)

The worst type of fool is a mocker. Mockers not only ignore correction but make fun of those who try to offer it to them. In 3:34 we learn that God "mocks mockers and he shows favor to the humble."

Above, we observed that, since wisdom is derived from experience and observation, it was natural for older people to be wiser than the young. Not all old people, however, learn from experience or their mistakes. They keep repeating them and become doddering old fools. Job's three friends are examples of such, as Elihu points out in the introduction to his speech (Job 32:6-8). Finally, and certainly most importantly, we must acknowledge that the foundation of wisdom is God. Wisdom begins with fear of the Lord, an attitude that leads the sage to listen to the words of God as they are spoken by the father. Woman Wisdom represents God and she is the one who teaches all the young men the lessons of life. Indeed, Proverbs 20:12 makes it clear that even the other sources of wisdom (experience and observation, tradition, learning from mistakes) is ultimately only possible because of God:

> An ear to hear and an eye to see—
> Yahweh made them both.

Our ability to observe, to hear the lessons of the fathers, as well as the criticism of our mistakes, is only because God has given us organs of hearing and seeing.

Everything must be understood in relationship to Yahweh. We must be humble, an attitude that comes from knowing that there is a greater power in the universe. Proverbs teaches that:

> Many plans are in people's hearts,
> but the advice of Yahweh, that is what will succeed. (19:21)

And so we look to the One greater than ourselves to provide the instruction we need to navigate life:

> To humans belong the plans of the heart,
> but from Yahweh comes a responding tongue. (16:1)

All true wisdom, knowledge, and insight—even that gained from other ancient Near Eastern wisdom texts—come from God:

> For Yahweh bestows wisdom,
> from his mouth come knowledge and understanding.
> He stores up resourcefulness for those with integrity—
> a shield for those who walk in innocence,
> to protect the paths of justice,
> guarding the way of his covenant partners. (2:6-8)

This further means that though Israelite sages can learn from Egyptian and other ancient Near Eastern wisdom, in the final analysis they would not count these pagans as truly wise. They are not fundamentally wise because they do not understand the most basic, important thing about the universe—that Yahweh is the Creator and Sustainer of it all.

Where Is Wisdom Found in Scripture?

Now that we understand wisdom and where it comes from, we turn now to ask where wisdom is found in Scripture. To answer this question, we must distinguish wisdom books (that is, books in which wisdom is a major concern) from books (and parts of books) which display some wisdom features. In our survey below, we will treat first those books in the Old Testament that might be called wisdom literature (Prov., Ecclesiastes, Job) and books (and parts of books) where we might see some of the features of wisdom (Song of Songs; Genesis 37-50; Psalms, Daniel). The following, however, should be considered a sampler of the latter category since space does not permit a full discussion of wisdom influence in the Old Testament. Finally, we will look at James as an example of a New Testament wisdom book.

Wisdom Books in the Old Testament

Proverbs: Normative Wisdom

When we consider wisdom in the Old Testament, we immediately think of Proverbs, which announces itself as a repository of wisdom (Prov. 1:1-7). The first part of the book (chaps. 1-9) contains speeches of a father to a son (e.g. 1:8-19) or of Woman Wisdom to all the men walking on the path of life (e.g. 1:20-33). The father's speeches typically have an exordium that calls the son to pay attention, and then he gives him motivation to listen, based primarily on self-interest. If the son listens, his life will go well, but if not, then he will run into trouble.

The father covers many topics but none more than women (see the bulk of chaps. 5-7). The son must avoid promiscuous women and have a robust relationship with his wife. This teaching parallels the admonition to avoid Woman Folly (9:13-18) and have a healthy relationship with Woman Wisdom (9:1-6).

The second part of the book contains proverbs, which are pithy observations, admonitions, and prohibitions that encourage wise behavior and

[handwritten marginal note: wise obser. on women]

discourage foolish behavior. The book ends with an acrostic poem on the "virtuous woman" (31:10-31) who is an embodiment of Woman Wisdom. It is interesting that in the Hebrew canon Proverbs is followed by Ruth, who is called a "virtuous woman" (Ruth 3:11), and then the Song of Songs which is composed of love poems in which the woman is the pursuer and the initiator of relationship.

There are three common misconceptions about Proverbs. I will address two of them in this section and the third later in the chapter.

The first misconception is that the proverbs of chapters 10-31 are secular in nature. That is, they have no theological significance. It is true that the Lord is only occasionally mentioned in proverbs (see 10:3 for instance), and most proverbs seem to be just good advice or observations as the following examples demonstrate:

A wise son makes a father glad,
    and a foolish son is the sorrow of his mother. (10:1)
A slack palm makes poverty;
    a determined hand makes rich. (10:4)

On the surface, it appears as if these proverbs have no theological value. The proverbs, however, should not just be read on the surface but in the broader context of the book. Above, we explored the significance of the choice between Woman Wisdom and Woman Folly. The reader must decide with which woman he would like to dine and develop an intimate relationship. We concluded that Woman Wisdom represented Yahweh and Woman Folly all the false gods that attempted to lure Israel away from the true God. The effect of this metaphor was to indicate that wisdom and folly are theological categories. This understanding carries forward to chapters 10 and following.

To apply this to 10:1, we would observe that a son who brings joy to his parents is wise and thus acting like a proper worshipper of Yahweh, while one who brought grief is acting like an idolater. In v. 4, laziness is presented as foolish behavior, again like those who do not worship the true God in contrast to hard workers who are acting like those who worship Yahweh. All the proverbs in chapters 10-31 must be understood in this sense.

We will use the proverbs cited above (10:1, 4) to illustrate the second misconception as well. It is incorrect to treat proverbs as if they are making absolute claims. In other words, proverbs are not always true. It is not always true that wise children bring joy to their parents. Sometimes it is a matter of wisdom for a child to bring grief to them. Let's say that an Israelite child's parents are Baal worshippers; they would be upset if their child did not follow them in their sinful religious practices, but doing so would not make the child wise. Or consider the claim of 10:4. Is it really true that lazy people are always poor? Not if they inherit a fortune from their parents. Nor is it always true that hard workers get rich. Hard working farmers might find their crops destroyed by a freak storm or some "injustice" (Prov. 13:23). But these proverbs are true most of the time and provide general direction to the majority of people on how to live to achieve a desired consequence.

In a word, timing is everything when it comes to the proverb. It is only true when applied in the right circumstance. This explains why the book contains what looks at first glance like "contradictory" advice:

> Don't answer fools according to their folly;
>> otherwise you will become like them yourself.
> Answer fools according to their folly;
>> otherwise, they will become wise in their own eyes. (26:4-5)

These are not mutually contradictory. They remind the reader that a wise person has to do more than learn the proverb[7]; they must be sensitive to the situation and know when to apply the right proverb. A wise person must know how to read people and situations as well as know the proverbs.

Ecclesiastes and Job: The Limits of Wisdom

Proverbs connects positive consequences with wise actions and negative ones with foolish behavior. Of course, life does not seem to work that way as the books of Ecclesiastes and Job make abundantly clear.

The Teacher in Ecclesiastes comments:

> Then I turned and observed something else under the sun. That is, the race is not to the swift, the battle not to the mighty, nor is food for the wise, nor wealth to the clever, nor favor to the intelligent, but time and chance happen to them all. (2:12-17)[8]
>
> Both I have observed in my meaningless life. There is a righteous person perishing in his righteousness, and there is a wicked person living long in his evil. (7:15)

For this reason, the book of Ecclesiastes raises question about the usefulness of wisdom. For instance, while wisdom has a relative value during life, death renders it ultimately meaningless (2:12-17). Thus, because wisdom does not necessarily lead to life's rewards and because death comes to the wise as well as the fool, the Teacher does not recommend a passionate pursuit of wisdom: "Do not be too righteous and do not be overly wise. Why ruin yourself?" (7:17).

Job too illustrates the limits of wisdom. Job is the very epitome of a wise man as Proverbs describes one. Job 1:1 (see also 1:8; 2:3) says that Job "was blameless and upright, one who feared God and turned away from evil." Even so, contrary to expectation, Job greatly suffers.

The bulk of the book of Job is a discussion of Job's condition. Why does he suffer and what should he do to make it stop? All the human participants of the book (the three friends, Elihu, and Job himself) present themselves as wise men who can diagnose the situation and recommend a cure. The book, it turns out, is a wisdom debate.

The well-known perspective of the three friends is that Job must be a sinner because if you sin, then you suffer. Therefore, if you suffer, then you are a sinner. Job suffers, so he must be a sinner. He can only alleviate his pain by repentance.

Job believes that his friends are right about how the world should work. He knows, however, that he is not a sinner. Therefore, his solution to his problem is to find God and bring a case against him. He should not be suffering because he is not a sinner and, therefore, God is unjust.

Elihu comes in toward the end of the book (chaps. 33-37) with the promise of a new perspective on the problem. He claims the spirit rather than age as the source of his wisdom (32:6-10). Nonetheless, as he gets into his argument, he soon starts repeating the same old retribution theology of the other people in the debate.

Of course, the book of Job does not wallow in the inadequacy of human wisdom. At the end, God asserts his wisdom and power in response to Job's restless questioning (chaps. 38-42) in a way that is anticipated in chapter 28, which concludes with the well-known and fundamental point that "the fear of the Lord is the beginning of wisdom." Job responds to Yahweh's speech by repenting (40:3-5; 42:1-6).

Old Testament Books with Wisdom Features

Proverbs, Ecclesiastes, and Job are the only wisdom books in the Old Testament, but a number of other books are related to the wisdom genre in one way or another. Indeed, wisdom is found extensively through the Old Testament, so much so that here we can only be selective and brief in our description.

Song of Songs

The Song of Songs is a collection of love poetry that celebrates God's good gift of physical intimacy between a man and a woman.[9] Some scholars have suggested that the Song can also be described as wisdom literature.[10] Of course, the Song is not explicitly didactic like Proverbs. It does not openly discuss wisdom like Ecclesiastes or Job. But if wisdom is understood to be the application of God's will to the nitty-gritty of life, then, as the Song describes love as intense, exclusive, and faithful in spite of obstacles, it may be seen as wisdom. Further, the relationship between the woman of the Song and the chorus is similar to that of the father to the son in Proverbs. That is, the woman teaches the daughters of Jerusalem in the way of love.[11]

Wisdom Psalms

A number of psalms have been rightly connected with wisdom. These psalms share themes with wisdom books. Psalm 1 is a classic example with its Proverb-like division of humanity into two categories, the righteous and the wicked. The righteous meditate on the law of the Lord, raising the question of the relationship between law and wisdom to be explored below. Psalm 1's placement as the first psalm puts wisdom in the mind of the readers from the very start. Indeed, much like Proverbs 9 (see above), Psalm 1 confronts the reader of the book of Psalms with a choice between righteousness and folly. In this way, it functions like a gatekeeper to the Psalms imagined as a literary sanctuary of intimate verbal fellowship with God.

Joseph and Daniel

The actions of godly characters of the Bible not surprisingly illustrate the principles of wisdom. In particular, Joseph and Daniel are examples. Indeed, it is not unusual for scholars to identify the texts that tell their stories as wisdom literature.[12]

One brief example will have to suffice. In Genesis 39, Joseph exemplifies the sexual ethics of Proverbs (see especially chaps. 5-7) by refusing to sleep with the "strange, foreign" woman, Potiphar's wife, who tries to lure him into her bed. Indeed, recognizing the connection between Joseph and the teaching in proverbs helps us understand that the rewards of wisdom are not absolute or mechanical. After all, the consequence of Joseph's refusal is contrary to what one might expect on a surface reading of Proverbs—he gets thrown in prison. But what looks to be punishment is actually a blessing in the broad scope of the story. His prison stay brings him into contact with the chief cup-bearer who ultimately brings him to the attention of the Pharaoh, a relationship that will put him in a position to provide resources for the family of God so it can withstand a horrible, prolonged famine.[13]

(margin handwritten note: Joseph ex.)

James: A New Testament Wisdom Book

Wisdom is not just restricted to the Old Testament. For illustration we turn to the book of James, a topic explored by Scot McKnight in this volume. James' connection to Proverbs and the Old Testament wisdom tradition is clearly seen in its statements about the source of wisdom, "that comes from above" (James 3:17). Those who lack wisdom are to ask "our generous God and he will give it to you" (1:5). In his practical instruction, James treats many of the topics familiar from the book of Proverbs, for instance, speech (3:1-12).

How Does Wisdom Relate to the Broader Canon?

The issue of wisdom's canonical significance is important for preaching. How does wisdom fit into the broader message of the Bible? What contributions does it make to theology? How does wisdom look forward to the New Testament?

Due to space constraints, we will only have the opportunity to briefly answer these questions. But we begin by acknowledging that wisdom's place in the broader canon has been seen as a problem. After all, the wisdom books have no explicit connection to redemptive history. Proverbs, Job, and Ecclesiastes do not mention God's great acts in history (e.g. the Exodus). These books are also characterized by an absence of explicit mention of the covenant, a pervasive metaphor of God's relationship with his people that permeates much of Scripture and is often the backbone of scholars' theology of the Bible.[14] Indeed, before Leo Perdue's helpful study, it was often thought that wisdom had nothing to do with the formal religious rituals of Israel.[15]

Once one realizes, however, that there is no single biblical-theological center in the Bible (like the great acts of God or covenant) but rather multiple trajectories through the Old Testament and into the New Testament, then one can more easily recognize how wisdom connects to the broader canon. I want to suggest three ways in which the wisdom tradition is situated in the canon.

Covenant Law and Wisdom

We have just observed that there is little explicit mention of covenant in wisdom literature. There is, however, a more subtle relationship through wisdom's connection to biblical law. Law in the Bible has a clear covenant context. God enters into a covenant with Moses at Sinai and gives them the law (Exod. 19-24).

God instructs Israel to proper behavior through his law. In this statement, we can see the connection with wisdom which itself is a form of instruction. Many years ago, Meredith Kline made the argument that wisdom related to the covenant through its relationship with law.[16] Law expresses the divine will for those who are in covenant with the great King and who have been the recipients of his gracious acts. Indeed, in the covenant/treaty form, the law is preceded by a historical prologue that recounts those great acts.[17] Of course, wisdom does not recount these acts itself, but with the canon the historical narrative functions as that prologue.

That wisdom and law are thus connected may be seen in a passage like Deuteronomy 4:5-6:

> Look, I now teach you these decrees and regulations just as the Lord my God commanded me, so that you may obey them in the land you are about to enter and occupy. Obey them completely, and you will display your wisdom and intelligence among the surrounding nations. When they hear all these decrees, they will explain, "How wise and prudent are the people of this great nation!"

There are differences between law and wisdom, to be sure. As we noted above, the instruction imparted by wisdom depends on the circumstances. Whether one answers a fool depends on the overall situation (Prov. 26:4-5). But one must never under any circumstances murder (Exod. 20:13; Deut. 5:17).

Some also argue that since it is the father who advises rather than God who legislates, the authority of wisdom is less than that of the law. But that appears to me to be doubtful, particularly when we observe that the father's advice is called "command" (*miswa*) and instruction (*tora*).[18] When the situation calls for the application of a proverb, then the proverb becomes a command, not just a "good idea." There is no difference in authority between wisdom and law. The father is a proxy for God in the book of Proverbs.

Thus, the first way in which I would situate wisdom in the broader canon is through its association with law, which itself is connected to the covenant.

Wisdom and Retribution Theology

The wisdom tradition also makes a significant contribution to the vexed issue of retribution in the Bible. We will start where we ended in the last section, with wisdom's association with law. We have observed that wisdom is connected, albeit subtly, with covenant through law. Of course, the covenant law is also connected with blessings and curses. The structure of the book of Deuteronomy clearly shows that if one keeps the law, then blessings will abound, but if one breaks the law, the corresponding curses go into effect (see in particular Deuteronomy 28).

In the book of Proverbs, the same dynamic pertains. Wisdom leads to reward, but rejecting wisdom and embracing folly causes disaster and ultimately death. Proverbs 22:6 provides a well-known example of the connection between wise behavior and reward:

Train up a child in his path;
    when they grow old, they will not depart from it.

The proverb connects the parents' behavior with reward. But is it true? Is it really true that godly parental training leads to godly children?

Indeed, the other two wisdom books largely question the idea that wisdom inexorably leads to good consequences or that folly results in trouble. Job does this through the narrative presentation of a man who is "blameless and upright" and "who feared God and turned away from evil" (Job 1:1), but suffered horribly, thus raising the question of retribution. The Teacher in the book of Ecclesiastes does so as well as he examines life "under the sun" and summarizes his conclusion in 7:15: "Both I have observed in my meaningless life: There is a righteous person perishing in his righteousness, and there is a wicked person living long in his evil." This leads him to the following startling advice: "Do not be too righteous and do not be overly wise. Why ruin yourself? Do not be too wicked and do not be a fool. Why die when it is not your time?" (7:16-17).

But is there a contradiction between Proverbs and Job/Ecclesiastes? Does the former actually say that wisdom will be rewarded without doubt and does the latter deny the same? The answer is no, if one reads Proverbs carefully. The proverb does not give guarantees. Proverbs 22:6, for instance, does not promise that if parents train their children in the proper way, they will automatically become godly. Rather, the proverb advocates the best course to a desired end, but it does not take into account all possibilities. That is, a well-trained child might come under the influence of evil peers (1:8-19). Parents need to do what they need to do, and if they do, then the desired outcome is much more likely but not assured.

The book of Proverbs indicates this through its frequent use of "better-than" proverbs.[19] These proverbs describe relative values and imply that the wise person will (at least sometimes) have to choose between these values.

> Better to have a little with fear of the Lord
>   than great treasure with inner turmoil. (15:16)
> Better to be poor and godly
>   than rich and dishonest. (16:8)

These proverbs demonstrate the sages' awareness that wisdom does not lead inexorably to wealth. Sometimes one must choose wisdom over wealth.

Thus, another important contribution that wisdom makes to the canon concerns the issue of retribution. The wisdom books grapple with an issue with which people struggled in ancient times as well as today. Why do good people suffer and bad prosper? Proverbs, Job, and Ecclesiastes give us a textual basis as we preach on this important topic.

Jesus, the Wise

Perhaps the most important component of the canonical context of wisdom for the Christian preacher is the question of how it relates to the New Testament. As an Old Testament professor, I want to emphasize the fact that, as B. Childs said, we must first understand the "discrete voice" of the Old Testament.[20] Otherwise, we may inappropriately smooth out what Brueggemann refers to as the "wild and untamed theological witness of the Old Testament."[21] In short, we must understand the wisdom in its Old Testament setting. But that is not the conclusion of the matter. As Christians, we must preach Christ from the Old Testament.

After all, Jesus insisted that his disciples read the Old Testament in the light of his coming:

> "Oh, how foolish you are, and how slow of heart to believe all that the prophets have declared! Was it not necessary that the Messiah should suffer these things and then enter into his glory?" Then beginning with Moses and all the prophets, he interpreted to them the things about himself in all the scriptures. (Luke 24:25-27, NRSV)
>
> "These are my words that I spoke to you while I was still with you—that everything written about me in the law of Moses, the prophets, and the psalms must be fulfilled." Then he opened their minds to understand the scriptures. . . . (Luke 24:44-45)

In my opinion each of the Wisdom books anticipate the coming of Christ in a particular way,[22] but in this chapter I will content myself by offering some reflections on a Christological understanding of wisdom itself. Above, we explained that the book of Proverbs presents its readers with a choice: to dine with Woman Wisdom or Woman Folly. To understand this moment of decision from a New Testament perspective, we must recognize the connection between Jesus and wisdom.

The New Testament presents Jesus as the epitome of wisdom. Even in his youth, Jesus was "filled with wisdom" (Luke 2:40). When he reached maturity and taught the crowds, they were amazed by his teaching since he showed unprecedented wisdom (Matt. 13:54; Mark 6:2). He even taught by parables, the staple teaching vehicle of the sage.[23] The people would have recognized Jesus as a wisdom teacher.

Even closer to the point, Jesus and the New Testament authors associated him with Woman Wisdom. For instance, Jesus responds to the critique of Jewish teachers by saying "wisdom is vindicated by her deeds" (Matt. 11:19, NRSV). In Colossians 1:15-20, much of the description of Jesus here echoes that of Woman Wisdom, especially the statement that he is the "firstborn of all creation" (1:15, see Prov. 8:22-31). The same may be said of the famous prologue to John where Jesus' relationship to creation sounds similar to that of Wisdom (see especially John 1:1-3).

The picture of Woman Wisdom (especially in Proverbs 8) is not a prophecy of Jesus but a metaphor of God as the teacher of his people. The association with Jesus in the New Testament means to inform his followers that he is the one in whom "are hidden all the treasures of wisdom and knowledge" (Col. 2:3).

Col 2:3

The implication of this association is that when we read Proverbs and are confronted with the choice between Wisdom and Folly, as Christians we understand that the choice is between Jesus (Woman Wisdom) and anything that would rival him as the most important thing in our lives.[24]

Conclusion

The purpose of this chapter was to provide a "lay of the land" of wisdom in the Bible. While later chapters will focus on more specific topics and speak more directly about preaching, it may be helpful to make explicit the major implications of the above survey for preaching from the wisdom literature.

First, it is vitally important to remember that the counsel provided by wisdom is not necessarily universally true and that the rewards and punishments associated with wise behavior are not promises. Preachers need to impress upon their congregation that it is just as important to learn how to discern "the proper time" as it is to know the content of the proverbs. To believe that the rewards and punishments of wisdom are guaranteed is to set people up for disappointment and the belief that God has been unfair (like Job and Qohelet). Even so, wisdom does normally lead to good results and provides a motivation for following the path wisdom encourages.

Second, the nature of the three main wisdom books requires thought about how best to preach them. The second part of Proverbs (chaps. 10-31), for instance, is a random collection of proverbs on a host of different topics, not in any systematic order. Rather than preaching on consecutive verses, Proverbs calls for topical preaching where the teaching on a single subject (say, wealth and poverty) are gathered together to give a full picture of the book's instruction on that topic. Since large parts of Ecclesiastes and Job present the perspective of human beings who are not aligned with the divine perspective of the book (presented by the second wise man and the Yahweh speeches), one must be careful to preach any particular passage in the context of the whole book (thus discouraging long series on those books).

Finally, the canonical perspective on wisdom suggests, even requires, Christ-centered preaching. The wisdom of the Old Testament, like all the other parts of the Old Testament, anticipates the coming suffering and glorification of Jesus (so Luke 24). It is not sufficient just to use the wisdom to encourage people to skillful living, or even to deepen their understanding of God in general. Faithful preaching of wisdom involves the presentation of the gospel.

While I have been unable to be exhaustive in my survey of wisdom in the Bible, I hope that I have given a sense of wisdom's rich witness to God and ultimately to Jesus Christ in this survey. In addition, I hope that this chapter serves to illustrate the rich life resources that the wisdom tradition offers not only to its ancient readers but also to those of our own day.

THE GOOD LIFE
Psalm 133

CALLIE PLUNKET BREWTON

En Route to the Sermon

This sermon was born of the pure joy of watching my children at play. They had a boat on a string that they kept dropping behind the chair in which they were standing. They would pull it up together and laugh with delight as they dropped the boat back behind the chair immediately. The game was simple and simply fun, and I thought how infrequently adults engage in a task together with that combination of laughter and concentration. Play is a means by which we prepare for adulthood and adult tasks, but it seems to me that, while we retain the skills of concentration that we have acquired through play, we put aside our capacity for delight as we tend to the labors of our adult lives. There are, of course, tasks that only a fool would view with elation, but there are also burdens that would be less weighty if we carried them with light hearts—or carried them with the help of a friend.

As I thought about how to communicate this truth in the pulpit, I remembered the wise words of Psalm 133, a wisdom psalm with delight at its core. The psalmist's exuberant vision of the joys of communal life is both infectious and challenging. Plays of word and sound as well as the similes that form the core of the psalm create an absolutely delightful experience for the sensitive reader, and its message is also didactic. Although its teaching method is unconventional, it provides guidance for the "skill of living," one of the central aims of wisdom literature in the Old Testament, as Tremper Longman helpfully points out. Having said that, the primary struggle for the preacher is defining what precisely is the wisdom of Psalm 133. The psalm resists paraphrase, and one only grasps its message through the experience of reading it. The sermon is, thus, rather more exegetical than is my preference, but I think it is only by progressing through the psalm that one has a sense of what it is trying to impart. As I said above, the psalm defies any efforts to state simply what it is about, but I think it is possible to say that the psalmist's ecstatic vision represents a challenge to us to match that description, to put the reality in alignment with the ideal. Life lived well is lived in community, and joy is at the heart of it. Wisdom, indeed.

The Sermon

> Ah! How good and how pleasant is
> The dwelling of kindred, all together—
> Like fine oil on the head,
> Running down over the beard,
> The beard of Aaron, running down
> Over the collar of his robes;
> Like the dew of Herman running down
> Over the mountains of Zion—
> There YHWH
> Commands the blessing:
> "Life evermore!"[1]

One of the shortest psalms in the Psalter, Psalm 133 is essentially a single sentence which revels in the life-giving power of community. Two similes form its core and build on each other: the image of the flowing oil "runs" down—to borrow the language of the psalmist—and into the image of the flowing dew of Mt. Hermon. The imagery is richly textured and manages to do more than merely *describe* the blessings of community. The power of the psalmist's language is such that it has the potential to draw the listener in, to enable her to *experience* the bliss of kindred dwelling "all together." Over the course of reading, one senses that the psalmist is almost breathless with excitement and joy: "Ah! How good and how pleasant!" the psalm begins. The conclusion is just as replete with joy as God commands "Life evermore!" in the final line.

At first glance, it seems strange that scholars have identified this psalm as belonging to the wisdom tradition of the Old Testament. Exclamations and images of beards wet with precious oil seem a little out of place in the wisdom writings. Perhaps more strikingly, the psalm seems to be empty of any prescriptive content: Isn't wisdom supposed to tell you what to do?

One might more easily identify Psalm 133 as a song of praise rather than instruction, but even when its tone or its form is didactic, wisdom is focused on "the skill of living," as Tremper Longman puts it. Living well in its fullest sense is the goal of wisdom, and Psalm 133 shares that goal. It begins by proclaiming that there is a particular way of living that is "good" (Heb. ṭôb) and "pleasant" (Heb. nā'îm), and by using these two words, it makes a claim for the benefits of a certain way of life. It seeks to impart certain truths about life, but the psalmist uses poetic language so powerfully that the listener is completely caught up in the beauty of the poem, scarcely aware that he is being persuaded of anything at all.

The psalm's initial exclamation leaves little room for dispute: "Ah! How good and pleasant is / the dwelling of kindred, all together." The Hebrew is wonderfully sonorous: hinnē(h) mah-ṭôb ûmah-nā'îm šebet 'aḥîm gam-yāḥad. The repetition of the h-sound creates the breathless sound of excitement, while the a-vowel dances through the two lines resulting in an auditory unity that underscores the unity of the "kindred, all together." Already, just by the act of reading the psalm and recreating the sounds represented on the page, we are caught up in its message of the bliss of communal life.

Communities of faith are so often fractious and difficult, and the joyful tone of Psalm 133 might ring false to our ears, made cynical by past experience; and yet, I think we become bitter about community when it fails us because our need for it is so great. Disappointment should not lead us to eschew life together but to strive to make it better, healthier. Communal life is the perfect environment for the growth of health and happiness in human beings, and the vision of Psalm 133 is an excellent starting point for all of us who long for the blessings that God gives us in the "dwelling of kindred, all together" because it offers a vision of community at its best.

One of the first glimpses of the psalmist's vision of community is the word "kindred." In Hebrew the word is 'aḥîm, which literally means "brothers," and, thus, its most basic reference is to family life.[2] The family unit of ancient Israel was intergenerational and interdependent—not the nuclear family of modern America—and it was the building block for all of society. The command of Deuteronomy 11:18-21 underscores the importance of the family for the theological well being of the people as a whole. It reads: "You shall put these words of mine on your heart and your soul . . . teach them to your children, talking about them when you are at home and when you are away . . . so that your days and the days of your children may be multiplied in the land . . . as long as the heavens are above the earth." The upshot of this command is clear: Israel cannot survive in the land, much less thrive, if the individual households of which it is composed do not function properly. In Deuteronomy, the emphasis is on the theological role of the family, but the theological function of the family is based on the physical reality of human existence in the ancient world. The care of the individual took place within the protective structure of the family, and human beings struggled mightily when this structure was damaged or destroyed. The desperate situation of Ruth and Naomi in the book of Ruth is a poignant case in point. Contemporary studies reveal that the family is still vitally important today, pointing to its role in the socialization and nurture of children, the overall health of adults, and the care of the elderly.

The connotations of "kindred" in the Old Testament do not end at the border of the family unit, however. Often familial terms are used metaphorically to look beyond even the borders of Israel, as in Amos 1:9. Indeed, family metaphors are used extensively throughout the ancient Near East to denote a political relationship. Kings who wished to emphasize their equality called one another "brother" and often more powerful leaders would be called "father."[3] In an analogous way, we greet each other as "brother" or "sister" even when we are not related by blood. The breadth of the connotations of "kindred" is narrowed only by our inability to imagine how tightly bound we are to the other human beings with whom we share our planet. The psalm itself at no point imposes limits or boundaries upon the reader's understanding of the nature of "kindred." Indeed, its imagery is wonderfully broad.

The two powerful similes of oil and dew flowing down in vv. 2-3a form the core of Psalm 133 as "the dwelling of kindred, all together" achieves a richness and a texture through imagery that a simple declarative statement could not proximate. The similes are bound together by the repetition of the word "running down," which occurs three times in these two verses: "Like fine oil on the face / *running down* the beard / the beard of Aaron, *running down* / over the collar of his robes // Like the dew of Herman *running down* / over the mountains of Zion. . . ."

The first substance "running down" is oil. In fact, the psalmist specifies that it is fine oil using the same word that describes the quality of communal life in the first line of the psalm: ṭôb. The goodness of community thus likened to the goodness of fine oil, as one scholar notes.[4] All of this goodness begins its journey on the face, recalling the assertion of Psalm 104:15 that the Lord made oil to "make the face shine." Olive oil was a source of wealth as well as pleasure in the ancient world, a reality we find reflected in many Old Testament texts, such as Proverbs 21:17 and Job 29:6. Oil on the head is also suggestive of anointing, a highly significant act whether in the context of the anointing of a king, prophet, or priest or as an act of hospitality—guests were sometimes honored by having oil poured on their heads.[5] The fact that it runs all the way down a man's beard is striking for the abundance that it suggests. Pouring so much oil on the head that it flows down over the beard is an excessive use of an expensive resource.

Excess appears to be the point, though. The goodness of community is overwhelming, overflowing. Like olive oil, it can make the face shine with gladness and help heal the soul (cf. Isa. 1:6). The richness of the imagery is almost over-stimulating and yet the poet cannot help but go even further with it. The beard that might belong to almost any man in the ancient world is now identified as the beard of Aaron, the first high priest and the brother of Moses! The image is glorious, and it is perhaps also a reminder of the Israelites' sacred calling. God is the one who made the people into a community, and their role is to be a means by which God blesses the rest of the world (Gen. 12:1-3).

The experience of blessing is sweetened in the second of the two similes of this psalm. While people who live in moisture-rich environments may not appreciate the value of a dew-laden leaf, the inhabitants of ancient Israel relied on dew as a source of water in their semi-arid climate. The image of dew that is so plentiful that one describes it as "running down" the side of a mountain represents the promise of fertile fields and orchards packed with fruit. The promise of agricultural abundance collides gloriously with the two places invoked by the psalmist: Mt. Hermon and Zion.

Visible from most parts of Palestine, Mt. Hermon is white-capped and lovely, and known for the quantity of its dewfall.[6] That such a dewfall would extend a hundred or so miles to the south—all the way from Mt. Herman to Zion—stretches the imagination, and yet such a stretch seems to be the psalmist's aim: the blessings of communal life can encompass vast distances. Fittingly, the final destination of this imagery is Zion, the place where God dwells with Israel (see Ps. 128, 134). It is from such a height that God sounds the high note with which the psalm concludes: "Life evermore!"

One of the chief aims of wisdom is a life well-lived, and it is to the "good life" that God commands us in this last verse of the psalm. The command is almost unnecessary, for we have been enticed with a vision of "the good life" that is absolutely gorgeous. "Taste and see that the Lord is good!" reads Psalm 34:9, and Psalm 133 urges us similarly to taste, to see, to touch, to smell, and to hear the goodness of community. The message of the psalm does not end there, however, for the psalmist also uses this abundance to persuade the audience to *be* all of these things, to develop a love that is as deep as the ties of blood and a bond that stretches as far as the east is from the west. The psalmist calls us to be the "good" oil, to anoint the heads of our neighbors, our "kindred," with the best that we have so that they are drenched with blessings. This, surely, is life well-lived. This, surely, is wisdom.

THE LORD SET HIS HEART ON YOU

Song of Songs 8:6-7

PAUL E. KOPTAK

En Route to the Sermon

This sermon grew out of the identification of the Song as wisdom literature alongside my own study of Woman Wisdom in the book of Proverbs. Once I began to think of the female lover as a kind of wisdom teacher, the concluding lines of the Song presented themselves as reflections on human experience that point to theological insights.

I've always been unhappy with claims that the allegorical readings that have sustained the church for centuries have to be rejected in the light of historical research, and I was greatly helped when I found that Paul Ricoeur's article on the "nuptial metaphor" fit well in that wisdom framework.[1] In his view, we do not run past the literal interpretation to allegory, but base a canonical reading upon it, looking to other texts that use the metaphor to describe human relationship with the divine Lord. This sermon is designed to affirm life-long commitments to love and to help listeners experience some of the emotional aspects of grace.

An earlier version of this sermon was preached at Trinity Evangelical Covenant Church, Oak Lawn, Illinois, in November 2009. The fifty-year old congregation had been graying until the community outreach of the pastor and a succession of pastoral interns attracted new members, many with young families. A Web site describes the church's worship as "traditional and relevant," using two hymnbooks, a choir, and other musical groups to provide a bridge for those with different experiences in worship. As guest preacher and with their permission, I departed from their practice of following the lectionary.

The Sermon

A couple once asked their pastor if portions of the Song of Songs could be read at their wedding. The pastor agreed, but marriage ceremonies aren't supposed to talk about what is going to happen afterward, so he left out the steamy parts. It wasn't until the couple was watching the video recording of the service three weeks later that they realized the Scripture reading had been censored! And so goes our uneasiness with this book of the Bible that praises the wonders of committed love, but needs editing if it is to be read in church. We cannot deny the beauty of words like:

> Place me like a seal over your heart,
>   like a seal on your arm;
> for love is as strong as death. (Song 8:6 TNIV)

The rabbis of old said of them, "All the ages are not worth the day on which the Song of Songs was given to Israel; for all the Writings are holy, but the Song of Songs is the Holy of Holies,"[2] and "Had not the Torah been given, Canticles would have sufficed to guide the world." It sounds as if they would have us read it more often than the occasional wedding—although they believed you had to be over thirty to do so. They read in Genesis as we do, that God created us to become one, to leave father and mother and "cleave." But we're still not so sure about moving from that general description to the frank and sensual imagery of the Songs. Like the pastor, we know what the honeymoon is about, but that doesn't mean we want to talk about it in a public setting.

That's probably why most interpreters and preachers throughout Jewish and Christian history have turned our eyes toward the more spiritual meaning of the poem, and we wouldn't want to be without their teaching. Bernard of Clairvaux preached eighty-six sermons on the first two chapters—in a mon- *Sigh!* astery. His message is worth hearing today: "What human affections have you ever experienced, any of you, that are sweeter than is now expressed to you from the heart of the most high?"[3]

Then the Rosetta Stone launched the translation of ancient literatures from Egypt and of Mesopotamia, and we realized that they too had poetry like this, in some cases even more explicit. And so we changed the way we read, hoping to get at what the poet originally intended. We received them as ancient love songs that tell us more about God's design for love and marriage than God's relation to humankind—more about how we are to love a life companion than how we are to return the love of God for us. Like Ancient Near Eastern love poetry, we came to see that these poems of Scripture are open expressions of desire, often presented in delicate images of nature. Well, "delicate" may be a matter of culture and taste—"Your eyes are like doves" still sounds pretty good today, but one can quibble with comparing a lover's hair to a flock of goats!

There is *mutuality*—each expresses desire for the other with gifts of praise. From the man: "How beautiful you are my darling! Oh, how beautiful? Your eyes are doves." From the woman: "How handsome you are my beloved! Oh, how charming!" (Song 1:15-16 TNIV). There is *bonding*—the woman has friends who ask: "How is your beloved better than others, most beautiful of women?" She answers them with more praise of his beauty and avows that there is no other for her (Song 5:9-16). "Therefore," says one scholar, "the biblical tradition celebrates sexuality as a gift that rejects the two extremes of asceticism and debauchery."[4] Debauchery treats sex like a commodity, an acquisition. Asceticism pretends we are too spiritual for that kind of thing. No, we affirm, this was all God's idea, wrapped up in all that God called "good." It only makes sense then, that this Bible book of love poems would lead us in honest reflection on sexuality and spirituality, and that its unnamed female poet who gets the first and last words can be our teacher. Moreover, let us listen to her as a teacher of wisdom. Teachers of wisdom (some call them sages), look at life and find lessons that can apply to daily living. They draw their lessons from nature and use poems, proverbs, and other observations drawn from everyday experience. Wisdom teachers sometimes seem more practical than spiritual—but their teaching is always theological. It always points to the wisdom of God.

In the book of Proverbs, this tradition is personified in Woman Wisdom, present at creation, who sets out a banquet to teach all she learned there about the way the world works (Prov. 8:1-9:12). That's why the young men are told to make wisdom a life companion using the words of love that appear in the Song (Prov. 4:3-9). She is not the only teaching woman in Proverbs, however. King Lemuel's mother warns him about dissipation, urging him to use wealth and power to speak for the poor and guarantee justice in the land. The concluding

poem praises the "woman of strength" for teaching and modeling the fear of
the Lord for her family (Prov. 31:1-31). All these teaching women of Proverbs
call us to lives of justice, righteousness, and equity as well (Prov. 1:3).

Justice is not at the forefront of the song, but what are we to make of her
claim, "Dark, am I, lovely . . . Do not stare at me because I am dark, darkened
by the sun," reporting the mistreatment of her brothers who make her work
in their vineyards (Song 1:5-6 author's translation). And what about her ini-
tiatives to seek and court her beloved? Renita Weems says this self-confident
woman is the only woman who speaks for herself in the whole Hebrew Bible.
Others are mediated by males who narrate the stories in which they appear,
but here she speaks for herself alone—and gets the most lines.[5] "I am dark
and lovely." She says it before her man ever gets the chance.

We listen in as she seeks out her love, offers her praise, and receives the
same from him, and then makes her request, itself a wise reflection:

> Set me as a seal upon your heart,
>   as a seal upon your arm;
> for love is as strong as death,
>   passion fierce as the grave.
> Its flashes are flashes of fire,
>   a raging flame.
> Many waters cannot quench love,
>   neither can floods drown it.
> If one offered for love
>   all the wealth of his house,
> it would be utterly scorned. (Song 8:6-7)

"Love is as strong as death"—Who can fight death and win? So also "Love is a
blazing fire" that "many waters cannot quench." Raging rivers cannot wash it
away. Her request is also a lesson, instructing us that the strong power of love
that draws couples together has the potential to keep them together. Humorist
Michael Perry found himself in love and thinking about getting married:

> I am not antimarriage, as my life is full of examples of married
> couples—my parents chief among them—who emanate a depth
> of calm with each other that is evident of what love can be when it

stops acting silly. . . . Sometimes I see the old man up the street going for his mail and I remember the day I sat with him and his wife in the Jamboree Days beer tent and he eagerly pulled out his wallet to show me a portrait of them when they met back in World War II—in the photo he is wearing a military uniform—and then I looked at them shoulder to shoulder, both coming in somewhere around a short five feet and grinning with their beers and I wondered what it was to tote that photo around for fifty-plus years and still be so proud to show it with your girl right there beside you.[6]

"Set me as a seal upon your heart"—*it's* a reference to the carved stone worn around the neck or on a ring that leaves a signature impression in wax or clay. Whether it refers to the stone or the imprint, doesn't matter, only that it says: "I will sign my name on your heart and your life, if you will do the same." A friend who recently lost her husband to a debilitating disease wants to start a work in his name to help others. She wants him to be remembered. I heard the story of a husband who insisted on staying with his dying wife, even though he was beyond exhaustion. "We'll call you," the hospital staff said. "Go and get some rest." *"No," was the answer. "She has been at my side nearly all my life; I'm not going to leave her now."*

"If one offered for love all the wealth of his house, it would be utterly scorned." Love is beyond price. "It is a commodity that cannot be bartered or bought. It is free but not cheap."[7] This is not to say lifetime love is simple, painless, or easy, or that sometimes it is just plain out of reach. But it is to say that *eros* not only attracts, it prepares the way for *philia* and *agape,* human love that gives us a glimpse of the friendship and faithfulness of God. There are other ways to understand that relationship, but with this one a wise woman teaches us about divine love that is passionate, committed, and singular.

Notice how well this woman's song of love sounds in harmony with the voice of Moses: "It was not because you were more numerous than any other people that the LORD set his heart on you and chose you—for you were the fewest of all peoples. It was because the LORD loved you and kept the oath that he swore to your ancestors, that the LORD has brought you out with a mighty hand . . . (Deut. 7:7). There's something here about the exclusivity of God's jealous love, itself a consuming fire, that runs throughout Deuteronomy (4:10-15,

39 cf. Exod. 20:5; 34:14). Early on I learned that this book of Scripture is the book of "one": one Lord, one place of worship, one instruction given through the one prophet, Moses. "Hear O Israel, the Lord is one" (Deut. 6:4-5).[8]

One love, the sage lover would add, love that commits to the exclusion of all others, encompassing all that we are. Malcolm Muggeridge recalled scanning the crowds at the train station for his wife: "What is love but a face, instantly recognizable in a sea of faces? A spotlight rather than a panning shot. This in contradistinction to power, which is a matter of numbers, of crowded scenes."[9]

No wonder the church has treasured the Song of Songs as a sign of God's love for his people. How many of us grew up singing, "I am my beloved's and he is mine—his banner over me is love"? We might debate the hermeneutics involved for the Christian education of our children, but the intention is spot on. This "nuptial metaphor" is something more than simple allegory.[10] The poetry is not *really* about God's love for Israel, or Christ the bridegroom of the church. It is about human sexual love, and yet the passion, jealousy, and strength of that love instinctively remind the Christian of the love of God.

If wisdom is a way of knowing that begins in common experience, we have found a great deal of it here. Wisdom looks at life-long love at its best and recognizes something of the order of creation, the way the world is supposed to work. We can leave the detailed explorations/discussions of sexuality and spirituality for another day. For now it is enough to remember that we relate to God in a way that is something like a marriage: joyful and exclusive, meant to go the distance. We might even draw from the Bible the word "covenant" and the image of bride (Jer. 2:1; Eph. 5:21-33; Rev. 19:6-8). And would it be wrong to say that the commitment goes both ways? We make a vow to love God with heart, soul, mind, and strength, but we do so because we have been loved: "The Lord set his heart on you and chose you. . . . It was because the Lord loved you and kept the oath that he swore to your ancestors" (Deut. 7:7-8).

"Set me as a seal upon your heart." There is too much "Jesus is my girl-friend/boyfriend" theology in Christian teaching and music today, and I'm not in favor of sentimentalizing the faith. But I do believe that this woman and her words of the Song are wise. That is, she observes with a careful eye and tells us something about the eternal value of passionate love, life-long love, love that does not give up, even when there is disappointment or even betrayal. "Love as strong as death"—even stronger. In the twelfth century Honorius of Autun imagined Christ saying: "Just as death overpowers all the mighty, and therefore is mightier than all, so too love is mightier than all— that has overpowered me who am the mightiest, and brought me to death for your sake."[11]

And so we read the Song of Songs for what it is, a song of love that points us to the enduring love of God, because "the LORD set his heart on you." Put another way: With the right teacher, our human experiences of love teach us about the love of God, and just as important, this everlasting love of God teaches us how to love another—for life.

ASTONISHED AND SILENT

Matthew 7:2

THOMAS G. LONG

En Route to the Sermon

The occasion for the following sermon was Lipscomb University's 2009 Conference on Preaching, the *Grande finale* for a series that provided fresh joy and stimulated essential homiletic creativity with its substantive presentations and interactions. The conference always opened and closed with worship, and this sermon was delivered at the concluding service.

More than a decade earlier Tom helped us launch the series of seminars and volumes on preaching, and it was altogether appropriate that he provide closure with this sermon whose audience was a community of preachers, oft nurtured by his work.

Long's sermon embodies Tremper Longman's notion that Jesus is the epitome of wisdom who amazed by his teaching and unprecedented wisdom. And in this sermon Long briefly holds the tension between the distinct understandings of the role of the ancient preacher *Qoheleth*, identified very differently by Longman and William Brown.[1] Although he underscores that Jesus's words "generated a crisis," Long eventually leans into Brown's "good news" and tacitly positive approach, reminding us that Jesus manifests the kingdom in the sermon's "second silence."

The sermon is surprisingly inductive and contains a healthy dose of narrative qualities. Filled with descriptive vignettes, its final sentence lands listeners—through common experience with the preacher—at the very location he has hinted at, alluded to, described, and referenced throughout the sermon. In the final and telling line, "astonished and silent," the congregation joins the preacher to *experience* the proclamation!

The Sermon

You have very graciously invited me here to preach a sermon. Now, a sermon, as we all know, is made out of words, and I have brought some words with me today. But even though sermons are crafted out of words, I think it important for us to remember that in sermons there are two powerful moments of silence.

The first silence comes at the very beginning of the sermon. You may not have noticed it a minute ago. It was brief and fleeting, but it was there. The Scripture lesson is read, the congregation sinks back into their seats, the preacher takes a deep and anxious breath, and there it is. It is so routine we hardly even notice this silence, but down at its depth it is an electric silence full of anticipation and expectation. What is going on in this silence? I think the African American church has it right when it says, in effect, "In that moment of silence for everyone, for preacher, for choir, for congregation, there is the wondering, 'Is there a word from the Lord?'" Amidst all the words of our culture that besiege us, is there a word that can cut through the clutter, a word that can make a difference, a word from beyond that can touch us and heal us, is there a word from the Lord? This question shouts in that silence.

I love the way that novelist and essayist Frederick Buechner has described this moment of silence. He writes,

> [T]he preacher climbs the steps to the pulpit with his sermon in his hand. He hikes his black robe up at the knee so he will not trip over it on the way up the steps. He feels as if he has swallowed an anchor.
> . . . The preacher . . . deals out his sermon note cards like a riverboat gambler. The stakes have never been higher. Two minutes from now he may have lost his listeners completely to their own thoughts, but at this minute he has them in the palm of his hand. The silence in the . . . church is deafening because everybody is listening to it. Everybody is listening, even [the preacher].[2]

The theologian Karl Barth also talked about this moment of silence at the beginning of a sermon when he noted that when the bells in the church ring and the congregation gathers, we do not come to hear about the cherry tree or the symphony or everyday life. In fact our gathering is a sign that "cherry tree and symphony and everyday life are possibilities somehow already exhausted."³ What hangs in the air is one question: Is it true? Is it true that God is present? Is it true that there is a word from the Lord today?

Now I know, I know, we preachers frequently squander the promise of this first urgent moment of silence. Two sentences into the sermon and the air of expectation has been let out of the room. This moment of silence anticipates a word from beyond, and we often fill it with a word from the all-too-familiar; this moment of silence cries out for a Word that brings life, a Word that changes everything, and we focus on the trivial. I think of Terry Waite, the Anglican clergyman who, in the mid-1980s, was assigned by the Archbishop of Canterbury as an envoy to Beirut to negotiate for the release of hostages. However, events went badly, and Waite himself was captured and made a hostage. For four years he was confined to a tiny cell in a Beirut prison, cut off from everything he loved—from church, family, civilization, home-land—isolated and alone. Over the years, though, he developed a relationship of trust with his guards. So much so that one of them was willing to do something very risky. He surreptitiously placed in Terry Waite's cell a transistor radio with one precious battery. For the first time in four years, Waite had the means for contact with the outside world. Careful to save the battery, Waite had to choose when to use the radio. He decided that the most urgent need he had was not for news or music, but for the gospel. Is there a Word from the Lord? So he waited until Sunday morning to turn it on. He tuned in the BBC to get a worship service, hungry for a word from God, hungry for the gospel, hungry for comfort. Imagine how he felt when the preacher began, "My theme for this morning is spiritual lessons from Winnie the Pooh." Waite said of this experience, "All I could do was laugh out loud so he did me a good service!"⁴

I think also of one of my students who was invited to preach a sermon at a worship service at the nursing home where she was serving as a student chaplain. This nursing home had worship in the big entrance lobby, and for the service it was crowded with elderly people, some with oxygen tanks, some in wheel chairs. One of the gifts that God gives to people of great age is the freedom to say and do exactly what they want, and sure enough, my student got a paragraph into the sermon when suddenly one of the elderly women present pulled the joystick on her electric wheelchair, turned it around, went back down the hall to her room shouting, "Blah, blah, blah!"

We preachers can squander the promise of that first silence, but it is amazing to me, even congregations that have been numbed into submission decade after decade come back the next Sunday and it's there: the silence of expectation, maybe this time.

But there is also a second moment of profound silence in preaching. If the first one comes at the beginning of the sermon, the second one comes at the end of the sermon. It is much rarer, in fact some people wonder if they have ever experienced this moment of silence at all. If the first moment of silence in preaching is the wondering, "Is there a word from the Lord?" the second moment of silence comes when the Holy Spirit has taken the fragile human words of the preacher and turned them, in fact, into the Word of God. When a word penetrates our existence; when a word separates life from death, wisdom from foolishness, blessing from curse, and our lives are touched and transformed; when the room in which the preached word has happened is breathless and still, and when there is the sudden awareness that the world has been drastically changed; when that happens, you can't simply pick up the hymnal and casually go into the next hymn. This is a moment like Easter, a moment when the light of the future is yet so bright, so full of promise and fear at the same time, we shield our eyes and close our mouths. This moment provokes astonished silence.

Matthew wants us to know this is the kind of silence that occurred at the end of Jesus' Sermon on the Mount. What Matthew says is, "When Jesus had finished speaking all these words, the crowd who heard him were astonished." The word "astonished" is, in Greek, even stronger. It's more like dumbstruck, flabbergasted, speechless. At the end of the Sermon on the Mount there was the silence of astonishment, dumbstruckness, flabbergasted speechlessness.

And Matthew wants us to know that this is not the only time this happened in the preaching of Jesus. In fact, it happened all the way through his ministry. It happened at the end of his ministry when he preached to the crowds in Jerusalem: they were dumbstruck by his words. It happened in the middle of his ministry when he was preaching to his hometown synagogue in Nazareth: they were flabbergasted at his wisdom. It happens here at the beginning of his ministry when he preaches the Sermon on the Mount: they were left astonished and silent. Matthew tells us the reason that this dumb-struck silence occurred was that Jesus did not preach like other preachers. He did not preach like the scribes; he preached with authority. The hungry desire for a Word from beyond was fulfilled in their hearing, and Jesus' preaching precipitated a crisis. If the first moment of silence is a wondering *if* there is a Word from the Lord, the second moment of silence occurs when, in fact, there *is* a Word from the Lord, a Word that turns the world over and creates a crisis.

Several years ago during the Sunday morning service in a church in Charlotte, North Carolina, the time came for the sermon. The prayer for illumination had been uttered, the scripture had been read, and the preacher was standing in the pulpit and about to open his mouth and preach, when suddenly a man in the balcony, a stranger nobody knew, stood up and said in a loud clear voice, "I have a word from the Lord." Heads swiveled around to see who this was who had intruded on worship. Whatever the man intended to say, whatever this word from the Lord was, no one ever got to hear it because two bouncers, disguised as ushers, bounded up the balcony steps like gazelles and muscled this guy out of the sanctuary and into the street.

I don't blame them; I fully understand the ushers' actions. The Apostle Paul said we ought to do things in worship decently and in order. This was out of order, and who knows? It could have turned out to be indecent as well. Who knew what this fellow had in mind? I don't blame the ushers at all for escorting this man to the street. But it does cause me to wonder a bit, because I am a preacher and almost every week I stand in a pulpit saying, in effect, "I have a word from the Lord." No ushers have ever bolted into alarmed action at my announcement; no one has ever muscled me out of the church. I wonder if it is because I, and many other preachers like me, have so often turned the silence of expectation into the sacrament of disappointment. I wonder if here, among the stained glass windows and the robes and the liturgy and the way we have preached, we have domesticated and tamed the gospel so that it can no longer provoke a crisis, so that the words, "I have a Word from the Lord," do not prompt the ushers to tense but instead tempt the congregation to relax and yawn.

Jesus did not preach like that. He did not preach like the scribes or the Presbyterians or the Methodists, the Lutherans or the Episcopalians. He preached, says Matthew, "As one with authority," which means his word generated a crisis. His preaching cleared the space of clutter and chatter, leaving a dumbstruck silence filled only with the largest of all human questions. What do we do now? How do we live? Who shall we be? That is the second silence in a sermon.

Now if we listen to the end of the Sermon on the Mount, we might not like what we hear because what provokes this second silence are hard and demanding words. Jesus does not come across as the cuddly, warm, inclusive Jesus we have come to love. He says instead at the end of the sermon, "Not everybody who says Lord, Lord will enter the kingdom of heaven, only those who hear these words and do them, only those who build their lives around them. There will be a lot of people who say, 'Lord look at me. I did wonderful things in your name. I was a very powerful person in terms of communicating what you wanted us to communicate. Look at me Lord.' And I will say to you, 'I don't recognize you. I recognize only those who have built their lives around the words that I have given, who have built their lives on solid rock. If you build it on sand, the winds will come and the storms will come and blow you away.'"

No way around it, these are words of judgment. I don't want to take the sting out of them, but I don't want us to misunderstand them either. While we often think of judgment as the mark of a punitive God and the playground of fundamentalists, in the gospel the judgment of God is actually a good thing, a promise that God will bring justice, will set things right.

One day I was walking across the seminary campus where I teach. One of my students hailed me.

"Dr. Long, could I speak to you for a minute?"

I said, "I'm going to get a cup of coffee, you want to go?" She did, and in the cafeteria she told me what was on her mind. She said she was serving as a field education student in a local church and that her supervising pastor was requiring her to preach next Sunday.

"Good," I said, putting down my coffee cup.

"No, it's *not* good," she said, shaking her head. "He is making me preach on the lectionary texts for Sunday."

"Good," I said again.

"No," she repeated, "it is not good. Have you read the lectionary texts for next week? They're all about judgment. I don't believe in judgment. I believe in grace, I believe in mercy. It took me three years of therapy to get over judgment. I am not going to preach judgment."

We talked about this for a while, with no resolution, and then we moved onto other topics. She began telling me about her family life. She and her husband have several children, only the youngest of whom, a teenage boy, was still at home, and he was giving them hell. He was into drugs, maybe dealing them, and in trouble with the police.

"Like last night," she said, "we were sitting at the supper table, my husband and I, and we had no idea where our son was. In the middle of supper, he comes banging in the back door, and I said to him, 'Would you like some supper?' He practically spit at us. He then stomped down the hall to his room and slammed the door.

"My husband got up and turned on ESPN," she said. "That is always his response."

Now it was her turn to put down her coffee cup. She looked at me with firmness in her eye. "I don't know . . . something got into me right at that moment. I'm afraid of my son, physically afraid of my own son. But something got into me and I got up from the table and I went down to his room and I pushed open the door and I said to him, 'You listen to me. I love you so much I am not going to put up with this anymore.'"

"Marilyn," I said, "I think you just preached a sermon on judgment."

God loves us so much, God will not put up with the foolishness in our lives. We have hungered for success and power and status, and Jesus says in this sermon that this is foolish and that God loves us so much God will not put up with this anymore. "Blessed are those that hunger and thirst for righteousness and justice." That is what makes life free and good. We Americans have been those who have trusted in military might and made war on others, and Jesus says that this is foolish and that God loves us so much that God is not going to put up with this anymore. "Blessed are the merciful . . . blessed are the meek . . . blessed are the peacemakers." The judgment of God is nothing more and nothing less than God's intention to set things right, in the world and in our lives. The judgment of God *is* the love of God. As one theologian put it, "Do not fear the wrath of God; fear the love of God, for the love of God will strip away everything that stands between you and God."

One of the ways we domesticate the Sermon on the Mount, one of the ways we diminish its power to render us speechless, is to think of it as a collection of religious rules and advice. "When you pray, do this; when you give alms, do that. . . . Do not worry about your life, turn the other cheek, do not judge others." Good sage advice, rules for living.

But Jesus is not talking about rules for coping in this world; Jesus is announcing the destruction of this world and the coming of God's reign.

To misunderstand the Sermon on the Mount as a series of rules is, by the way, the same thing we often do to the Ten Commandments. We tend to think of the Ten Commandments as ten things we'd really like to do, but that God doesn't want us to do. So to please God, we should not do them. But that misses the point, misses the way the commandments begin: "I am the Lord your God. I brought you out of slavery into the land of freedom and this is the shape of freedom. I love you so much, I am not putting up with your enslavement any more. I, the Lord your God, am setting things right. I am setting you so free you don't even have to have any other gods. You have been given so much you are free not to covet what is your neighbor's. You are free to have the joyous rest of the Sabbath day and to keep it holy."

This is not a list of rules; it is the shape of freedom; it is the quality of life in a world remade by the judgment of God.

So it is with the Sermon on the Mount. These are not words of advice; they are words of life and death, words that create a crisis, words that stun us into speechlessness as we contemplate the world we have so carefully built, the world in which we have invested, the world we have so dearly cherished falling into the sea like a plywood shack in a flood

As the theologian Paul Tillich put it many years ago:

> We can be cynical . . . only so long as we feel safety in the place in which our cynicism can be exercised. But if the foundations of this place and all places begin to crumble, cynicism itself crumbles with them. And only two alternatives remain—despair, which is the certainty of eternal destruction, or faith, which is the certainty of eternal salvation. "'The world itself shall crumble, but, my salvation knows no end,' says the Lord."[5]

To cling to the old structures of death, war, and greed is to live in a world that is passing away, to occupy a house with no foundation, a dwelling slated for condemnation. This is not God's world, and as Jesus says, even the pious who still cling to this world will be unrecognizable: "I never knew you." I recognize, said Jesus, those who are shaped by this freedom and belong to God's new world.

And there is astonished silence as we imagine the collapse of a world that once seemed so stable, a house so compelling and attractive. But then, even as we stand speechless, the silence is broken by the first words of Easter, "Do not be afraid." Do not be afraid because even as our foolish house crumbles in watery ruins, there stands a house built on the solid rock of Jesus' own Word, and the door is open, and the voice of Jesus is beckoning, "Come to me, all you that are weary and are carrying heavy burdens, and I will give you rest."

When my wife and I moved to Atlanta eight years ago, we shopped around for a church. We finally decided we would join a congregation in downtown Atlanta. We liked the worship, we liked the commitment to mission, and we decided to join. The minister invited us, and all the others who were joining that particular season, to come and meet with the church officers on a Wednesday night for dinner. So we did. We were gathered in the fellowship hall around a square table, and when dinner was done, the pastor said, "I would like to go around the table and ask each person joining the church to say why you are joining this church."

We did and each of us said the kind of things one would expect. One person said, "I'm a musician; this church has one of the finest music programs in the city, and therefore I'm joining." Another one said, "We've got two teenage daughters, and the youth program here is fantastic. That is why we're joining." Still another person said, "I didn't like the minister in the church I belonged to, and I like the minister here a lot. I'm going to join."

Then it got around to a man I'll call Samuel. His story was that he was high on crack cocaine on the streets, stumbled into the church's outreach center, and begged to be helped. The director of the center said, "We've spent our budget for this month. I can't get you into a treatment program until next month. But if you will stay with us, we will stay with you." She then took his hand, they knelt on the carpet of her office and prayed together. He stayed and got into the treatment program.

"I've been sober for three years now and the reason I'm joining this church is that God *saved* me in this church!" he exclaimed. The rest of us looked at each other sheepishly. We were there for the music and the parking; he was there for the salvation.

A few weeks later, there was a little squib in our church news letter that said Samuel was now an inmate in one of the local county jails. I thought to myself, "Samuel and I joined the church together; we are brothers in Christ." So, I went to see him. After going through three metal detectors, I found myself on the opposite side of a thick plate glass window holding a telephone and looking at Samuel in an orange jail jumpsuit. He was holding the other phone.

"Samuel," I said, "how are you?"

"By the grace of God," he said, "I'm doing all right."

"What happened?"

"I was working in the outreach center," he replied, "counseling people, people like myself, people off the streets, telling them they could do right. But then I realized I hadn't done right myself. I had a warrant for my arrest out here. It was an old warrant, years old; it would have never caught up with me, but I knew about it. So on Christmas Eve I turned myself in." But then Samuel's face brightened, "I will be out by Easter! I cannot wait to worship at church on Easter. But in the meantime I've got an outreach center going here in the jail. A lot of these people can't read or write, so I write letters to their sweethearts and wives telling them that they miss them and love them. Every night we have a prayer meeting in my cell. Not many come, but we pray for the other prisoners and the guards."

I looked through the plate glass at my brother in Christ, Samuel, in the jumpsuit of a county prisoner, and I saw one of the freest human beings in the world, a man who is building his life not on sand, but on the rock of the gospel.

In the presence of such a free and joyful life, so filled with the promise of God's new world, I was astonished and silent.

Chapter

TWO

PROVERBS, PERSUASION, AND PREACHING

Glenn D. Pemberton

Unique in the Old Testament, only the book of Proverbs explicitly expresses its compositional purposes, its reason for being.[1] Unlike their canonical brothers and sisters, the sages adopt a simple rhetorical strategy: tell your audience what you intend to say, then tell your audience what you said you would say. Proverbs achieves the first of these goals through a series of purpose statements in its opening verses:

> to learn about wisdom and instruction,
> to understand words of insight,
> to acquire instruction in wise dealing:
> righteousness, justice, and equity,
> to give shrewdness to the simple,
> to the young – knowledge and prudence
> (let the wise listen and add learning
> and the discerning gain skill)
> to understand a proverb and a figure
> the words of the wise and their riddles. (1:2-6; author's translation)

In essence, the sages assert a character development program built on a theological foundation: the fear of the Lord (1:7). Presupposing that the reader already lives by faith in relationship to God, the book sets out a curriculum that interlocks intellectual growth with ethical virtue.

Intellectually, the sages challenge the reader to learn the content of wisdom (1:2a) and to grasp the meaning of these sayings, proverbs, figures, and riddles (1:2b, 6). As is often pointed out, wisdom is not a matter of high intelligence; nor is folly the result of low I.Q. The sages' teaching, however, does consist of content that must be mastered in recall, understanding, and application.

Ethically, an integral part of the sages' program is instruction in wise behavior toward others, expressed by the three terms: "righteousness, justice, and equity" (1:3). At first glance this triumvirate seems out of place in a wisdom text, even more so in Proverbs' programmatic prologue. These terms reverberate the common prophetic declaration: "Let justice roll down like waters, and righteousness like an ever-flowing stream" (Amos 5:24; cf. Mic. 6:8). But surprisingly and perhaps indicative of a greater commonality between sages and prophets than we have often recognized, these three terms and related ideas appear frequently in Proverbs. "Righteousness" (*zadik* or *zedek*) occurs most often (over seventy times), "justice" (*mishpat*) twenty times, and "equity" (*mesharim*) five times (as a verb or noun the related term "upright, straight" [*yashar*] occurs over thirty times). The aim of Proverbs is to form intellect through wise content and deploy this intellect in ethical behavior—complete character formation.

Toward these ends the primary contours of the book are equally clear. Proverbs consists of two distinct movements or sections: 1) chapters 1-9 speak to the reader through a series of ten lectures or speeches originally addressed to "my son" or "sons" and five interludes, four of which personify wisdom as a woman, and 2) chapters 10-31 present numerous individual proverbs along with a few longer forms, including the final acrostic tribute to the "woman of valor" (31:10-31).

What Proverbs seeks to accomplish seems clear enough: wisdom is a conversion of thought and action that results in character transformation. But *how* the book achieves its goals is less often considered, and worth our effort to understand. How does Proverbs persuade the reader in favor of its program? And how might their efforts to persuade intersect with our own persuasive efforts in preaching from this text? How indeed, when Proverbs' product (character formation through intellectual development and ethical virtue) faces stiff market competition from easier to acquire and less expensive alternatives? The investment of energy to achieve the good life Proverbs envisions is significantly greater than what the alternative rhetoric proposes. I take it to be no happenstance that immediately following Proverbs' statement of purpose (1:2-7) that the first father-son speech admits the presence of competition that offers the son excitement, fast money, friends, and community (1:11-14). Why wait when you can have it all and have it now? With anti-wisdom there is no need for discipline, persistence, patience, or (most of all) character formation. The good life is only a moment away. Can wisdom possibly win? How does a sage convince anyone to choose a path that is more difficult, more strenuous, and more expensive—a longer route to what appears to be the same end? How does one persuade when the central message is a cross not a crown?

In what follows I examine the three major genres in the book of Proverbs (the lectures and interludes of Proverbs 1-9, and the short sayings of Proverbs 10-31) and offer a few observations about how the sages attempt to persuade the son and reader in favor of wisdom. Since their task remains as our task in preaching and their opposition remains as our opposition, we should gain some insight from this study to improve our textual understanding and aid our persuasive attempts in favor of wisdom.

Persuasion in the Lectures of Proverbs 1-9

I

Hear, my child, and accept my words,
that the years of your life may be many (4:10)

Each of the ten father-son speeches begins with an introductory appeal for the son (and now the reader) to "listen," "pay attention," or "not forget" what is about to be said.[2] And each of these appeals includes at least some reason for such an initial hearing. For example, the third lecture begins:

My child, do not forget my teaching
but let your heart keep my commandments;

for length of days and years of life
and abundant welfare they will give you. (3:1-2)

Or in the seventh lecture:

My child, be attentive to my words;
incline your ear to my sayings.
Do not let them escape from your sight;
 keep them within your heart.
For they are life to those who find them,
and healing to all their flesh. (4:20-22, NRSV)

We might be tempted to dismiss these opening appeals as little more than formulaic introductions; after all, most speeches begin with some attention-getting device. However, in four of the ten speeches most of the lecture is devoted to the sole aim of gaining the son's attention; little instruction exists in these four speeches.[3] Consequently, the initial efforts to acquire the audience's attention may not be the result of mere habitual formula, but a matter of high priority and genuine challenge. It may sound simple, but the first task in persuading in wisdom's favor is to gain an authentic hearing. As preachers and parents of teenagers understand, wisdom has little chance in a world of competing voices unless we create a hearing opportunity.

Achieving an initial hearing in the lectures of Proverbs 1-9 varies based on the rhetorical situation of the speaker and audience. In 1:8-19 the alternative rhetoric is so compelling that it must be deconstructed in order for the son to give attention to wisdom. So the father and mother expose the alluring invitation for the son to join friends in an exciting adventure for easy money in an egalitarian community ("one for all and all for one") for what it really is: suicidal greed (1:16-19). The second speech confronts an apparent impatience for results with the assurance that wisdom's rewards are real and substantial (2:12-22), but they require an intense commitment for the long haul (2:1-11). Another lecture recognizes the speaker's lack of standing (ethos) in the eyes of the audience and the hurdle this creates for genuine hearing. As a result the father draws on the words of the grandfather in order to get the son to listen, a savvy ploy then and now (4:1-9). Finally, in 4:10-19 the audience appears to have high regard for the speaker, but complacency regarding listening and staying the course of wisdom. So the speaker draws on their prior relationship

(4:11) along with asserting lavish promises and dire warnings to once again attain their attention (4:12, 18-19).

All of these lectures share a common concern for genuine *listening*. Each speaker appears to understand the unique circumstances that threaten an authentic hearing. Each speaker discerns the world of competing voices that offer newer, quicker, and easier ways to "the good life." And each speaker knows that unless we are able to slice through the noise and gain an audience for our teaching, the path of wisdom will see few footsteps.

II
I came to a fork in the road
and I took it.
—Yogi Berra

The ability to gain another person's attention is an exercise of power, albeit a rare power. How effective speakers handle such power may reveal as much about their character and their "product" as what they claim. In Proverbs 1-9, once the father gains the son's attention, he tells the truth about wisdom—and nothing but the truth. Wisdom is more than a means to an end, a way to get the good life. Wisdom is more than an end in itself, the destination at which one declares, "Now I am wise!" Instead, wisdom is a practice (as in practicing medicine) or a vocation (a chosen manner of living). Or in the prevailing metaphor of Proverbs 1-9, wisdom is a road on which we travel.

A path is created by constant foot traffic, much to the chagrin of landscape designers and the delight of hikers. During our years in Colorado, I had my share of experiences navigating mountain trails. Sometimes the path unfolded like a map, a clear route from beginning to end. Most of the time, however, it was not so easy. I was forced to discern the best direction, take it, and stay on course to arrive at the lake or back at home. A map helps; a reliable guide is even better. Good guides have experience and know the trail so that they keep their charges safe to the end. Refusing the aid of a guide or a map and asserting self-reliance (I detect an audible sigh from some), or falling into the hands of a disreputable guide is a matter of life and death in the mountains. A trail may be difficult to navigate, hold hidden dangers, or be deceptive, leading to nowhere.

Although a world away from the Rocky Mountains, the sages draw on the image of the path to explain truth about wisdom. As a way of life, wisdom is a manner in which one decides every day to live, not a once and for all time decision. A person must choose each day to continue this walk. Consequently, frequent admonitions urge the son to stay on the good path or make his own paths true.

> Therefore, walk in the way of the good,
>   and keep to the paths of the just. (2:20)
> Let your eyes look directly forward
>   and your gaze be straight before you.
> Keep straight the path of your feet,
>   and all your ways will be sure.
> Do not swerve to the right or to the left;
>   turn your foot away from evil. (4:25-27)

And in a similar fashion other texts warn against taking the wrong road or walking with the wrong people.

> My child, do not walk in their way,
>   keep your foot from their paths (1:15)
> Do not enter the path of the wicked,
>   and do not walk in the way of evildoers. (4:14)

The sages also warn about the route that leads to an unexpected destination. In these texts, the "other" woman (any woman other than the son's wife) enters the picture as an unreliable guide and one who is deceptively deadly:

> Her feet go down to death;
>   her steps follow the path to Sheol.
> She does not keep straight to the path of life;
>   her ways wander, and she does not know it. . . .
> Keep your way far from her,
>   and do not go near the door of her house. (5:5-6,8)
> Do not let your hearts turn aside to her ways;
>   do not stray into her paths.
> For many are those she has laid low,

and numerous are her victims.
Her house is the way to Sheol,
    going down to the chambers of death. (7:25-27)

While the "other" woman leads to death, the sages assert that wisdom, the instruction of the father and mother, will save a person from taking the wrong path and its consequences (2:12,15). In addition to listening, the son must trust with all his heart "in the Lord" who "will make his paths straight" (3:5-6).

This, then, is the truth about wisdom. Once the sages do the heavy lifting to gain a hearing they do not "sugar coat" the hard truth about what they offer. There is no bait and switch scheme to get the son to commit to wisdom, only later to discover its true nature; such a practice is the method of the wicked men and "other" women in Proverbs 1-9, not the sages. Nor does the father try to make wisdom appear easier, as if wisdom could be purchased for three easy payments of $19.95 (plus shipping). Or that once received wisdom will change your life in seven to ten days or your money back. Instead, they tell the truth: wisdom is a way of life, a life-long journey of character formation.

III

The path of the righteous is like the light of dawn,
which shines brighter and brighter until full day. (4:18)

While wisdom is not the way to immediate gratification, the lectures of Proverbs 1-9 do not undervalue wisdom's benefits. Quite the opposite, the sages connect their teaching with many rewards. They promise that those who choose wisdom will receive pendants and adornments for their necks (1:9, 3:22) and a garland or even a "beautiful crown" for their heads (3:9). They promise that on this path a person may walk and even run without concern for tripping over hidden obstacles (3:23, 4:12). But ultimately the sages make it clear that the decision for or against wisdom is a decision between life and death, a choice for life that is genuinely living, or for life that is a living death. The long-term value of wisdom is beyond anything; wisdom is life.

Consequently, we overhear the father urge the son to accept his words and keep them with diligence because

They are life to those who find them,
    and healing to all their flesh. (4:22)

or so that

> When you walk, they will lead you;
>> when you lie down, they will watch over you,
>> and when you awake, they will talk with you.
> For the commandment is a lamp and the teaching a light,
>> and the reproofs of discipline are the way of life. (6:22-23)

And while this path may not offer quick access to the "good life," at least those who choose wisdom are not dying for their choice. Because death is the true destiny for those who refuse to accept wisdom.

> For human ways are under the eyes of the Lord,
>> and he examines all their paths.
> The iniquities of the wicked ensnare them,
>> and they are caught in the toils of their sin.
> They die for lack of discipline,
>> and because of their great folly they are lost. (5:21-23)

Or in the father's story of the young man who became involved with an "other" woman:

> Right away he follows her,
>> and goes like an ox to the slaughter,
> or bounds like a stag toward the trap
>> until an arrow pierces its entrails.
> He is like a bird rushing into a snare,
>> not knowing that it will cost him his life. (7:21-23)

The path of wisdom is the way to life—genuine, full, and complete. And though at first it may not appear to be so, every other trail leads to death—a night of the living dead.[4] So the sages' task (and our own) is nothing less than convincing those who hear us that what we teach *is life*. Of course, such a task demands that our proclamation from week to week is, in fact, life-giving.

Persuasion in the Interludes of Proverbs 1-9

Interspersed among the ten lectures, five interludes further the efforts to persuade the reader in favor of wisdom. In these texts, with the exception of 6:1-19, wisdom comes to life as a woman in order to make her own appeal. Woman Wisdom, however, is not the only woman in Proverbs 1-9. The sages do not operate in a vacuum, but in the real world of competing voices. And so another woman or group of women is also in competition for the son's favors: dangerous women who threaten the demise of the son (e.g., 2:16-19, 7:6-23).[5]

I
A wife of noble character who can find? (31:10)

While the literature on Woman Wisdom is vast and provides many insights into her presence, one persuasive aspect is fairly obvious: Woman Wisdom is *a woman*. In a book with explicit interest in persuading young men (1:4), it should not be surprising that wisdom is portrayed as a woman. As one who observes young people every day on a college campus, I can testify that a sure way to get a young person's attention is to talk about the opposite sex. And just as we might expect, Proverbs 1-9 presents this woman as *the one* a young man should pursue. After an initial declaration of "blessed" for anyone who finds wisdom the poet dazzles the reader with her value:

> for her income is better than silver,
>> and her revenue better than gold.
> She is more precious than jewels,
>> and nothing you desire can compare with her.
> Long life is in her right hand;
>> in her left hand are riches and honor.
> Her ways are ways of pleasantness,
>> and all her paths are peace.
> She is a tree of life to those who lay hold of her;
>> those who hold her fast are called happy. (3:14-18)

It is possible that the poet has in mind a patron-client relationship with Woman Wisdom. The key terms, however, make me think of a more intimate setting. She is "more precious" than anything (or perhaps anyone) the son might desire. More evocatively, the son should "lay hold" of her and never let her go ("hold her fast").

Along these lines, a little later in the text the father takes up the personification and urges the son to "Say to wisdom, 'You are my sister,' and call insight your intimate friend" (7:4). Similar terminology appears in the Song of Solomon to denote a romantic, even marital relationship.[6] In other words, the father and mother present wisdom to the son in the form of a desirable woman and urge him to marry this woman—to make her his life. She alone has the capacity to bless him beyond his wildest dreams—in contrast to the other women who lurk and lead to death (e.g., 2:16-19, 7:6-23). In this way marriage to Woman Wisdom is comparable to the metaphor of the path or life-long journey.

The possibility of life spent as one flesh with wisdom comes to a grand finale in Proverbs 31, the well-known ode to the woman of valor. Here the sages describe the ideal wife in terms reminiscent of the description of Woman Wisdom in Proverbs 1-9. She is beyond any realistic portrait of an ideal wife, never sleeping (31:15, 18), working non-stop (31:13-16, 18-19, 24), and always blessing her husband, family, and community (31:11-12, 20-21, 27-28). She embodies the fear of the Lord (31:30). Certainly, we should all seek to follow wisdom's example. But the key idea in this concluding chapter is the celebration of the many good things this woman (wisdom) will have done for the young man—if only he has made her his wife.

II
Before I formed you in the womb I knew you,
and before you were born I consecrated you;
I appointed you a prophet to the nations.
Jeremiah 1:5

The persuasive quality of Woman Wisdom is not exhausted with the idea of an attractive and available woman. In her first appearance in the book, Woman Wisdom speaks with a voice reminiscent of Israel's prophets:

How long, O simple ones, will you love being simple?
How long will scoffers delight in their scoffing
    and fools hate knowledge?
Give heed to my reproof;
I will pour out my thoughts to you;
    I will make my words known to you. (1:22-23)

Like a prophet she expresses dire consequences for those who have refused to accept her words. Because she has tried to help them but been rejected (scorned), she will laugh when calamity strikes (and it will). Only then will those who reject her turn back and call for help, but then it will be too late. They had their chance to accept her counsel; now they will suffer the fate of their decision (1:24-33). Wisdom is a woman to be reckoned with, a powerful prophet who speaks for God.

III

Before the mountains had been shaped,
before the hills, I was brought forth . . .
When he established the heavens, I was there . . .
then I was beside him, like a master worker.

8:25, 27a, 30a

Woman Wisdom, however, is even more than a prophet. In chapter 8, another text with vast secondary literature, wisdom initially takes a royal persona. She speaks of "noble things" (*negidim*, 8:6a) with an honesty that refuses to stretch or bend the truth (8:6-9). She possesses "good advice and sound wisdom" (8:14a), along with honor and "enduring wealth" (8:18), while Wisdom herself is of far greater value than gold, silver, jewels, or any other point of comparison (8:10,11, 19). And it is through Wisdom's insight and strength that she claims:

By me kings reign,
    and rulers decree what is just;
by me rulers rule,
    and nobles, all who govern rightly. (8:15-16)

Wisdom is not just the good woman who stands behind every great man. She is the insight and power operant in every upright throne, presidency, or leader.

But there is still more to be said for Woman Wisdom, much more. In 8:22-31 her story takes a remarkable turn. First, she "was given birth" by God before the world began (8:24-25). Some translations are somewhat unclear that the Hebrew term in verses 22 and 24 (*khyl*) commonly denotes the process of labor and birth.[7] Second, as the daughter of God, Wisdom was at Yahweh's side during creation (8:27-31). Her precise role is ambiguous due to uncertainty surrounding the key term *'amon* in verse 30. Proposals are unusually diverse: master worker, craftsman, confidant, sage, infant, ward, growing up, or continually present—just to mention a few options. Within a context that has mentioned the birth of daughter wisdom prior to creation (8:22-26), the idea of "infant" or "growing up" fits the context—with the consequent sense in verse 30 of something like a "bring your daughter to work day," with "little Wisdom" playing, dancing, and taking great joy in her father's creation (vv. 30-31). But while the nuance of the image may be unclear, the persuasive quality of the personification is not. Because of Wisdom's divine essence and her presence at creation, the sons should accept her instruction. She was there at the beginning and knows how the world works. So she concludes:

> And now, my children, listen to me:
> > happy are those who keep my ways.
> Hear instruction and be wise,
> > and do not neglect it.
> Happy is the one who listens to me,
> > watching daily at my gates,
> > waiting beside my doors.
> For whoever finds me finds life
> > and obtains favor from the Lord;
> but those who miss me injure themselves;
> > all who hate me love death. (8:32-36)

From the mundane to bold acts of imagination the sages make every attempt in the early chapters of Proverbs to persuade the sons and the readers to choose the way of wisdom. In the lectures they work to gain a hearing, tell the truth about wisdom, and enumerate the benefits of this way of life. And in the interludes wisdom comes to life as an eligible and highly desirable woman for marriage, a prophet who speaks for God, and God's daughter who was present when the world began. The sages have made their case for wisdom, though they have presented little of wisdom's actual content. Presupposing a favorable response to their appeal, the content of wisdom awaits the reader in Proverbs 10-31.

Persuasion in Proverbs 10-31

A word fitly spoken is like apples of gold in a setting of silver.
Proverbs 25:11

At the Conference on Preaching at Lipscomb University, we discussed the persuasive qualities of the sayings in Proverbs 10-31 by first asking participants to share memorable proverbs—a request supported by numerous contributions. Although hardly scientific and fully aware of the significant cultural differences between ourselves and ancient Israelites, what we observed from this exercise provides an entry point for understanding how proverbs persuade.

I
My Grandfather used to say,
"Study long, study wrong."

First, a proverb influences us because of who spoke it to us. It was remarkable how often a conference participant shared a proverb in our session or later in writing—only after first telling who said it to him or her. Perhaps I prompted this attribution by asking the audience to write down proverbs that they remembered from their parents or grandparents. But I do not think these attributions were solely due to my request: 1) because not all of the shared proverbs stemmed from the sources I mentioned, and 2) because of the stress several participants placed on the identity of the speaker. A proverb prompts memory and the voice of an authority. So it was an *English teacher* who warned, "Mess with the bull and you get the horns," a *grandfather* who said, "Study long, study wrong," and a *great-grandfather via a mother* who hurried the family with "People won't care what you look like, but they'll remember you getting there late." Whether the source of our memory actually coined or originated the saying is irrelevant. In fact, I observed that in some cases individuals remembered the same proverb through different voices. One person's mother and another's father both said, "Whether you think you can or you think you can't, you are probably right." Others vividly recalled parents and grandparents who had favorite biblical proverbs. Obviously the parent or grandparent did not coin the saying, "Trust in the Lord with all your heart and lean not on your own understanding," but it was through these people that the proverb took on meaning for the daughter or son, not its mere existence in the biblical text. The important thing—what makes a proverb persuasive— is the authoritative voice of the speaker. To be fair, at the conference we did have at least one person who recalled a proverb from a disrespected authority (a former coach); so we should take our point with moderation. Nonetheless, like many other forms of communication, a proverb comes to life and persuades through personality and our esteem for the speaker; a saying from a less respected source is unlikely to carry the same weight.

II
Stick to the wicket
and the runs will come.

Second, we observed that proverbs are deeply rooted in and reliant on cultural values and references. In my classes on Wisdom Literature at Abilene Christian University, I frequently begin with the same exercise of sharing favorite proverbs. Given university student instincts, the class often turns to the funniest or catchiest sayings they can remember. So we swap proverbs, listen, and laugh until we turn to our international students, who had sat politely but quietly while their American colleagues spoke. But now, with broad smiles and their own laughter they recite sayings from their homeland—first in their native tongue of German, Japanese, Spanish, and Portuguese. And then, although these students are fluent in English, they stumble over their translations: "It means something like . . . but that's not exactly it . . . in German it sounds different. . . ." Meanwhile, their American colleagues now sit quietly. Never has the dictum "To translate is to lie" been so eloquently demonstrated. Consider the following examples:

> *Mokopi o na le marago a malele* (Botswana)
> A beggar has a long bottom (must be willing to wait)
> *Allen Leuten recht gutan*
>   *ist eine Kunst die niemand kann.* (German)
> Making it right for everyone is an art that no one can do.
> *Mas sabe el Diablo por Viejo de que por diablo* (South American)
> The devil knows more because he is old than because he is the devil.
> *Hecha la ley*
>   *hecha la trampa.* (South American)
> As soon as the law is made, the trick is made.

Spoken aloud, each of these proverbs has a rhythm or even rhyme; but when we hear a translation we are left cold. A translated proverb may be true enough, but it lacks appeal. The media of sound and rhythm are lost, impossible to convey in another language.

Culture, of course, stretches well beyond language to include a group's values, practices, and much more. And so, consequently even English proverbs (for English speakers) are subject to a loss of meaning due to cultural slippage. For example, a colleague at the conference mentioned a proverb I had heard once before:

> A whistling woman and a cackling hen
> come to no good end.

The rhyme is obvious to me, but why a whistling woman should meet the fate of a cackling hen is part of American culture that predates my time. A variant of the saying simplifies the idea:

> A whistling woman will never marry.

I suspect this second version is a later attempt to update the proverb for an audience removed from cackling hens. It explains the enigma of the proverb and in the process loses much of the original appeal. Or to repeat the proverb from the heading of this section:

> Stick to the wicket
> and the runs will come.

This saying appears to be English (literally), but its meaning was a bit beyond our befuddled American audience (especially this American).

While not all proverbs engage language, sound, and unique cultural references to the extent of these examples, the observation nonetheless stands: culture plays a pivotal role in the persuasive quality of proverbs. In fact, proverbs are often so embedded in culture that even the most precise transplants will leave meaning and, thus, persuasiveness behind. I may want my students to set aside all distractions and just keep trying, but if they do not understand the game of cricket, telling them to "stick to the wicket" is unlikely to be of much help. Or I might have liked to encourage my daughter (when she was much younger) to exercise good manners, but to speak to her of whistling women and cackling hens would have only caused her to lose all decorum as she rolled about on the floor in laughter.[8]

III

Like a dog that returns to its vomit
is a fool who reverts to his folly.
Proverbs 26:11

Third, from examples given at the conference we observed that proverbs often convey their message in enigmatic ways to capture the hearer's imagination. It may be humor or a striking image that stirs reflection, or it might be a powerful truth expressed in such a memorable way that the proverb evokes internalization that ultimately shapes character. To take a few examples from the sublime to the graphic:

> He who sweats in peace
>> will not bleed in war.
>> (Asian)
> You cannot wake one who pretends to be sleeping.
>> (Navajo)

> The rich rules over the poor,
>> and the borrower is the slave of the lender.
>> (Prov. 22:7)

> Give a pig and a boy everything they want,
>> and you'll end up with a good pig
>> and a bad boy.

Whether proverbs cause us to laugh so hard we cannot catch our breath or are breath-taking in their simplicity and insight, everything relies on the hearer catching the enigma. Some denote this feature as the "gap" between the lines of the proverb; how are these two or three statements connected? What is the linking idea? But however we may describe it, like a joke or parable, if a speaker has to explain the enigma then the proverb has lost its power. If our hearer does not understand such ideas as sweating in peace, pretending to sleep, or enslaving debt, then the sayings above do not work. Or if they have never seen a fat pig or a dog eat its own vomit, the proverbs miss their mark. The moment we explain a joke, it is no longer funny; the moment we explain a proverb, it loses much of its power to persuade.

What we have just said about how the sayings of the book of Proverbs go about their task of character formation makes our task of preaching from this text enormously difficult. Other than a general attribution to Solomon and a few other ancients, unless the voices of parents, grandparents, teachers, or others of high esteem have brought us these sayings, the assortment of sentences in Proverbs 10-31 comes to us apart from any influential guide. And at least for most people these days, a claim that the saying comes from Scripture does little to help. Instead, these sayings originate in an alien language and culture, both of which must be translated. Even then, often times our hearers (or we) will not catch the enigma hidden in the ancient text so that we find it necessary to explain the riddle. Must we destroy the proverb in order to preach it? Other difficulties, not explored here, also abound: the general rather than absolute nature of proverbs (e.g., 22:6), the challenge of knowing when a proverb intends to describe the world without affirmation and when it means to prescribe what should be (e.g., compare 17:8 to 10:2), or the wisdom we need to know when a proverb applies and when it does not (e.g., 26:5-6). Perhaps, in the words of another shared saying:

> It is better to remain silent
> and be thought a fool,
> than to open one's mouth
> and remove all doubt.

Preaching from Proverbs is not for the faint of heart.

Better is the end of a thing than its beginning.
(Ecclesiastes 7:8a)

The sages of the book of Proverbs were engaged in what they took to be a life or death struggle for the character and, therefore, the destiny of the reader. To suggest that their concern was merely to provide insider information for how to get ahead in life, be happy, or have more wealth is to seriously misread Proverbs and misunderstand the idea of wisdom. True, wisdom may lead to such benefits but only secondarily. The path of wisdom is a life-long course of character development that changes a person from the inside out. And because transformation is their goal, the sages engage in what may be aptly described as a battle against all comers.

   The results of our brief investigation into the persuasive qualities of the genres of Proverbs may have unearthed no dazzling new discovery. Instead, we have discovered the sages work to be *haba na haba Ujaza kibaba* ("little by little fills the bucket"). Find a way to solicit an authentic hearing, speak the truth about the path of wisdom, and convince the audience that the difficult trail is the way to life. And whether drawn from Israel's past, her surrounding world, or a courageous act of vivid imagination, when wisdom comes to life as a woman in Proverbs 1-9, her presence rearranges the discursive field of battle. Desirable for marriage, a prophet who speaks for God, a queen, and Yahweh's daughter present at creation—she invites and draws the son into a new world of possibility. But even then, once the son chooses wisdom over folly, the sage's task is not done. The sage in Proverbs never stops teaching the way of wisdom, engaging culture with effective tools and techniques, limited only by the character of wisdom herself.

THE BEGINNING OF WISDOM
Proverbs 1:1-8

THOMAS G. LONG

En Route to the Sermon

Tom Long's sermon contrasts living "the good life" with living "a good life." Glenn Pemberton would identify "the good life" as a description of what the gang offers in Proverbs 1:8-19, power and material wealth. In contrast, "a good life" is what wisdom offers. Living a good life is by far the more difficult path to follow but results in deeper satisfaction and a richer relationship with others and with God. In this sermon Long identifies "a good life" with the most common saying in the book of Proverbs, "the fear of the Lord." The fear of the Lord is a difficult relationship by which to live. Contrary to what we might hope, Long maintains that the concept does involve "gut-clinching dread." It means that "the stakes are high" when it comes to choosing the path of life we will follow. The fear of the Lord removes us from the center of life and puts God at the center. It means that our Christianity is not just a ritual or a Sunday event. Rather it shapes all of our thoughts and actions. It is, as both Pemberton and Long assert, to practice a life style.

With faithful imagination, Long drives us deeper into the experience of faith to show how it manifests itself in wisdom and how Christianity looks when it is a practice. This sermon was preached at the Conference on Preaching at Lipscomb University, October 2009.

The Sermon _____

Several years ago, a young man who had just graduated from an Ivy League school and who was venturing out into the world for the first time on his own, wrote in the *New Yorker* about some of apprehensions. He said that he felt fully prepared to live the good life, a life "full of bay windows and summer vacations and dinner out whenever," but that he hungered for more. I not only crave *the* good life, he said. I also want to live "*a* good life, at peace with [myself]."[1] *The* good life . . . *a* good life.

Well, guidance on how to live *a* good life is precisely what the Book of Proverbs claims to provide. In fact, these opening verses sound, according to Old Testament scholar Christine Yoder, like a blurb on the dust jacket of a book at Barnes and Noble.[2] Read this book, they exclaim, and you will learn how to be wise, savvy, fair, balanced, and righteous—strategies and techniques for living *a* good life. Indeed, if Proverbs were a Barnes and Noble book, we would probably find it shelved in the self-help section, right between *Who Moved My Cheese?* and Donald Trump's *The Art of the Deal*.

Except . . . for that last verse of the prologue, "The fear of the Lord is the beginning of wisdom." The fear of the Lord is the dominant theme in Proverbs. It is all through this book; the phrase appears fourteen times in thirty-one chapters. It begins the book, and it ends the book. It is the meter to which the music of Proverbs is sung, the parentheses that bracket all of its teaching. According to Proverbs, there is no wisdom, there is no living *a* good life, outside of the fear of the Lord. The fear of the Lord is the beginning of wisdom.

When we run across that phrase "the fear of the Lord," we usually hasten to say that "the fear of the Lord" doesn't really mean "the *fear* of the Lord," being afraid of God, cowering in dread before the divine presence . . . it means something kinder and gentler . . . something like awe or reverence. The awe of the Lord is the beginning of wisdom. True, but maybe we move a little too quickly here. There is in the ancient term "the fear of the Lord" at least an element of gut-clinching dread, and perhaps it ought to be in our theological repertoire, too. Proverbs wants us to know that wisdom is not kid stuff, the stakes are high, and there is reason to be afraid, very afraid. Not afraid of an angry and vengeful God, but, perhaps the best way to put it is, to be alert to God's power and presence and to be afraid of what life would become, who *we* would become, were life not infused with God's mercy, providence, guidance, and care.

One ancient devotional tradition in the church, the *Ars Moriendi*, or "Art of Dying Well" tradition, imagined what terrors would unfold were God's mercy and protection not surrounding us. This devotional tradition imagined a conversation between Satan and the dying person:

Satan: You're frightened, aren't you?

Dying person: Yes, I am frightened, but I am trusting my savior who calms my fears.

Satan: Oh really? You think you are going to be rewarded by this Jesus, don't you? You who have no righteousness.

Dying person: Christ is my righteousness.

Satan: Oh ho, Christ is your righteousness? You think Christ will welcome you to the company of Peter and Paul and the apostles? You who have sinned over and over again?

Dying person: No, I am not going into the company of Peter and Paul. I am going into the company of the thief on the cross, who heard the promise, "Today, you will be with me in paradise."

Satan: Legions of demons are salivating, waiting for your soul.

Dying person: And I would be hopeless and fearful before that, if the Lord had not already crushed your tyranny.[3]

To have the fear of the Lord is to know God's power, a power we desperately need to free us from the snares of sin and death.

To have the fear of the Lord is to know that the stakes are high. But, to have the fear of the Lord is *also* to know that God cannot be compartmentalized in Sunday morning, by theological schools, or through religious devotions. God *wanders*, as Proverbs is eager to tell us, through the pathways, marketplaces, and family rooms of our lives. God is concerned about our prayers and liturgies. But, God *also* cares about weights and measures, honesty in speech, and words of kindness spoken to a neighbor.

In Richard Lischer's wonderful book *Open Secrets*, he tells about the first church he served as a pastor, a small Lutheran congregation in the rural Midwest. He recounts how, behind the altar, stood a stained glass window, one he calls "our best window." The window showed a graphic depiction of the trinity, a triangle of lines connecting Latin words for Father, Son, and Holy Spirit. Lischer says that the light shone through this window on all of their important services and ceremonies. They worshipped under this window, consecrated marriages under this window, and buried the dead under this window. Then he comments:

> An aerial photographer once remarked that from the air you can see paths, like the canals on Mars, that crisscross pastures and fields among the farms where neighbors have trudged for generations, just to visit or help one another in times of need. These, too, are the highways among *Pater, Filius,* and *Spiritus Sanctus* grooved into human relationships. The word "religion" comes from the same root as "ligaments." These are the ties that bind.[4]

If our doctrines are to become more than creeds in a book, they must become wisdom, the ligaments that tie our lives together. The fear of the Lord finally governs how we shape our everyday lives of faith. I read recently of a little Roman Catholic congregation in the English village of Morebath.[5] This parish had a priest who served them faithfully for nearly fifty years, and he kept a detailed journal chronicling life in the church and village. And what were the people of the parish doing? The ordinary things that church people do. Some women were sewing a new set of black vestments for their beloved priest, and others were boiling beeswax to make candles for the masses. Still others were tending a flock of sheep dedicated to the parish, the wool being sold to supplement the church budget. And the whole congregation was divided into groups, committees actually, and each was assigned one of the statues of the saints. The groups cleaned and tended to the statues, and one Sunday a year, each committee's statue was honored in worship.

But then, the English Reformation occurred, and overnight the little parish in Morebath went from being Catholic to Protestant. Out went the black vestments, the beeswax candles, and the statues. And parish life waned, because Christianity was now being interpreted as a set of *ideas* rather than a set of practices. Faith lost its shape, lost its grounding in everyday life, lost its capacity to form wisdom.

The fear of the Lord also drives us deeper into life, makes us unwilling to live only at the surface level. The way the prologue puts it, the fear of the Lord gives the wisdom needed to plumb riddles and parables, to be discerning.

When I was a student serving as a CPE chaplain at an Atlanta hospital, one night I was the chaplain on call. I received word that I was needed on a certain floor, and I went. What had happened was that a patient, a middle-aged woman, had gone into cardiac arrest, and the emergency team had rushed into her room to attempt to revive her. The family had been shooed away to the waiting room, and there is where I found them. We talked and prayed together, waiting through tense and anxious moments. Finally, a young and frightened resident physician came to the family room and said, "I'm sorry. We did all we could. We have called her physician to come talk to you. He's on his way." Members of the family began to sob in deep grief.

In about twenty minutes, the physician arrived, entered the room, and gave a stiffly delivered medical school lecture on what had killed the wife and mother of this family. He then turned on his heels and left. I prayed once more with them, and then they left the hospital to travel home in sorrow.

It was now quite late, and I went to the hospital vending room to get some coffee. To my surprise, I found someone already there, sitting at a table nursing a cup of coffee. It was the physician. He looked up at me, recognized me from the family room, and he said, "I killed her." He then told me that he had ordered some blood work to be done. The results were on his desk, and he looked at them on his way out the door to play golf. Her tests results were normal, so he called the nurses' station, took her off some medications, and headed for the links. "I should have known," he said, "that her chemistry could not have returned to normal so quickly, but I was in a hurry. I was looking at another patient's blood tests. I made a mistake, and I killed her."

"Oh no," I said, stupidly. "You didn't do anything wrong. It could have happened to anyone."

I wish I could take back those words. This physician was trying to discern wisdom, was trying to claim the language of confession and sin, and I tried to snatch it away. My words deprived him of the depth to which wisdom was calling. He was not trying to get off the hook, he was trying to figure out how he lost his way, trying to solve a riddle, how to confess his sin.

The fear of the Lord is the beginning of wisdom. The fear of God leads us to a kind of wisdom that enables us to know what counts in life, what truly matters and what will pass away. In Saul Bellow's *Mr. Sammler's Planet*, Sammler gazes at the face of his dead friend, Elya Gruner, as he prays. His prayer is full of the wisdom of God:

> Remember, God, the soul of Elya Gruner, who as willingly as possible and as well as he was able, and even to an intolerable point, and even in suffocation and even as death was coming was eager . . . to do what was required of him . . . . He was aware that he must meet, and he did meet—through all the confusion and degraded clowning of this life . . . the terms of his contract. The terms which, in his inmost heart, each man knows . . . For that is the truth of it—that we all know, God. . . .[6]

CAUTION: CONTENTS MAY BE HOT

Proverbs 3:1-26

KARL J. MCLARTY

En Route to the Sermon

Because Proverbs has long been a favorite of mine, I had used it often in classes at church, but I had struggled to give it center stage in my preaching. I decided in the fall of 2009 to preach a series of Sunday night sermons on Proverbs. Cloverdale Church of Christ in Searcy, Arkansas, has an older demographic on Sunday nights due to the success of small groups among our younger members. This allowed the sermons to be more directed at those seeking to give wisdom than the actual recipients of wisdom. This was the kickoff sermon on November 15, 2009.

I leaned heavily upon the question posed by Glenn Pemberton in his essay at the beginning of this chapter. The question is, "How do the sages of Proverbs convince readers to choose wisdom?" I sought to capture the pathos of that question through the eyes of the individuals who had raised the young man and were facing the moment of "cutting the apron strings" and letting him stand on his own. Pemberton touched on three types of material found in Proverbs: lectures, interludes, and short, pithy sayings. In the lecture material I found validation for the emotions of the parents, and therefore sought to capture their attention with this in the first move of the sermon. In the sages parents can find a sympathetic ear and a resource for wisdom in the challenges of parenting. I strove to make parents feel a sense of camaraderie with the sages in their shared struggle to impart wisdom. Based on this kindred struggle, parents would wish to know more about this neglected book that acknowledges the joys and heartaches of all parents who watch their children leave the home.

Between the first and second types of material, I inserted two items of my own to clarify the place of wisdom in the Bible, which is more often mined for exciting narratives or revealed laws than wisdom's insights into the "skill of living" or "how to navigate life well."[1] The contrast between Wisdom and Torah was an insight I found in Walter Brueggemann.[2] Wisdom does not come packaged in what most often sells, but it has a value of its own that can attract and stand the test of time. The second item I inserted was the place of wisdom in reaching that stage of life called manhood. In our culture there is no definitive "rite of passage," but that doesn't stop every young man from seeking what it takes to be viewed as a man and no longer a boy. Wisdom is a crucial element to the transition.

In the second material by Pemberton, I found the personification of wisdom as a woman to be a successful assault on every barrier that would normally be raised against sapiential wisdom. As he pointed out all the ways the sages worked this metaphor, I began to consider ways that I could do this in order to accomplish the same result. Although the first move of the sermon targeted the parents, it also gave the young man a place in the sermon that now was moved to the front and center.

The journey image at the sermon's end was not from the third material, short, pithy sayings, but was a return to the lectures. The sages explained that wisdom was not a destination but a path, a road, a trip. I felt that the road-trip of life was capable of bringing all the pieces together. This also brought the sermon back to the living room where it began. Now the parents know they have a resource in Proverbs, and young persons have been given a new appreciation for this book in navigating their future challenges.

The Sermon

"My son, do not forget my teaching, but keep my commands in your heart . . ." (Prov. 3:1) and "My son, preserve sound judgment and discernment, do not let them out of your sight . . ." (Prov. 3:21). We are separated by several millennia and cultural differences, but there is the sound of parental pleading that comes through loud and clear. The young man is leaving home to explore a large and dangerous world. The parents' concern wells up and cries out, "Take care, drive safe, and don't be reckless," but the son sees only friends, car keys, and freedom waiting outside the front door. Desperation mixes with expectations, and the room is full of transmitters sending to a receiver that is set on another frequency. Mom looks to dad with a "Don't let my baby go out the door without a few more words," to which dad signals back, "I'm doing the best I can, Dear, but he is growing up fast." A timeless and natural rite of passage has again occurred, demanding more than a few words at the moment of departure. Can anything be effectively said? Voice another concern? Sound another warning? Set out one more insight? Just more acts of desperation from the parents heard as another lecture by the youth. Yet, the sages of Israel had a few more ideas that were consistent with the teachings of home, while playing to the age-relevant concerns of the youth.

The sages had their work cut out for them at the wisdom school of Israel. The freshman class would have been restless and over confident like every class before and after them. The first seven verses of Proverbs reads like a syllabus and sound like a great idea for a continuing education program for senior citizens. The class on Torah would be much more to their liking. Plagues on Egypt, conquest of the Promise Land, a small boy with five stones and a sling defeating a giant Philistine are stories that capture the imagination and fire the spirit with honor, sacrifice, and courage. In addition, Torah speaks to the presence of God in the darkest of times. When all seems lost, God fights for Israel and the enemy is overthrown! These are not just interesting topics for study; the young pay money and give up free time to experience these stories. How can wisdom compete?

Last week I sat in my blue recliner and noticed a children's book resting on the arm. I picked it up and began to reread the familiar story of *The Gingerbread Man*. When the gingerbread man spoke, I could hear the voice of the same character in the movie *Shrek 2*. The character was the same, but the book and the movie were completely different. In *Shrek 2* the hero has been separated from his wife by the scheming of a fairy godmother and her complicit son, Prince Charming. As the plot builds to the climax, the gingerbread man helps Shrek create a supersized gingerbread man. Together the good guys charge the castle facing strong opposition until, under a barrage of steaming milk, the gingerbread man dies in service of good and defeat of evil. The story was like Torah with the hero facing overwhelming odds and yet with the loyalty of friends, courage, and conviction of the right, good overcame evil in an unexpected denouement! This is the gingerbread man that sells movie tickets and DVDs. But that isn't the gingerbread man that has been a children's story for hundreds of years. The gingerbread man is about wisdom and folly. A small cookie comes to life and eludes all efforts to be captured and eaten by his sheer foot speed. Soon his mocking cry, "Run, run as fast as you can, but you can't catch me, I'm the gingerbread man" falls on the ears of the fox. The fox is patient and calculating and the foolish young cookie accepts a river crossing on the back of the fox. Before the two cross the river, the young cookie is eaten. "For the waywardness of the simple will kill them, and the complacency of fools will destroy them" (Prov. 1:32). If a wisdom story of a cookie can be hijacked by Hollywood, what is wisdom to do in the face of great stories from Torah? In addition to appearing, in contrast, boring, wisdom has even been accused of being heavy on anthropology and light on theology. God is the hero of all the stories of great reversal, but wisdom advises against placing oneself in positions that are high on risk and low on odds. The young men, who are already suspicious of a class that seems to be low on adrenaline and risk, are now armed with a scriptural reason to object to wisdom. The sages may be down, but don't count them out. Notice the attraction of wisdom.

Two men and a boy walk into a bar. No, this is not the start of a joke, but the midpoint of the movie "Second Hand Lions" starring Michael Cane, Robert Duvall, and Haley Joel Osment. Garth and Hub are two old bachelor brothers that have been left with a great-nephew Walter. Walter's mother has made poor choices in life and as a result Walter doesn't know what it means to be a good man. While eating at the bar, some young men begin picking on Hub who in self-defense beats them all up. He then takes them to the house and gives them an unusual speech. Holding fresh steaks on their black eyes, Hub speaks about honor, courage, loyalty, and much more. We don't get to hear the "everything you need to know about being a man speech," but what little we do stirs something inside of every man. Boys don't want to just grow up, they want to be men and be recognized as worthy of respect by others. Walter begins to seek the opportunity to hear that speech, and little by little he is given the pieces in their appropriate time. The sages predict a similar moment of embarrassing discipline and rebuke for the students of Proverbs (3:11) but promise that God is making men out of them (v. 12). There will be pain followed by insights and for the ones who humbly accept God's wisdom, God will say, "That's my boy."

Then comes a brilliant marketing strategy by the sages. Wisdom is personified as a woman that the young man is to pursue (3:13). She is accessible to all but found only by those who are diligent. In a world where money can buy anything but time, she can accomplish more (v. 14). She is more desirable than anything a young man could imagine (v. 15). In an age where men crave to be respected by their peers, she will bestow honor (v. 16). She will provide the good life if you only will hold on to her (vv. 17-18). The tide of wisdom appears to be turning at this point. Maybe wisdom isn't so bad; maybe the book of Proverbs could bear some looking through.

Next, the sages spring the surprising fact that wisdom is not static. There is a journey to be taken and wisdom goes along as the expert guide (3:23-26). It is said that old men speak of the past because it is all they have and young men speak of the future for the same reason. Miley Ray Cyrus' hit song "The Climb" captures the enthusiasm and need to have a journey worthy of the energy and determination of every young person.

The ministry staff tries to get together on Thursdays for a cup of coffee and a time of swapping stories, sharing insights, and strategizing. The coffee house last month had gotten new paper cups that were very colorful. As I waited for the others to arrive, I began to study the cup, noticing that it told a story. The picture began with a young man sitting alone at an outdoor coffee house enjoying a cup of coffee. His hands are on the cup, but his eyes are looking to the right. I slowly turned the cup counter-clockwise to see what was eliciting such attention from this young man. Two young women are sitting a few tables away and are returning the gaze. In fine print below the women is the statement: "caution: contents may be hot." I laughed to myself wondering if such a placement for a warning about the temperature of my coffee was coincidence. Thinking about this imagery in Proverbs, I know that one woman is Wisdom, but I'm not sure if the other is her roommate Prudence (8:12) or her friend Understanding (3:13).

And so we watch our young adult walking through the door that will lead to a world of so many possibilities. We know in our heart we must say something, but what is going to be heard at such a time as this? "Don't play in the street," "Brush your teeth before bed," "Always say thank you and please" have all been good advice but are not suitable for this moment. Most of our wisdom has been to protect the child from mistakes that could have negative long-term consequences. Now we look on and know that a new vision of an old wisdom is needed to outfit the young man to face the world. Now is the time to hear the sages and point to a life with wisdom, a life which first of all includes the promise that God is going to be making a man of you that will make the world a better place. Secondly, it is a life ruled by God's creation, Lady Wisdom, who is attractive, challenging, and worthy of your greatest attentions. Lastly, it is a life that will be a journey demanding decisions, determination, and discernment if you are to succeed. In short, point the youth to wisdom and say, "If you can handle it, get wisdom. But realize that you are taking the difficult road and will need to dig deep in your soul to endure. God has built the world with wisdom and has offered that same wisdom to you if you are willing to accept the challenge. You may need to give up everything else in order to gain wisdom, but you won't mind when you understand the fear of the LORD (2:5). There in his presence you will realize that nothing compares to the wisdom of God. So step out the door and walk in wisdom if you dare. Just remember, "Caution: contents may be hot."

THE PROVERBIAL DEAD END STREET

Finding Wisdom at the End of Our Rational Rope

(Proverbs 14:12; 16:25; 30:1-4)

KEVIN J. YOUNGBLOOD

En Route to the Sermon

Glenn Pemberton's insightful essay on the rhetoric of Proverbs raises the question of how wisdom's voice is to be heard above the competing voices in the marketplace promising the same thing wisdom offers but at a fraction of the cost and time. Wisdom fights an uphill battle in her effort to draw those who are young and inexperienced away from deceptive promises of shortcuts to the good life which seem to come from every direction. Her strategy, however, is not to engage in a price war with those offering bargains on a rich and fulfilling life. Rather, Wisdom wages a rhetorical war on such offers, exposing the lethal fallacy of the world's cheap substitutes for genuine sagacity and integrity. Proverbs 14:12, repeated in 16:25, serves as a striking example of Wisdom's rhetorical strategy.

This proverb is like the recent Office Max commercial that tells the story of a local barber who suddenly finds himself competing with a national chain. Across the street, the national chain begins offering haircuts for only $5.00. Of course, he cannot engage in a price war with such a marketing giant without losing his shirt. Not to be outdone, however, he wins the rhetorical war by purchasing supplies at Office Max to make a sign of his own: "We fix $5.00 haircuts."

The inexperienced may experiment with life's shortcuts, but inevitably they will be disappointed and come looking for the solution to their dilemma. Proverbs capitalizes on the experience of those who have been down the shortcut and know that it leads nowhere. Thus, my sermon on Proverbs 14:12

relies heavily on Pemberton's insights into Proverbs's rhetorical strategy and how this strategy contrasts with that of the competition.

Pemberton notes that the prevailing metaphor in Proverbs 1-9 is the "path or road on which we travel." I believe that this is true not only of Proverbs 1-9 but all of Proverbs, and I exploit this metaphor as a rhetorical strategy throughout the sermon, much as Proverbs does. In fact, I use Proverbs 1-9 as well as Proverbs 30-31 as a kind of hermeneutical framework within which to understand the sentence sayings that span the chasm between these two collections of longer sayings.

Pemberton reveals a key difficulty in preaching the sentence sayings of Proverbs when he observes: ". . . often times our hearers (or we) will not catch the enigma hidden in the ancient text so that we find it necessary to explain the riddle. Must we destroy the proverb in order to preach it?" He has well expressed the frustration that many literarily sensitive preachers feel when confronted with the task of turning an aphorism into a sermon. The two genres are not exactly compatible.

I have tried to retain the rhetorical power of the proverb by allowing surrounding proverbs to serve as interpretive aids. Since my proverb occurs twice, I play on the different nuance it has in its different environments. It occurs first in a collection focused on the righteous/wicked, wise/foolish, diligent/lazy oppositions. These oppositions in the surrounding proverbs certainly color the way one reads Proverbs 14:12. Its second occurrence (16:25), however, is in a collection focused on proper relationships between king and subjects, including proper relationships between the divine king, Yahweh, and his covenant people. In this setting, the proverb takes on a slightly different hue. Thus the flexibility of the proverb is highlighted as is the need for careful application appropriate to the situation.

Finally, I connect the proverb to portions of Proverbs 1 – 9 and Proverbs 30 – 31 via the road/path/journey metaphor to further elucidate its depth. Since these two sections frame the sentence sayings and elaborate on the themes and metaphors compacted in the aphorisms, they serve as an effective hermeneutical tool while keeping the proverb intact. Of course, a certain amount of explanation is inevitable in a sermon, especially when much of the proverb's rhetorical power is evident only in the original Hebrew. Nonetheless, I hope that by employing this strategy I have successfully heeded Pemberton's warning concerning the danger of destroying a proverb and undermining its rhetorical power.

The Sermon

I can remember when I was a boy in grade school how much I enjoyed going on field trips. On mornings of a scheduled field trip, my mother did not have to wake me up. I would bound out of bed at the first sound of my alarm clock, shower, dress, pack my lunch, and head for the bus stop all without so much as a word of exhortation from my parents. One field trip in particular was especially exciting to me. I was eleven years old and had developed a deep interest in aviation, in planes of every kind. Model planes cluttered the surfaces of the shelves in my room, and the air smelled of model glue. A half-finished model plane sat on my desk. On this particular morning we were taking a field trip to the municipal airport in my hometown where a professional pilot would give us a tour of the 747 planes that he flew for Delta Airlines. I was ecstatic; I could hardly sleep the night before.

I will never forget the feeling I had the next morning when it was finally my turn to enter the cockpit of that 747 plane; the pilot only allowed three of us at a time into the cockpit. It was as though I had entered the inner sanctuary, the Holy of Holies. A dizzying array of fascinating instruments came into view as I ascended the three steps into that sacred space. It was such a collage of technology that I had difficulty focusing on any one thing, but then an especially peculiar little gauge caught my eye. It was a small ball suspended behind the glass of the gauge that wiggled with the slightest movement in the plane. The top half of the ball was blue and the bottom half was black with little yellow notches stretching vertically across it. I pointed to it and asked the pilot what it was called. He said that it was an artificial horizon. Its name was even more intriguing than its appearance. I asked, "What does it do?" To my surprise the pilot told me that the instrument's sole function was to tell him which way is up and which way is down. I was completely unprepared for such a simple answer. Why was such a complicated instrument necessary for determining something as obvious as which way is up and which way is down?

The pilot recognized the puzzled look on my young, naïve face and proceeded to explain in terms that an eleven year old could understand. He told me that when a pilot is flying high in the air he sees nothing but white puffy clouds all around him. Suspended so high above the earth, the pilot has no sense of gravity and therefore nothing within him can tell him which way is up and which is down. Only that funny little two-toned ball on the plane's dashboard gives the pilot any sense of up and down. He proceeded to illustrate the importance of that little instrument by telling me the story of a friend of his who served as a jet pilot in Vietnam. His life came to a sudden and tragic end one night when he crashed his plane full speed into the ground beside a freight train because he thought that the red flashing light on the end of the freight train was the wingtip light of his buddy flying next to him. In his weariness he had ignored his artificial horizon, trusting instead his own perception of up and down.

Recently, I remembered the pilot's sobering story as I was reading Proverbs 14:12. Here the sage says, "There is a way that seems right from a human perspective but its destination is the highway to death" (author's translation). What is true of the pilot in flight is equally true of us all when navigating the hairpin twists and turns of life in this fallen world. We have no inherent sense of direction on which to rely. We are badly in need of a moral/spiritual version of the artificial horizon. Unfortunately, we humans are not only directionally challenged in the spiritual sense, we are also blind to our moral disorientation and therefore convinced that we know where we are going. We are like the man who refuses to stop and ask for directions and winds up getting hopelessly lost.

It is precisely such delusions that this succinct, hard-hitting proverb is designed to shatter. We must be careful, however, how we hear this proverb. A proverb can appear to be straightforward, even simplistic upon a first hearing. In fact, some of them are so black and white or so pedantic as to appear to be cliché. Don't be fooled, however, by this proverb's brevity or its stark assessment of the lethal implications of trusting one's own instincts. Beneath the surface of this proverb lies subtlety and keen insight that can only be perceived after extended meditation.

A professor of mine once said that proverbs are like hard candy; they are not meant to be chewed up and swallowed in a moment. They are meant to be savored. They have to sit on the tongue and slowly dissolve in order for their full flavor to be experienced and enjoyed. Let it sit in your right cheek for a while as its complex mixture of sweet and sour seeps into your mouth. Then roll it over your tongue to the left cheek and see what different nuances of flavor emerge. In other words, take time to linger over the details of the proverb. *How* the proverb means is every bit as important as *what* the proverb means. Let's hear it again but this time with one of its significant subtleties accented: "There is a *way* that seems right from a human perspective but its destination is the *highway* to death"

I deliberately stressed the words "way" and "highway" for two reasons. First, the two terms are the same Hebrew word; however, in the first line of the proverb the word is singular while in the second line it is plural. You may be wondering why your English translations don't reflect this subtle shift from the singular to the plural. The reason is that the plural in Hebrew does not always indicate quantitative increase. Sometimes it conveys qualitative increase, a qualitative increase that is hard to express in English translation. The point of this subtle shift is not that the one way that seems right at the outset turns into a fork in the road or splinters into several roads heading toward different destinations. Rather the point is that this innocent looking, simple shortcut, this one-way road that looks so promising and easy to navigate and so predictable actually turns into a multi-lane superhighway with heavy traffic traveling at such speeds that you find yourself trapped, caught up in the momentum of a stampede headed for a cliff. Jesus made a similar point in Matthew 7:13 when he said, "For the gate is wide and the way is easy that leads to destruction, and those who enter by it are many" (ESV). The shortcuts of life may appear straightforward and promising, but more often than not they come to a dead-end, literally. It is far better to stay on the clearly marked path.

This brings me to the second reason for stressing the two words "way" and "highway." Proverbs 14:12 develops an already well-established metaphor in Proverbs—the journey metaphor. In fact, the entire book of Proverbs portrays itself as a pathway through life paved with aphorisms of various sizes, shapes, and colors, often mismatched, often ill-fitting which can make walking the path tricky. One must watch his step lest he trip over the odd, seemingly random collection of proverbial sayings supposedly designed to lead to the good life. Since Proverbs 14:12 is relying on this established metaphor, it is not really free standing. It does have a context, or perhaps better, contexts.

The proverb's immediate context is Proverbs 10:1-15:33 a collection of Solomonic proverbs focusing on the oppositions of wisdom/folly, righteousness/wickedness, wealth/poverty, pride/humility, and laziness/diligence. Within this context Proverbs 14:12 makes the point that the vices of folly, wickedness, greed, pride, and laziness may seem at the moment like a desirable short cut to the good life, but ultimately these paths lead to ruin.

Significantly, the aphorism of Proverbs 14:12 is repeated verbatim in the next collection of Solomonic proverbs, Proverbs 16-22. This collection focuses on the proper conduct of kings and the proper relationships between kings and subjects, including the proper relationship between humans and their divine king, Yahweh. In this context the proverb highlights the difference between the divine and human perspectives and underscores the point made in Isaiah 55:8 where Yahweh says, "My thoughts are not your thoughts, neither are your ways my ways, declares Yahweh. For as the heavens are higher than the earth, so are my ways higher than your ways and my thoughts than your thoughts."[1] The difference between the divine and human perspectives is then illustrated through a number of aphorisms that challenge human assessments of what is and is not desirable. For example, humans normally consider hunger an undesirable state, but Proverbs 16:26 points out that it is an excellent source of motivation for the worker and saves him from idleness. Verses 27-30 describe a number of vices that seem clever to their practitioners but ultimately have a destabilizing effect on the social and cosmic orders. Finally, 16:31 turns the human perspective on aging on its head. While we view gray hair as a sign of encroaching infirmity, God sees it as a crown of glory—as evidence of longevity due to wisdom and righteousness.

So, depending on where you are in your wisdom journey, the proverb may take on new, subtly nuanced, significance. Nonetheless, regardless of its context the proverb still warns against a naïve confidence in human perception, in our fallen sense of direction that inevitably leads us astray. Thus the proverb underscores the significance of the journey metaphor that is so ubiquitous in Proverbs. This journey began in Proverbs 1-9, the first collection of wisdom sayings in the form of speeches that a father delivers to a son regarding various life skills essential to his son's material and spiritual success. In the midst of these speeches, the father warns the son, "Trust Yahweh with your whole heart, and do not rely on your own insight. In all of your travels acknowledge him and he will straighten your paths" (Prov. 3:5-6, author's translation). Thus from the beginning this path was marked with warnings about choosing our own way, seeking short-cuts that take us off the beaten path.

The journey ends in Proverbs 30-31, a kind of epilogue that summarizes and clarifies the key themes of the book. As we near the end of this proverb paved road, we hear a fellow traveler named Agur (meaning "I wander" in Hebrew) express a similar sentiment when he confesses:

> "I am exhausted, O God. I am exhausted, O God, and at my wits' end because I am too brutish to be a man. I do not even possess human discernment. I haven't learned wisdom; nor have I acquired knowledge of the holy one. Who has ascended to heaven and descended again? Who has gathered the winds in his fist? Who has wrapped the waters in a cloak? Who has secured all the corners of the earth? What is his name, or what is his son's name? Surely you know!" (Prov. 30:1-4, author's translation)

This is not what we hoped to hear after enduring this long journey through proverbs. We had hoped to hear confirmation that we had arrived, that at the end of this difficult road paved with one-line aphorisms we had finally found wisdom. Instead, we hear the frustrated rant of a man who at the end of his pursuit of wisdom has discovered only how ignorant he really is. We may be tempted to be discouraged at this point, to think that the journey was in vain. Agur confirms what the proverb says. There is a way that seems right from a human point of view but its destination is disappointing, even lethal. Not even a book like Proverbs can lead to wisdom if it is not read under divine guidance.

At this point, however, I cannot help but feel that there is a flaw in this proverb. Even after hearing it in its various contexts and appreciating its diverse hues which are like a ray of light hitting a glass prism and scattering into an array of colors, the proverb still has the quality of the famed oracle at Delphi. It is a catch 22 when you really think about it. Is it not the case that all roads ultimately end at the grave? Is it not the case that the sage dies just as surely as the fool? Do the righteous not suffer decay just like the wicked? The proverb implies that there is an alternative route, a path that leads somewhere other than death. Yet, Proverbs offers no guarantees of eternal life or of life beyond the grave. Is this proverb simply sending us on a fool's errand? Will we like Agur reach the end of our road in despair?

Consider Jesus, for example. I cannot imagine a wiser or more righteous person. Yet, look where his path took him. His path ended in a horrible, ignoble death. If Jesus' path ended in death, then what hope do we have of avoiding that fate? But did Jesus' path really end at the grave? If we believe the biblical story we would surely have to answer "No!" It is true that Jesus' path led to the grave but that is not where his path ends. Jesus ploughed *through* death; he blazed a trail leading *out of the grave*. Perhaps this proverb can only be fully appreciated in the light of Christ's finished work. As Paul says, ". . . our Savior Christ Jesus . . . abolished death and brought life and immortality to light through the gospel . . ." (2 Tim. 1:10, ESV). When we read this proverb in the light of Jesus' resurrection we see it in a whole new light. The proverb does not promise that we can find a path that avoids death, a path *around* the grave that bypasses it altogether. Instead, it means that Christ has made a way, in fact he *is* the way that passes through death but does not end there. He is the path that breaks through the grave whose destination is the eternal life found in the presence of his Father.

To what extent the sage responsible for composing Proverbs 14:12 could have anticipated Yahweh's solution to the problem of death is impossible to say. He likely could have never envisioned a savior like Jesus, but that is precisely why this proverb points so profoundly to Christ. Nothing about Jesus' way seemed right. Everything about his entrance into this world and his journey through it seemed wrong from a human perspective. It did not seem right that the Son of God should be born in a barn and spend his first night in a feeding trough. It did not seem right that he should piddle away all of his time with prostitutes, tax collectors, and other miscreants. It did not seem right that he should antagonize the respectable, religious people. It certainly did not seem right that he should end his life hanging on a criminal's cross. Everything about Jesus' way is counter-intuitive. Yet, his way is the only way that does not end at the grave. His way exposes just how disoriented we are, how off track we are in our thinking about everything. He showed us that our religious shortcuts to God only led us farther and farther away from him. He showed us that our shortcuts to life via material gain and hedonism only drains us of true joy. The gospel, as it were, reveals the implied corollary to this proverb: there is a way that seems wrong from a human point of view, but its destination is the path to everlasting life. Or as Paul so eloquently put it:

> For the word of the cross is folly to those who are perishing, but to us who are being saved it is the power of God. For it is written, "I will destroy the wisdom of the wise, and the discernment of the discerning I will thwart." Where is the one who is wise? Where is the scribe? Where is the debater of this age? Has not God made foolish the wisdom of the world? For since, in the wisdom of God, the world did not know God through wisdom, it pleased God through the folly of what we preach to save those who believe. For Jews demand signs and Greeks seek wisdom, but we preach Christ crucified, a stumbling block to Jews and folly to Gentiles, but to those who are called, both Jews and Greeks, Christ the power of God and the wisdom of God. For the foolishness of God is wiser than men, and the weakness of God is stronger than men.[2]

Then perhaps Agur's words near the end of Proverbs are not so despairing. After all, he does recognize the limitations of his own wisdom and raises the most profound question of all biblical revelation: "Who has ascended to heaven and descended again? . . . What is his name, or what is his son's name?" His name is Yahweh and his son's name is Jesus, "in whom are hidden all the treasures of wisdom and knowledge" (Col. 2:3). Follow him; for he is the only path that does not *end* in death.

VANITY OF VANITIES:
Ecclesiastes and Wisdom's Discontents

Thomas G. Long

Canon and Community

The main emphasis of this essay is not to provide insights for preaching on the book of Ecclesiastes, although there will be a smidgen of that along the way. Mainly I want to think about what it means for preachers that Ecclesiastes is in the biblical canon at all. I am persuaded that its presence makes a difference, not only in the shape of the canon, but also in the shape of the preaching ministry.

Here are two homemade images of the biblical canon. First, the canon can be imagined as a vast church choir. If we stand too close to some of the singers in a church choir, we hear dissonance. A few singers are unable to carry the tune, keep rhythm, or maybe are slightly off pitch. Likewise, there are some portions of the biblical canon, perhaps even some whole books that, if one stands too close to them, what protrudes are the dissonances. Luther famously thought that the book of James was a dissonant "epistle of straw," out of pitch with the grace of the gospel, and Luther would not have grieved had James left the choir loft. But instead of standing close to the biblical choir, it is perhaps more productive to listen from the back of the church because, given a bit of distance, the voices that sounded so discordant close up now create intriguing counter tones, their very dissonances making the harmonies of the canon far more interesting.

Another homespun image for the canon is to imagine that the canon is a kind of family. Like most families, the biblical canon has its share of eccentrics, but the very presence of these eccentrics, and the room made for them by the other relatives, makes a family what it is. Trying to negotiate the differences, the discrepancies, even the dysfunctionalities in a family is a very important dynamic of family life. The fact that a family of diverse writers and communities created the canon, and the resultant diversity of the canon, works to shape the diversity of the church today and enriches the kind of vocalization we give to biblical multiplicity when we preach.

The annotator of the Gospel of Matthew in the Discipleship Study Bible, commenting on the Beatitudes, says that these are apocalyptic imperatives, that is to say, the readers and hearers of Jesus' words are being ordered to be poor in spirit, to mourn, to be meek, to hunger and thirst for righteousness, and so on. "The reward," this commentator goes on to assure us, "will be the kingdom of heaven in the future and the establishment of a community set apart to and for the righteous work of God in the present."[1]

This is a fairly standard interpretation of the Beatitudes, and I don't want to minimize it. There is truth here, but the inevitable result of such a reading is to receive the Beatitudes not as a blessing but as a hopelessly demanding, and finally condemning, ethic. For most of my Christian life I have understood the Beatitudes precisely this way, as a kind of comprehensive checklist of moral virtues that each Christian is responsible for living out. Taken seriously as imperatives, the Beatitudes convey the hard truth that one is supposed to be poor in spirit, meek, pure in heart, and all the rest. To fail to fulfill each and every one of these virtues means that one fails the ultimate moral test, namely, that one is not "perfect as your heavenly Father is perfect" (Matt. 5:48). Who can even come close to achieving this?

However, I now understand the Beatitudes differently, as a kind of blend of apocalyptic speech and more down-to-earth wisdom literature addressed not so much to discrete believers but to a community of faith, in essence to a congregation. Understood this way, they carry a different, more hopeful import. They are still demanding, to be sure, but the Beatitudes are not commands addressed to super-Christians to become what they are not, demanding that they strive toward virtues they don't have, but an encouragement to faith communities to make room for virtues that the Spirit has already placed in their midst. The Beatitudes are descriptions of the various voices in the choir, the members of the family of God we are called to incorporate, tolerate, and even celebrate. Understood this way, the Beatitudes have a different sound. "Blessed is the congregation that makes room for those among them who are poor in spirit. Blessed is the congregation that makes room for those among them who mourn. Blessed is the congregation that makes room for those among them who are meek and those who hunger and thirst for righteousness."

We have in the congregation where I worship a woman I will call "Sarah." Sarah is absolutely zealous for social justice. Now our congregation is one where commitment to social justice is highly valued, but, when it comes to the justice issues of the day, Sarah is, as Paul once described himself, "as to righteousness under the law, blameless." She is zealously engaged with every social justice issue imaginable. Every Sunday she's got a petition to sign, a march she wants us to be involved in, a public outrage she wants us to protest, an urgent letter she wants us to write to congress. Sometimes, to tell the truth, Sarah's single-mindedness irritates the heck out of me. But it would be a tremendous loss were Sarah to become discouraged and drift away. Blessed is the congregation that makes room for Sarah because she hungers and thirsts for justice, for righteousness.

We also have "George" in our congregation who has no observable political edge but who is a person of gentleness and meekness. He serves as the unofficial greeter every Sunday, embracing first-time visitors as if they were long-lost brothers and sisters. No one makes more palpable the hospitality of Christ than George, and "Blessed is the congregation that honors meekness." Without people like George, we would lose our agape love; without Sarah we would lose our prophetic zeal. Somehow, negotiating a congregational life that makes room for both Sarah and George and the many others who, in their own ways embody the different virtues named in the Beatitudes, enables us to be a blessed community. None of us is, unto ourselves, whole, but together we are "whole, as our heavenly Father is whole."

In short, the church is a family of diversity in the same way that the biblical canon is a family, and I think the model of the canon negotiating relationships among the diversities that are found there is an important one for the church and also for the pulpit. When it comes particularly to Ecclesiastes, it is a most interesting entry into the family of the canon, because it is a book both of wisdom and counter wisdom. What this means is that Ecclesiastes is a wisdom book in the sense that it employs the vocabulary of wisdom, it incorporates the this-worldly grounding of wisdom literature, and it employs the literary tropes of wisdom. But it is also counter wisdom in the sense that Ecclesiastes takes on the assumptions and presumptions of the wisdom tradition found, say, in Psalm 1 or in Proverbs. The author of Ecclesiastes is a kind of saboteur of conventional wisdom, but sabotage done as an inside job, canonically speaking. I think this is a particularly timely moment for the pulpit to consider seriously the fact that we have saboteurs of conventional wisdom in the canon of Scripture right at the point that the pulpit in America is, as I see it, making a shift in the preferred sermon genre, right before our very eyes, from narrative to wisdom.

From Narration to *Phronesis*

A year or so ago, I had a piece of pedagogy in my basic preaching class blow up in my face. What happened was I played the tape of a sermon I'd been using for several years that I think is an absolutely exquisite example of narrative preaching. It's done by one of America's most famous and celebrated preachers. You would know his name if I mentioned it. This particular sermon ends with four gemlike narratives, each one of them subtly ratcheting forward the argument of the sermon to a stunning denouement Every time I've used this sermon in class students are not only moved by it, they are struck by the beautiful artistic quality of its structure. It is a tour-de-force of narrative preaching.[2]

Well not this time. In fact my students said, "That was kind of boring." "Why did he tell all those stories? I kind of got it after the first one." The students surely missed some of the subtleties of the sermon design, and their reactions could have been merely the expressions of just one class with its own peculiar chemistry. But in some ways I wondered if I was watching the canary die in the coal mine, a younger generation of beginning preachers growing impatient with the primary methodology of preaching that has been in place in the American pulpit for fifty years: narrative preaching.

Soon after this classroom experience, I was talking to an Episcopal priest who told me that a new associate pastor, a young woman, had just joined their church staff. She was scheduled to preach her first sermon in her new position, and she asked this older priest to take a look at her manuscript for any suggestions he might have. He read the manuscript and thought it was good, but also thought that it displayed the dense content often typical of a newly minted seminary trained preacher. So he told her as diplomatically as he could, "This is a fine sermon but it needs a little light and air in it."

She became slightly defensive and asked him to say more clearly what he meant. "Well," he said, "what I'm trying to say is that your sermon has a lot of strong content but it doesn't connect to life very well."

She continued to resist, saying she still wasn't sure what he meant. "What I'm really trying to tell you," he explained, "is you need to put some stories in your sermon."

"Ah, I thought so," she replied. "I think we have a generational issue here. Stories mean something important to you and to your generation. They don't mean nearly as much to my generation."

I don't think the change in sermon genre going on in our time is only a generational issue, but I do think many preachers are sensing that the older narrative forms of preaching, so delightful for a previous time, are beginning to wear thin, and that many preachers are moving to a different genre: *phronesis* or wisdom preaching.

If narrative preaching emphasized imagination and illumination, wisdom preaching focuses on what could be called Christian *savoir faire*. Many sermons today are less about the grand themes of biblical narrative or the epiphanies that occur in moments of peak experience and much more about practical everyday wisdom. How do you deal with life? How do you handle a lifeless marriage? How do you engage children who don't respond to you? How do you bring some meaning and purpose into a vocation? If a previous generation of American Christians had grown weary of instruction and hungered for a profound sense of delight, it could be said that our generation of over–stimulated, media-saturated congregants hungers for the knowledge and know-how to live a faithful and satisfying life.

Counter Testimony

The move from narrative to wisdom preaching in our culture reveals one of the first connections between our situation and the presence in the biblical canon of Ecclesiastes. This biblical book represents in some ways the failure of narrative; it is an expression of protest by and for people for whom the dominant faith narrative has ceased working and for whom the reigning story of faith has been disrupted. The author of Ecclesisates, Qoheleth, is much like Job here. For Job, the loss of confidence in the old narrative has happened in a very dramatic and traumatic way. For Qoheleth, the same collapse has occurred through the grinding away of a life honestly observed, resulting in a cynical, worldly wisdom. Neither Job nor Qoheleth is able fully to participate in the broad narrative movement from creation to consummation that constitutes the prophetic and gospel literature. For them, the cherished faith story has ceased to give structure and meaning to their lives.

How many people in our congregations are in precisely in this same position? To be sure, there are many of the faithful who are confidently "marching to Zion" as they always have, and that is a beautiful thing, but a good many people in the pews are just trying to make it through the night. For them, finding their place in some overarching narrative is a very difficult, if not impossible, achievement now. The question on their minds is not "How do I live out the Great Commandment?" but rather, "How do I plan this one day in a way that gives meaning to my life?"

We can observe an example of the new appeal of Christian *savoir faire* by exploring a statement from the Letter of James: "How great a forest is set ablaze by a small fire! And the tongue is a fire . . . . With it we bless the Lord and Father, and with it we curse those who are made in the likeness of God. From the same mouth come blessing and cursing. My brothers and sisters, this ought not to be so" (James 3:5bff). When I first began my ministry thirty-five years ago, if I would preach on a piece of ethical instruction like this text, people's eyes would usually glaze over. But now, if I preach on a text like this in some creative and pragmatic way, people lean forward because there is a new awareness of what we don't know, a new hunger to find some pattern for living that makes practical and spiritual sense, and people want to know how to organize their lives.

My oldest child is now in her late thirties, and we have, for the last dozen years or so, been getting to know each other as adult to adult. Many parents of older children will recognize the joy of this season in life, a time finally to get to relate to one's children not as parent to child but as adult to adult. However, in order to get to such a relational place, one often has to retrace the path through some treacherous territory and to relive some painful experiences. In one conversation I had with my daughter, she remembered a time when she was an adolescent, and she and I were tangled in a father-daughter, parent-adolescent dispute. In the middle of the firestorm, she recalled that I said to her, "You're nothing but trouble to me!" Now, that is not the kind of thing I would say. I don't remember saying that. But she does, and twenty years later she is still trying to pull that poison dart out of her soul. So when James says be careful about the tongue, I now lean forward myself. I want to know in practical terms, as a matter of wisdom on the ground, how to use my tongue.

When Dietrich Bonheoffer was the principle of a seminary in Finkenwalde, he made a wise and practical ethical rule for the community. No one in the community, Bonhoeffer said, was to mention the name of anyone else in the community unless that person was present to hear it, even if the intent was to say something good. How would that rule go over in a congregation today? What if the pastors and officers were to say, "No one in this congregation may mention the name of anyone else in the congregation unless that person is present to hear it, even if the intent is good?" Gossip would go out the window, even gossip in the name of prayer ("I think we ought to be concerned about the Millers. I have, uhmm, heard some things. Let us pray for the Millers"). Eberhard Bethge, who was a student at the Finkenwald seminary in those days, admitted that the community utterly failed to carry out Bonhoeffer's rule, but that their constant attempts to follow it transformed the community nevertheless.

There are those moments in church history when the people of God need to be formed and reformed in terms of practical wisdom before they can resume living the narrative and continue the march to Zion. The church needs the language and wisdom of the faith to fortify them so that their marching legs are ready to go.

There is a small town near where I live that has a Baptist church with a very fine choir. Several years ago the choirmaster and music director at this church received a notice in the mail from the Episcopal National Cathedral in Washington, DC. There are more services of worship at the National Cathedral every week than the Cathedral choirs can serve, so the notice indicated that choirs from local congregations would be welcome to apply to sing a service at the Cathedral. The choir director of this Baptist Church decided that it would be a wonderful experience, and a fun trip, to take his choir up to Washington and to let them sing at the National Cathedral, so he applied. His choir was accepted, but it was not for one of the main Sunday services. The response to the invitation had been strong, many choirs had applied, and the only slot available for this Baptist choir was a Sunday afternoon evensong.

So the choir director told his choir, "Good news. We're going to Washington to sing at the National Cathedral, and we're going to sing evensong."

Somebody on the back row voiced the question on everybody's mind, "What's evensong?"

The choir director replied, "I knew you'd ask that," and he passed out copies of the music and text of the evensong service. He told the choir that they we're going to rehearse this service for the next several weeks, but he added, "We're not just going to do it at choir practice. I want you every night to pray this service at home. Before you go to bed, read the words of this service prayerfully."

The service includes this prayer, "Blessed are you, O Lord, creator of the changes of day and night, giving rest to the weary, renewing the strength of those who are spent, bestowing upon us occasions of song in the evening, creator of changes day and night. Giving rest to the weary, renewing the strength of those who are spent." So the choir prayed this every night, and they sang it together every Wednesday.

Then Hurricane Katrina hit the Gulf Coast. Suddenly, refugees from Katrina were streaming away from the Gulf coast and seeking shelter in neighboring areas, including the small town in Georgia where this Baptist church was located. Many communities recoiled at the intrusion of these refugees, fearful that this massive influx of desperate people would overwhelm their economy and their community resources. But in this little town there was a group that organized a place of hospitality for the refugees. It was the choir of the First Baptist Church, "Giving rest to the weary, renewing the strength of those who are spent," living out the practical wisdom formed by the practice of learning and praying the language of worship.

The Cynical Preacher Qoheleth

The first contribution, then, of Ecclesiastes to our preaching today is that this book is a piece of wisdom literature, and as such it is written for people for whom the grand narrative has been temporarily disrupted, for people who cannot readily march to Zion until they are formed in practical wisdom, until they are deepened in practice and get their language straight.

But the second contribution Ecclesiastes creates for preaching today runs in a different direction. Yes, Ecclesiastes is wisdom, but Ecclesiastes is perhaps the most pessimistic and cynical book in the Bible. Before we consider what that cynicism and pessimistic attitude might mean, we should remind ourselves that at some point, and the exact point is disputed, an editor assigned the name "Qoheleth" to the narrator of this book, meaning "teacher" or "preacher" ("The words of Qoheleth, the son of David . . ." Eccles. 1:1). Something in this book connected with the preaching role; something in this book connected with leadership in the faith community.

Perhaps one thing that connected is that the kind of pessimism and cynicism we find in Ecclesiastes is an occupational hazard of preachers. For example, here is what Qoheleth says: "In my vain life I've seen everything. There are righteous people who perish in righteousness, and there are wicked people who prolong their life in evil doing" (Eccles. 7:15). What pastor has not, in the depths of her or his soul, looked out at the congregation and said the same. There is a woman out there who has lived a faithful and loving life, but her kids are on drugs and now she's got pancreatic cancer and is dying in pain. And there is another guy who comes once every six months to church, puts five dollars in the plate, whose kids are getting into Harvard, and he's giving them a Lexus as they go. Which of us has not wondered about that, muttered under our breath, "In my vain life I've seen everything. There are righteous people who perish in righteousness, and there are wicked people who prolong their life in evil doing"?

Or listen to this: "I hated all my toil in which I'd toiled under the sun seeing that I must leave it to those that come after me. And who knows whether they will be wise or foolish, yet they will be master of all for which I've toiled and used my wisdom under the sun. This also is vanity" (Eccles. 2:18-19). To paraphrase: "I've worked my tail off to get this congregation straightened out, but I just know that some idiot is going to follow me and destroy the whole thing, everything that I have built. This is all vanity."

This is bitter stuff, and, frankly, I do not want Qoheleth as my full-time pastor. The Book of Ecclesiastes is, hopefully, not who most preachers are, but it is where honest preachers go on occasion in the dark night of the soul. I don't want to hear from the pulpit the ceaseless stream of Qoheleth's cynicism, the endless deconstruction of tradition, the constantly deferred meaning. This may earn tenure at the university, but I don't want a steady diet of this from the pulpit. Nevertheless, most pastors can recognize Qoheleth moments in ministry.

Beyond the raw cynicism of the book, Ecclesiastes' structure provides a big swath of sayings bounded by an *inclusio*. Ecclesiastes begins, "Vanity of vanities" and it ends the same way: "Vanity of vanities." Read from beginning to end, then, Ecclesiastes is unyielding cynicism, an unrelieved cry of vanity. But to this material is appended an epilogue, and almost all scholars agree this epilogue is penned by a separate hand. In the epilogue, an adult suddenly enters the room to say, "Okay, we've heard enough, the end of the matter, all has been said; fear God and keep his commandments." When the main body of Ecclesiastes and the epilogue are taken together, a long stretch of cynicism leads, abruptly perhaps, but inevitably to a word of faithful commitment: everything's been heard, keep the commandments. This blending of perspectives in Ecclesiastes opens up two main ways to think about the book, and I think preachers should resist a hasty choice between them. They're in tension with each other, but both of them are insightful and valuable.

The first way to understand Ecclesiastes is that the book's body and epilogue are at cross purposes: cynicism collides with faith. The epilogue is treated as a welcome trumping of the negativity of the first part of the book. Seen this way, the long section before the epilogue is nothing more than a gloomy meditation on the emptiness of life by a confused and despair ridden pseudo-sage. Thank God, then, that the epilogist finally shows up to kind of put an end to the matter.

I had a personal experience with this collision of views several years ago when my father got very interested in our family genealogy. He began to do research, and he discovered that a strand of our family, the Griers, had moved from Pennsylvania into rural Greene County, Georgia. There they established a homestead and, by all reports, did many wonderful and productive things. Eager to visit this old homestead, my father located an old sage in Greene County, the unofficial local historian and master of lore, who reputedly knew where every family cemetery in the county was located. "Do you know the whereabouts of the Grier family homestead and cemetery?" my father asked him.

"Yep, I do," the old man said. "It's out there by the Georgia railroad in the pine trees. I can take you there." So my father and I drove out to Greene County and met the local historian. He guided us down the rural highway by the Georgia railroad and seemingly out in the middle of nowhere, he ordered us to stop the car. We got out, walked across a field and into the pine trees. Suddenly there was a clearing, or what had once been one. Nothing was there but scrub brush and pine needles, but in generations past a home had stood in this place. We went to the edge of the clearing, and the old man pointed to the ground. "They were buried here," he said. Sure enough, while there were no markers or tombstones, there were clearly depressions in the earth, places where old graves had sunk under the wearing of the rain and the wind. The Grier burial ground.

My father and I stood looking at this soil that contained our ancestors, having almost a mystical experience. Finally I pulled away from the graveyard, leaving my father still standing there in silent reverie. I walked over to the local historian, who was watching us from a distance. When I drew close, the old man said, "You know what this teaches me?"

I said, "No. What?

"It tells me that you ought to get all you can get while you can get it because when it's over, it's over. All that's left is a bunch of soft places in the mud."

I should have said, "Thank you, Qoheleth." Out there in a Georgia pine grove, we were experiencing the same collision between cynicism and reverence, between the ethics of *carpe diem* and the honoring of ancient tradition, that we find between Ecclesiastes' body of material and epilogue.

To take this collision-oriented approach to Ecclesiastes provides two important insights about preaching. The first insight is that it takes a long

time in Ecclesiastes until the epilogue shows up, and this is no mere coincidence. The epilogue does not appear at the end of the first chapter, but arrives
only after many pages of "vanity of vanities," which means there is a tolerance in the biblical canon, and thus in the family of God, for cynicism and
skepticism that endures for a long time. There is no premature cessation of
the despair and cynicism of Qoheleth. In this sense, Ecclesiastes is structured
a bit like the lament psalms, which usually turn to praise, but not until there
has been verse after verse after verse of lament.

The second insight from this more despairing look at Ecclesiastes is that
the despairing tone in the main body of the book gives voice to the views and
feelings of many people in the church, who would say what Qoheleth says, if
they could find the courage to speak. This is their book, the articulation of
the broken moments in their lives and in the broader life of congregations.
Theologian Edward Farley once wrote of what he called a "nasty suspicion"
among theologians—and I would say congregations as well—that behind
the liturgy, the preaching, the creeds, and the theology of the church there is
nothing real; that preachers are in effect, stock brokers selling stock on nonex-
istent corporations. Behind all the pious talk of the preacher is nothing, "but
the stockbroker himself."

Now most church goers would probably not articulate quite that degree
of suspicion, but along comes a novel like *The Da Vinci Code* or the announcement of the Discovery Channel that they have found the bones of Jesus under
an apartment building in Jerusalem, and something is aroused in a lot of our
best and brightest lay people, a suspicion that the mythologies of the Christian
faith have been a kind of false stock and underneath it there is a more plausible, reasonable explanation for the Christian faith. This reminds me of a little
boy who came home from school one day angry because he had discovered on
the playground that Santa Claus was not real, that he had been deceived, and
that all of those presents under the tree had actually been placed there by his
parents. He barged into his home and angrily lectured his mother for having
misled him, and then he stormed away toward his room. As he walked away,
he turned back and said, "And another thing. I'm going to get to the bottom
of this Jesus business too."

There are a lot of people in our congregation who believe that underneath the preaching, the biblical theologizing, the creedalisms of the church,

there is a more plausible, less mythical "Jesus business" that can be gotten down to. They want to see Jesus unprotected by his Sunday school body-guards. Therefore they rejoice over Qoheleth's poking of the tradition. Vanity of vanities. Preachers today need to remember that this view of the faith is not finally alien to us. It is, after all, in the canon, and it is to be responded to with respect, with pastoral care, and, if the structure of Ecclesiastes gives us any instruction, with great patience.

There is also the voice of the brokenhearted in here. The very first Sunday I ever preached as a student pastor, I was standing at the door after the service, as nervous at the door as I had been in the pulpit, trying to figure out how the sermon had gone. Coming out of the church was a woman who was the mother of a child with cerebral palsy. She had had many anguished and ter-rible experiences concerning the health of this child. As she came to the door, she took my hand and said, "I really loved the last hymn." Nothing about the sermon, just "I really loved the last hymn."

To tell the truth, I was so narcissistically self-absorbed in concern over my sermon, I couldn't remember what the last hymn was. So I told a white lie. "Yes, I did too," I said. "It's one of my favorites."

She threw my hand down and stomped away, muttering, "It was a ter-rible hymn." As soon as I could, I went with trepidation back into the church and found a bulletin. The last hymn was "God Will Take Care of You." The Qoheleth in her said, "Vanity of vanities. God is not taking care of me." In the canon, and in the family of God, there is a place for her voice to be responded to, to be listened to, to be included.

The voice of Qoheleth is the voice of the disillusioned and despairing. I remember as a young minister going to an annual gathering of my denom-ination. I can no longer recall the exact issue being debated at the meeting, but I still burn with the disillusionment of realizing that beneath the language of "doing the will of God" and "prayerful discernment" was a raw and mean racism being slathered over with the language of piety. After five days of having my naïve views of the church punctured, I came home with my BS detector set on stun. If somebody had said to me on the way home, "God loves you," I think I would have spit at them and ordered them to prove it. It is a strange but real comfort to know that Qoheleth's BS detector is also set high. There are pastors and congregants who have been disillusioned by the corruptions of the church they have seen, and they (hopefully) temporarily don't believe any of it. Their (and our) disillusionment finds expression in the canon. A place is made for it. A pastor once told me of a woman in his congregation ravaged by the hell of depression. "What kept me alive," she told him, "was reading Ecclesiastes. I couldn't have made it without Ecclesiastes."

The second approach to Ecclesiastes is somewhat different. Yes, Qoheleth is cynical. Yes, he looks vanity in the face and calls a spade a spade. But in Qoheleth there is a tacit positive theology, almost a proto-incarnational theology at work; that whatever meaning in life and joy in God is to be found here and now, on the ground of real life and experience, and not in speculation. It is, in a sense, a license for us to proclaim, "Do not look for the joy of the kingdom in the next pasture. Look for the joy of the kingdom in the place where you have been set. The joy of the kingdom is not in the ideal of holy matrimony but in repairing *this* broken marriage, not in the wistful hope of perfect offspring but in dealing with *these* troublesome children, finding meaning not in some heavenly bye-and-bye but in finding meaning in *this* day and in *this* work, doing our best to patch things up and being reconciled with *that* real neighbor on the other side of the fence.

The two approaches to Ecclesiastes, the cynical and the more positive, are beautifully described in two excellent commentaries. Tremper Longman's *The Book of Ecclesiastes* in the New International Commentary Series[3] is more representative of the first approach to Ecclesiastes. For Longman, Qoheleth is an unrelievedly despairing figure for whom "life is full of trouble and then you die." Death, moreover, is the end of the human story, and God is "distant, occasionally indifferent, and sometimes cruel." He says that when Qoheleth calls on his readers to "fear God," he means fear in the worst sense, "that of fright before powerful and dangerous being, not respect or awe for a mighty and compassionate deity."[4] Only at the end of the book, in the epilogue to be exact, does Ecclesiastes find its true ground. According to Longman, when we arrive at long last at the injunction to "reverence God and keep God's commandments," we realize that the cynical rantings of Qoheleth are meant to be received as "a foil, a teaching device, used by the second wise man [the author of the epilogue] in order to instruct his son (12:12) concerning the dangers of speculative, doubting wisdom in Israel."[5]

William Brown's *Ecclesiastes* in The Interpretation commentary series is representative of the second approach to Ecclesiastes. While acknowledging the power of reading Ecclesiastes as a paean to "nothingness," Brown suggests another, more canonical and hopeful way of understanding Qoheleth. "If anything, Qoheleth emphasizes the 'seeking dimension' that is essential to faithful inquiry. As a seeker, Qoheleth sees himself on a journey toward understanding the totality of experience under God . . . ."[6] Qoheleth will not be distracted by poetry; he turns his eye to this life, to the material reality of the world in front of us. He will not turn away his gaze, and as such he is a witness to the hope that "there is something *within* this 'total nothingness,' not behind it or above it, that adumbrates the new creation."[7]

These two commentaries, and the approaches they represent, convey to preaching not an either-or choice but two perspectives on a great canonical text. Holding both approaches not as hard demands for decision but as differing perspectives on Ecclesiastes, we can see in this book both the practical wisdom so eagerly sought in our time and the counter-wisdom that keeps preaching honest to the real experiences of people caught up in life's ambiguities. Today's preachers need the ancient preacher Qoheleth reminding us that Jesus, too, manifested the kingdom at tables where people "ate and drank and enjoyed themselves" (Ecc 8:15). Today's preachers also need the more cynical voice of Qoheleth, reminding us when our rhetoric soars above the realities, that "all is vanity."

As such, Ecclesiastes, I believe, finally teaches the preacher humility. Especially in a time when people want to be taught, there is a temptation on the part of us to become the overconfident voices of authority. Ecclesiastes reminds us that anytime our sermons drift into saying, "Now the Bible clearly teaches," we're fudging. As a matter of fact the Bible is completely clear about almost nothing. Even those things about which the Bible seems crystal clear turn out to be far more nuanced, complex, and mysterious than they first appear. The Bible is full of gaps and concealments that have to be negotiated by the readers and hearers. Guesses have to be made. Admissions of the limitation of our knowledge have to be confessed. The drama of reading the complexities and ambiguities of Scripture replicate our coming to faith.

So, preach wisdom, but be sure to remember only God is truly wise and our wisdom is provisional. When human wisdom presumes to be permanent, we have once again fashioned a golden calf.

WHERE IS OUR *POSITION* ON DISASTER?

Job 1–4

DAVID FLEER

En Route to the Sermon

For more than a quarter century Tom Long's work has informed and challenged my preaching, from creating an attention to literary genres to nurturing appreciation for rhetorical issues at stake in the text and sermon. His essay in this volume provides the muse for the sermon that follows which encourages a "saboteur of conventional wisdom."

Long suggests that Ecclesiastes shape the pulpit and wryly observes that its epilogue arrives only after many pages of "vanity of vanities," hinting at a tolerance in the biblical canon, and thus in the family of God, for prolonged skepticism. The sermon follows this plot line, and invites Qoheleth into the world imagined in Job where it entertains a cynical critique of the disasters which are daily broadcast into our living rooms.

Long further encourages us to hold in tension Ecclesiastes' voice of the disillusioned with its tacit positive theology because practical wisdom is so eagerly sought in our time and we need a counter-wisdom to keep our preaching honest before those caught up in life's difficulties. The sermon finds in Job's beautifully monstrous description of calamity and pain a direction for living into the troubles that surround us.

The sermon's occasion was the week of the earthquake in Chile (February 2010), just over one month after the Haitian earthquake, and in the wake of a national discussion of popular Christian interpretations of the events.

The powerful pericope at the sermon's heart (Job 1:13-19) is one that demands more performance than telling or even description. It has such magnetic pull that passive, objective, caustic resistance to engagement can be reversed by its reality.

If "All the world's a stage, and most of us are desperately unrehearsed," as playwright Sean O'Casey once said, then Scripture is our script and "church" is our rehearsal. In such a scenario, this particular sermon orients to reality, converses with the cast about the project ahead, and invites an "uncommon wisdom" in the throes of disaster.

The sermon initially identifies us with Eliphaz, as distant critics who please ourselves with financial donations and relieve guilt and prevent lasting involvement by casting Pat Robertson as scapegoat. But, with the help of Job, the sermon finally refuses to escape and instead pushes us into the world, "girding up our loins," prepared for faithful and wise action.

The Sermon

Step with me onto the stage. Listen! Someone is describing unfolding disasters:

> Now on the day when Job's sons and daughters were eating and drinking wine in their oldest brother's house, a messenger came to Job and said, "The oxen were plowing and the donkeys feeding beside them, and the Sabeans attacked and took them and killed the servants with the edge of the sword, and I alone have escaped to tell you."
>
> While he was still speaking, another came and said, "The fire of God fell from heaven and burned up the sheep and the servants, and I alone have escaped to tell you."
>
> While he was still speaking, another came and said, "The Chaldeans formed three bands and made a raid on the camels and killed the servants with the edge of the sword, and I alone have escaped to tell you."
>
> While he was still speaking, another came and said, "Your children were eating and drinking wine in their oldest brother's house, and behold, a great wind came from across the wilderness and struck the four corners of the house, and it fell on the young people . . . and they died . . . and I alone have escaped to tell you."[1]

This isn't the only time we've been privy to images of tragedy. How often have we screened the visual news of a jarring calamity?

- Katrina's Flood
- 9/11
- Indonesia's Tsunami
- Haiti's Earthquake
- This week's Catastrophe in Chile

Seems like the onslaught never ends.

But the question I pose this morning is, "What biblical text frames the way we think about catastrophe?" Or, "From which vantage do we gaze?" That is, "where is our *position* on disaster?"

Not too many decades ago, every preacher worth "his salt" had an "Earthquake Sermon" tucked in the back of his Bible, ready at a moment's notice. Tornado or flood, didn't matter, blizzard or hurricane, the sermon could identify the signs of God's wrath.

For example, "There is no *divine* visitation which is likely to have so general an influence upon sinners as an earthquake." So proclaimed John Wesley two centuries ago.

John Wesley made it plain, "God grabs our attention with an earthquake. Nothing like it." Kind of a "Red sky at night, sailors' delight, red sky in the morning, sailors take warning" approach. No clearer notice from the Almighty than an old fashioned earthquake!

But after the recent catastrophes in Haiti and Chile, "the Earthquake Sermon" doesn't sound quite as orthodox as Wesley. Sounds more like Eliphaz, whose position on disaster starts with the biblical proverb, "Those who sow iniquity harvest *trouble*" (Job 4).

"You want to know what stance to take?" Eliphaz asks. "I'll tell you why disaster strikes. People reap what they sow. Build a flimsy apartment on a fault line and don't be surprised when your poor engineering and stupid geography cause people to get hurt. Same is true spiritually. Bargain with the devil, and be prepared to pay the piper. Those who plant iniquity harvest *trouble*."

Seems like we've heard that recently.

"Something happened a long time ago in Haiti," Pat Robertson informed the television audience. "They were under the heel of the French, Napoleon the third. They got together and swore a pact to the devil and said, 'We will serve you if you will get us free from the prince.' True story. And so the devil said, 'Okay, it's a deal.' The Haitians got themselves free, but ever since, they have been cursed by one thing after another."

Or, so the televangelist explained the "back story" for the Haitian earthquake.

What "disaster perspective" do *we* take?

Pat Robertson has been pretty quiet in the days since the Chile catastrophe. But, his "Earthquake Sermon" was enough to fuel the blogosphere and Facebook with a bevy of condemnations.

"I am a Republican and a Christian and Pat Robertson does not speak for me."

Some even rekindled their belief in hell, just so Pat might be an occupant! Others kindly dismissed him: "Pat needs to retire."

But, what of *us*? What "disaster position" do *we* take as the tsunami is being tracked on our television's screen? Where do *we* stand when an international disaster creates again "a viewing experience," ripe for CNN's Situation Room?

"Hi Wolf, I am standing in front of the damage in Santiago?"

"Reporting from Honolulu as they brace themselves for the tsunami."

"Looters are raiding the appliance store across the street, as we speak, Wolf."

What "disaster perspective" do *we* take?

This week I told a group of graduate students that I was preaching today from the tragedy in Job. "Really?" one questioned. "Don't you think the congregation wants a *break*? Maybe a diversion from all they've seen on the TV?"Others nodded to agree.

Maybe.

After Haiti, I was impressed with our immediate responses. With a click and a credit card, soon we were watching relief agencies digging through the rubble. Our disaster money in action.

But, researchers say that we may have *selfish reasons* for helping others.

Brain scans by a team of neuroscientists at the National Institutes of Health found that when a research subject was encouraged to think of giving money to a charity, parts of the brain lit up, the parts normally associated with selfish pleasures *like eating and sex*!

The neuroscientists think that

- altruism carries its own rewards,
- "sacrifice" is a huge source of satisfaction,
- the most selfish thing we can do is help other people.[2]

After first blush, really? Giving money to Haiti relief is on the same "satisfaction team" as *food and sex*? No wonder we were pleased to click and send a little financial help . . . . *the first time!*

But, after the initial wave, the disaster grew and compounded with multiple aftershocks. Floods turned to looting. Earthquakes ended in violence. Haiti is followed by Chile. After six weeks, more than one million Haitians remain homeless. Many are living in plastic tarps, with floods and hurricanes on the horizon. Food, water, and medical care all remain problems. Haitians are still choking in rubble and staggering obstacles remain.

That wears on the pleasure factor! Like Eliphaz, we have only so much patience for this kind of stuff.

Maybe the grad students were right. The joy of giving doesn't last long. We need a break.

So, is *this* the "position" *we* take? Change the subject? Look away, as we sit in our arm chairs before the television? *Our* family, *our* health, and *our* community all still in one piece.

The students advise:

- we want a diversion,
- we can only absorb so much,
- focus on a praise inspiring Psalm,
- turn the channel!

What "disaster position" do *we* take?
Wait!
What if we pursue another alternative?

Step with me onto Job's stage, whose tragedy is described in a way that moves us—not to release endorphins of pleasure or divert our attention, *but into its rhythms and themes.*

Because Job's story isn't meant to create the objective distance that accommodates someone's theological assessment. Nor is Job written for our viewing pleasure, like high definition TV. It's live theater and invites us into its reality, sucking us in with its blossoming detail, its ballet of movement.

Four messengers whose four messages four times conclude, "I alone have escaped to tell you" (1:16, 17, 18, 19), underscore the completeness and finality of the tragedies they describe.

Three times the messengers report is introduced, "And while he was still speaking" (1:16, 17, 18), knitting together the disasters, overlapping them, compounding them, multiplying their impact and the horror of their news. "Everything gone. And, now the children."

Listen to the pattern of the disasters' source:

- the *Sabeans* attack,
- the *fire* falls,
- the *Chaldeans* pillage and murder,
- the *wind* strikes.

The form—human, natural, human, natural—weaves perfectly, like an orchestra of melancholy strings, like the prolonged cry of a bugle, music in the saddest key.

And into this form fits the content of disaster. Possessions, wealth, and, most devastating of all, family, all gone. "And I alone have escaped to tell you."

Here we stand, on the stage, in the midst of the cataclysm where everything looks different.

Within the envelopment of a collapsed building, the mother's fingers touch her lips, the father's face is sober, his eyes mist, hearing the doctor describe the option of amputation to remove their child, pinned under a fallen beam.

Beside us, women with arms open, eyes clenched shut, grieve over the dead.

Tragedy, loss, and horror, in person and up close.

Step in, but watch yourself because Job isn't a still shot, it has movement!

- The *tragedies* move. The disasters have trajectories: first wealth, then family, then health, all lost.
- Nor is Job's *reaction* a single photograph. Job's *response* has movement.
  - "In all of this Job did not sin"
  - Later, "In all of this Job did not sin . . . with his lips"
  - Later, "And then Job opened his mouth and cursed the day of his birth . . . . 'God damn the day I was born'" (3:1).

- Eliphaz and his friends' *response* evolves, as well. The first week of silence and weeping soon turns to challenge and harsh critique after Job's graphic complaints (Job 2, 4).

From breeze to squall, the rushing winds of Job are spinning and turbulent: from storm to typhoon, a vortex of reality.

A stark contrast to Robertson and Eliphaz who are distant and objective and judging, claiming to see what they cannot see and to know what is beyond their knowledge . . . .

And . . . stark contrast to us when we sit in front of television's screen. On the sofa with Eliphaz. Distant and objective "evaluating" all that is before us and pleased to find in Pat Robertson a diversionary culprit to judge.

But if our faith is more *performance* than *proposition* and if *how we live* means *more* than *what we think*, then we will step onto the stage and move into the scene.

Because tomorrow's late breaking news will unfold fresh disasters from afar: forest fires, mud slides, a university shooting. Unemployment will rise, foreclosures increase, "For Sale" signs will line our business streets.

But *this time* we'll not point our finger at the usual suspects: insurance companies, the poor, or the "other party" which forces us to remain objective and inactive and angry and judgmental.

This time we'll step into the winds of Job, armed with a theology and faith that remembers Eliphaz, at his best and wisest, held his mouth shut, wept and kept a long silent vigil.

Television cameras pulled out days after Katrina while the problems continued. Haitian coverage is already on the wane. Broadcasts from Chile will last only as long as networks think we *want* to watch.[3]

But we will continue to work with God's wisdom and courage.

And tomorrow morning something else will recur that we've not previously seen, nor have yet had eyes to see. Unfolding continuing disasters, *untelevised and always invisible before:*

- Inescapable systems of poverty,
- Famine-ensuring international trade,
- Institutions that exclude,
- Schools that fail,

- All previously beyond our view.

Motives are seldom visible—but systemic calamity should always be clear.

So, *this time* we will allow ourselves to be pulled into the world Job imagines, no longer distant, no longer judging, no longer blinded by our pleasures and privilege.

This time with eyes to see and wisdom to act in faith,

- we will position ourselves in the painful realities before us,
- we will roll up our sleeves
- as we pledge to live in God's position:
  - identifying hidden systems of oppression,
  - committed to relieving the pain.

﹏QOHELETH'S QUESTION﹏
(Ecclesiastes 1:12—2:26)

KEN DURHAM

En Route to the Sermon

This sermon on the "Royal Experiment" of Ecclesiastes 1:12–2:26 is an attempt to capture something of the witty, acerbic, Eeyore-like flavor of not only the dissatisfactions of Qoheleth but much of the wisdom literature. It seeks to speak both to the Christian insider with more questions and doubts than she's dared raise within her church circles and to the searching skeptic distrustful of the easy, chirpy optimism he thinks to be the Christian gospel (a person Thomas Long characterizes as having "a highly-developed BS-detector"). This text offers a prime opportunity to demonstrate, as Long has done in these lectures and in *Preaching from Memory to Hope*, how startlingly-candid and wonderfully-diverse the biblical canon is—broad enough to give voice to a wide range of spiritual strivings, and blunt enough to capture the ear of today's budding cynic.

We first trace Qoheleth's trip through the royal buffet line, following a sermon scheme suggestive of Long's "episodic" alternative to the narrative style so popular over the past generation. "What really satisfies? This? Let's taste and see, shall we? Nope!" Again and again. If "authenticity" is indeed the coin of the realm in the post-modern marketplace of values, then a sermonic journey in search of the really Real should have possibilities.

Regarding my choices of other voices within this sermon, if Frederick Buechner resonates with some older Christians like myself, then the late David Foster Wallace surely does so with younger seekers. Wallace has become one of today's most admired "saboteurs of conventional wisdom" (Long's phrase describing the wisdom writers). In the selection from his celebrated Kenyon College graduation address, he virtually reiterates, item by item, Qoheleth's buffet menu of dead-end entrees: money, things, sexual allure, power, and intellect.

A bruised and woozy society trying to rebound from what *Time* magazine has called "The Decade from Hell" needs what Ecclesiastes brings: a fresh, forthright, and potentially-healing word to people grown more suspicious than ever of a Christian narrative that says God wants us all to be healthy, wealthy, and wise. Qoheleth disrupts that notion with a vengeance: "I had all that, and more . . . and I hated my life! The answer, the really Real, must be found elsewhere."

The suggestion of three "gifts" of God through the Teacher is meant to reawaken listeners to how much life and currency the Living Word has yet in it: to build empathy for the restless skeptic, to critique masterfully the trivialities that masquerade as truth, and ultimately to lead to the Source of true satisfaction.

David Hubbard (*Ecclesiastes, Song of Solomon* in The Preacher's Commentary series) suggests an apt doorway to the sermon's final movement—a movement to the gospel of Jesus, "the Greater Wise Man." The world-weary woman at the well in John 4 appears as a smart but unfulfilled everywoman/seeker who has quite unexpectedly stumbled upon the Christ who can satisfy her deepest thirst, and ours. She has, impossibly, become a guest at the King's Buffet! Only by the Spirit, she discovers, can the spirit be fed, and filled.

The Sermon

Qoheleth's question. It just keeps coming up.

It surfaces in the film *Zoolander*, an over-the-top spoof of the world of high fashion models. One day the pathologically-narcissistic Derek Zoolander has a (fleeting) epiphany. He asks his fellow models, "Do you ever think that maybe there's *more* to life than being really, really, really, ridiculously good-looking?"

Closer to reality, you hear Qoheleth's question in a *60 Minutes* interview with Patriots quarterback Tom Brady. "Why do I have three Super Bowl rings and still think there's something greater out there for me?" Brady wonders. "It's got to be *more* than this." Steve Kroft asks, "What's the answer?" Brady shakes his head. "I wish I knew."

What's Qoheleth's question? Peggy Lee nailed it years ago in her sultry song "Is That All There Is?"

Is there *more*? More than looking really, really good? More than winning the ultimate football game? More than indulging our every whim and fancy? (Some of us might say, "Give me a few years of indulging and winning and looking really, really good, and I'll get back to you on that.")

Qoheleth's question is found in Scripture in a book that explores it from every conceivable angle. It's ancient Hebrew "wisdom literature"—three millennia old—which may not be just the most contemporary book in the Bible, it may be the most contemporary book on our bookshelves. It's Ecclesiastes.

The King's Buffet

Who's Qoheleth? He's the voice of Ecclesiastes. His name translates to "the Teacher" and he's identified as "son of David, king in Jerusalem" (Eccles. 1:1) So naturally we think of King Solomon the Wise. But this collection may come from a later period, so we could be hearing from a compiler of Solomon's wisdom.

But what's meant to be clear to us is that this is the voice of someone who has the position, power, and occasion to try it all, a sumptuous buffet of princely prerogatives: higher education, fleshly delights, grand building projects, anything money can buy. And try it he does, with a purple passion.

Let's look at Qoheleth's quest (what some Bible scholars call "The Royal Experiment") and see how it turned out.

Higher Ed (Eccles. 1:12-18). "I devoted myself to study . . . and increased in wisdom more than any of Jerusalem's former rulers" (Eccles. 1:12-16), Qoheleth modestly confesses. Here's a man who knows the value—and cachet—of a really, really good education. (I'll bet he enjoyed being called "The Teacher.")

But education can make fools of us. Like the prominent professor who visited the bishop. "Welcome, Mr. Smith!" the bishop said, "Won't you take a chair?" "That's *Dr.* Smith," his pedigreed visitor huffed. "Oh, forgive me," said the bishop. "Please, take *two* chairs!"

Seeking after wisdom is much to be valued, surely. (This is, after all, "wisdom literature.") It's the theme of Proverbs: "Blessed is the man who finds wisdom" (Prov. 3:18). But Qoheleth discovers the mixed blessing that is education: "with much wisdom comes much sorrow" (Eccles. 1:18) The more we learn, the wider our eyes are opened to the world's folly and madness and pain and sorrow. Wiser but sadder. Some things, it turns out, just can't be fixed with a proper explanation.

The Good Life (Eccles. 2:1-3). "Next, I tested pleasure—laughter, wine, the embrace of folly" (2:1-3) Onward through the buffet line! Qoheleth clearly knows how to have a really, really good time, the kind a royal budget can subsidize. But all that fun, and the wine that fuels it, doesn't deliver the expected payoff, apparently. (It's a wise person who discerns the difference between the Good Life and a good life.)

We mustn't get too ascetic here. Our God is the creator of every earthly delight, a reflection of the Creator's good nature in this good world. God invented all pleasures! And C. S. Lewis reminded us, badness is only goodness spoiled.

But Qoheleth finds that pleasure for its own sake—artificially generated by chemicals or sheer excess—"accomplishes nothing" (2:2). The morning after always comes, and any sense of well-being conjured the night before has vanished with the sunrise, leaving him as empty as before. If not with Peggy Lee, then Qoheleth surely would sing along with Mick Jagger: "I Can't Get No Satisfaction."

Projects (Eccles. 2:4-6). "I undertook great projects" (2:4). Qoheleth decides to leave the party and become a renowned builder, an architect of splendid projects: mansions, vineyards, gardens, parks, reservoirs. Perhaps he'll find himself in aesthetics.

On a recent visit to New York, my wife and I passed by the very conspicuous Trump Tower on Fifth Avenue. Like Trump Towers in Chicago, Toronto, Las Vegas, Dubai, and elsewhere, it's a really, really large monument to one man's remarkable sense of self.

But maybe the Teacher is after more than mere artistic self-aggrandizement ("something people will remember me by"). He's making the world a greener, lovelier place, and that's a good thing, right? But alas, he sees his grand projects as just more examples of what he calls (nine times in Ecclesiastes) "chasing after the wind"—the same wind that eventually erodes all our monuments.

Stuff (Eccles. 2:7-11). Predictably, the Teacher's quest drives him to hyper-accumulation: "I amassed stuff—really, really lots of stuff—herds, flocks, silver, gold, slaves" (2:7-8). He's the patron saint of conspicuous consumption—"I denied myself nothing." And though there's a certain "delight" in his manic pursuit of the Israelite version of the American Dream, still Qoheleth's question hangs in the air: Is that all? Isn't there *more?*

Having run the buffet table, he renders his verdict on his Royal Experiment: It's not working. "Meaningless!" (2:11), "Vanity!" It's a word (*hebel*) meaning "empty, senseless, vapid" he'll repeat no fewer than thirty-eight times.

Our bummed-out Teacher closes the chapter with more of his glass-half-empty reflections. You can strive for wisdom, but fickle fate ultimately overtakes wise and fool alike, and both are soon forgotten (2:13-16). You work like a dog to build something good, but in the end you can't take it with you, and it's left to somebody who never broke a sweat (2:18-21). Toil all day, toss and turn all night, and that's pretty much it (2:22-23).

Tell us how you really feel, Qoheleth! And he does: "I hate my life!" (2:17).

Frederick Buechner sums it up as only he can: "If you decide to knock yourself out getting rich . . . all you have to show for it in the end is the biggest income tax in town and a bad liver; and when you finally kick the bucket, the chances are that your dim-witted heirs will sink the whole thing in a phony Florida real estate deal . . . . If you decide to break your back getting a decent education and end up a Columbia Ph.D. and an advisor to presidents, you'll be just as dead when the time comes as the high school drop-out who went into sausage-stuffing, and you'll be forgotten just about as soon." [1]

This Is God's Word?

So. What do we make of all this negativity? Hardly sounds like Scripture! Well, it does, actually. It sounds like many of the psalms, those we call the "laments." Long before we had the Blues, we had the laments of Israel: prayer-songs from people in pain, beseeching their God, "What's the deal? Life isn't fair! How long will this go on? Lord, I protest!" Almost half the psalms are laments.

It seems that in the infinite wisdom and grace of God, it was ordained that holy Scripture should give expression not only to our highest aspirations and deepest affections, but to our most intense experiences of frustration and failure as well. (And for a God who welcomes my rants and interrogations as I grapple with it all, I say, praise God!)

I don't want Qoheleth for my primary theologian or my spiritual formation director, but I'm grateful for some substantial gifts that God conveys to us through him. I'll suggest three.

First: *Credible common ground for today's seeker.* Research reported in 2009 that almost three out of four unchurched adults under the age of twenty-nine characterize us insiders as "out of touch with reality."[2] Ouch! Outsiders aren't convinced that we're in tune with many of the real questions and struggles so conspicuously present in our world. And if they feel we've never wrestled with the fallen angels, then where, pray tell, is our common ground? How will today's church engage today's cynic?

One contemporary author warns of a chic contemporary cynicism of ironic detachment (embodied in Jerry Seinfeld's TV character)—the fashionable skepticism that avoids at all cost any appearance of taking anything seriously.[3] But such cynicism is not life-engaging, much less life-giving.

Qoheleth's, however, is the voice of someone fully engaged with life and its Creator. "Bring it on!" he says, as off he goes in search of the really Real. His voice in our Scripture gives us credible common ground upon which to engage the mind and heart of today's honest seeker . . . while helping us draw closer to many of our neighbors in our grasp of their restlessness and frustration.

Second: *A keen social critique.* Qoheleth's a brilliant social critic. He candidly probes the merits of the very gods (money, sex, power, education) that beckon us down paths of trivial pursuit. He reminds me of David Foster Wallace, a gifted but conflicted writer who, plagued by severe depression, took his own life in 2008. In 2005, Wallace challenged Kenyon College students to choose their gods carefully:

> This, I submit, is the freedom of a real education: You get to decide what to worship. In the day-to-day trenches of adult life, there's actually no such thing as atheism. There's no such thing as not worshipping. Everybody worships. The only choice we get is what to worship. And an outstanding reason for choosing some [concept of God] to worship . . . is that pretty much anything else you worship will eat you alive.
>
> If you worship money and things . . . you'll never feel you have enough. Worship your own body and sexual allure and you'll always

feel ugly, and when time and age start showing, you'll die a million deaths before they finally plant you . . . . Worship power—you'll feel weak and afraid, and you'll need ever more power over others to keep the fear at bay. Worship your intellect, being seen as smart—you'll end up feeling stupid, a fraud, always on the verge of being found out.[4]

And Qoheleth sayeth, Amen.

And third: *A hunger for the Real Buffet.* David Hubbard has written that wisdom literature can help point us to "the greater wise man, and the greater wisdom."[5] That's where I'd like us to end up today. With Jesus.

What Qoheleth reminds us as he moves us through the royal buffet line of education and pleasure and projects and acquisition is that these are all ultimately unsuccessful saviors. Deliverers who don't deliver. Because they can't, not at the level of our deepest need. That's why it's not working.

Jesus met a woman at a well. And they had this breathtakingly honest, substantive conversation about hunger and worship and marriage and eternity. And the promise he made her that day was that he would—personally and perpetually—give her . . . satisfaction.

"Everyone who drinks this water will be thirsty again, but whoever drinks the water I give him will never thirst. Indeed, the water I give will become in him a spring of water welling up to eternal life" (John 4:131-14). He later identifies that "living water" as God's Holy Spirit (John 7:37-39).

What I believe it is that you crave—Mr. Zoolander, Mr. Brady, Ms. Lee, Mr. Jagger, et. al.—is something absolutely and fundamentally *spiritual.* We're spiritual beings, you and I, in constant need of spiritual filling. And the pleasure we all seek—forever unsatisfied until we know it—is God's pleasure in us. But we can know it. Because God took on our flesh. And took on our sin. So we would never have to be burdened by unbearable burdens or content with meager satisfactions.

Is there *more?* Oh yes. There really, really, really is. Come to the feast.

FROM OCCUPATION TO VOCATION
ECCLESIASTES 5:8-20

JERRY TAYLOR

En Route to the Sermon

It is my practice to allow the text to firmly settle in my mind. Once the text settles I meditate upon it while walking, driving, or waiting in line at the store. Throughout the day I pay close attention to statements, experiences, and encounters with the expectant hope that they will shine new light upon the text. This contemplative process generates thoughts and ideas that serve as sermonic insights and provide a contemporary flavor to the scriptural passage.

I found it challenging to develop a sermon from the genre of wisdom literature. Wisdom literature seems less narrative than other genres in Scripture. It would have been less difficult had the text in Ecclesiastes been similar to the gospel narratives. The gospels contain well structured narratives that effectively energize the human imagination.

However, Tom Long's comments on the move from narration to *phronesis* helped me appreciate the need to do more preaching from wisdom literature. He claims that a younger generation of preachers has grown impatient with narrative preaching. As the impatience grows, many preachers are moving to a different genre: *phronesis* or wisdom preaching. Long defines wisdom preaching as helping the audience make sense of spiritual truth and how it fits into everyday life.

If preached effectively, Ecclesiastes 5:8-20 yields great wisdom that brings meaning and purpose into a person's life regarding work, money, and vocation. In light of America's present economic crisis and high unemployment, wisdom preaching has the potential of having a positive impact on the nation as a whole. This is especially true in light of Long's belief that

Ecclesiastes is written for people for whom the grand narrative has been temporarily disrupted.

The Sermon

Desperate craving for wealth and possessions is fuel that adds fury to the blazing flames of oppression. In a world pregnant with the twins of greed and violence, injustice struts about as a proud father awaiting the birth of his offspring. Injustice has a long lineage of descendants that span across all generations of human history. Injustice is as ancient as the human family.

The wise man says in Ecclesiastes 5:8, "If you see the poor oppressed in a district, and justice and rights denied, do not be surprised at such things; for one official is eyed by a higher one, and over them both are others higher still."

In some nations the government is the greatest arena for injustice, the place where it finds the most effective expression. In some countries the government is totally corrupt. In those nations government is nothing more than a cleverly devised system of organized crime backed by military power and the threat of police brutality.

In the wake of the major economic collapse of 2008 and the massive bailouts of major corporations, many Americans view the federal government of the United States of America as a corrupt enterprise. The economic collapse revealed that authorized officials in the banking industry as well as in the government had been co-opted by the spirit of capitalistic greed.

Bankers and politicians encouraged the average American to adhere to the seducing spirit of greedy consumerism. The advertising industry effectively aroused an internal state of discontent in the American soul. Unbridled commercialism awakened in Americans an untamed aspiration to higher standards of luxurious living.

The free market was flooded with goods, products, and services that were anything but free! Great profits went into the pockets of those who participated in the business of manufacturing America's discontent.

- What happens to a person when the gateway to the spirit of acquisition is completely open and undisciplined?
- What happens to a nation that is cleverly seduced into being a gluttonous and consumer-oriented society?

- What happens to a culture that adopts a "Wall-E World" mentality that sees super-sized consumption as its only purpose for existing?
- What happens to the moral fiber of the American family when entire households become chronically addicted to the economic enterprise of spending, borrowing- and debt?
- What kind of moral climate is birthed in America when unsupervised greed on Wall Street has illegal intercourse with unsupervised consumption on Main Street?

Ecclesiastes 5:11 says, "As goods increase, so do those who consume them." As goods increase, desire increases. Greed is an ever-expanding trait. The "gold rush" eventually grows into a "mad rush." Someone has wisely observed that we start out wanting silver. Next we want gold. We move from wanting gold to desiring land. Our desire for land becomes a desire to possess and own the people who live on the land. We must ask ourselves how much of the world's content is required to satisfy the internal discontent that has been stirred within America's soul?

The Wise man says in Ecclesiastes 5:12, "The sleep of a laborer is sweet, whether he eats little or much, but the abundance of a rich man permits him no sleep." The person who has managed to become rich spends the balance of his or her life worrying about losing it all. They keep one eye on their abundance and the other eye on their neighbor.

The thought of losing wealth and standing among the nations of the world makes America anxious. America's feeling of national insecurity constantly keeps her threat level on high alert. The wise man cautions that such fear can easily lead to a disposition of irrational protectionism.

Fear-based hoarding leads to a constrictive and destructive pattern of behavior that threatens a nation's healthy survival and innovative creativity. America's best offering to the world is not money, power and wealth. Instead the best offering America can make to the world is its vocational commitment to seeking justice, truth, liberty and integrity.

The wise man says, "Whoever loves money never has money enough; whoever loves wealth is never satisfied with his income." The insatiable love of money and wealth creates unethical competition, greed, and overconsumption. These things can cause the complete impoverishment of a nation's soul.

Edward Deci explores this behavior in his book entitled *Why We Do What We Do?* He says that "politicians and economists call for more spending to boost the GNP, while on the other hand critics and psychologists argue that affluence impoverishes the soul." He states further, "It seems that people who are the healthiest focus on developing satisfying personal relationships, growing as individuals, and contributing to their community."

When Americans care more about money, wealth, affluence, and consumption we sadly become like the people described in James Pattern and Peter Kim's book, *The Day America Told the Truth.* According to these authors, about twenty-five percent of our citizens would be willing to abandon their entire family to receive ten million dollars; about seven percent would be willing to kill a stranger for that amount; and three percent would be willing to put their children up for adoption.

These statistics are evidence that some Americans care more about becoming millionaires than they care about the higher ideals of life. As money becomes America's god, liberty, truth, compassion, and community will all be sacrificed on the altar of greed. When Americans are devoted to money their faith suffers during severe economic downturns.

America today is in the tight grips of a frightening financial crisis. Fear has carjacked Wall Street and seems intent on driving a panicked economy into a state of nervous depression. The unemployment rate is rising each day. Jobs are being cut like amputated limbs overtaken by diabetes. Americans are frustrated and angry because they can no longer depend on having a steady source of income.

Many of the material things Americans once possessed are now being repossessed by the banks. Others who still have employment live with the constant anxiety of losing their jobs and their possessions.

In Ecclesiastes 5:13 the wise man describes such a situation as a grievous evil under the sun. He says, "I have seen a grievous evil under the sun: wealth hoarded to the harm of its owner, or wealth lost through some misfortune, so that when he has a son there is nothing left for him."

America's economic crisis forces us to ask an important question. What is our understanding of the relationship between money, consumer goods, and work? As American consumers we have been subversively conditioned to place the greatest value on commodities. In Ecclesiastes 5:11 the wise man puts goods and consumerism in proper perspective. He says, "As goods increase, so do those who consume them. And what benefit are they to the owner except to feast his eyes on them?" The wisdom of the New Testament writer of the book of James reminds us that we can never satisfy the lust of the eyes and the lust of the flesh.

This brings us to a second significant question. How do the desires for riches and the abundant lifestyle impact the American attitude towards work? We are taught early to get a good education so we can "land" a good job. A good job will in turn provide us with a good income. We are subtly taught to seek work not for work's sake but to seek work for money's sake. When we seek work solely for the sake of making money we are best described by the wise man's words in Ecclesiastes 5:17. He says we spend our life doing work in hopeless darkness, filled with great frustration, affliction, and anger.

This verse should help Americans see work not as an occupation but as a vocation. A vocation is a calling to care about a specific work our creator has us equipped for. The work becomes bigger than a job or position of employment. Our vocation becomes the avenue through which the soul finds its truest expression of love for God and the neighbor. Vocation is not primarily viewed as a source of income but as an opportunity for the "outflow" of God's love into the world.

The wise man says in 5:18 that it is good and proper for a person to find satisfaction in his toilsome labor under the sun during the few days of life God has given. He says further in verse 19, when God gives a people wealth and possessions, and enables them to enjoy them, to accept this portion and be happy in their work—this is a gift of God.

Adequate compensation follows the faithful exercise of one's vocation. As Jesus says, all these other things will be added unto us. It is when vocation occupies us that God keeps us occupied with gladness of heart. Our hearts are occupied with gladness because we understand that we may experience job change or even job loss, but we never lose our life's work. There are no layoffs when it comes to one's vocation.

When we are engaged in a meaningful vocation our work becomes more like a paid vacation. Walking worthy of our vocation removes all anxieties about our career. On the one hand, a career can be controlled, obstructed, and undermined by others. On the other hand, only you are in control of your vocation.

We leave jobs behind and we change careers, but there is no force on earth that can end our vocation. Careers are human inventions, but vocation is God given. Career is what you do but vocation is who you are. A career without a vocation becomes the greatest producer of discontent. A career without a vocation turns work into an occupation that ultimately feels like incarceration.

Chapter
FOUR

PREACHING WISDOM FROM THE FLIPSIDE

ALYCE M. MCKENZIE

Wisdom as Paradigmatic Theme for Preaching

Some years ago, when I lived in Pennsylvania, my daily commute took me past a billboard with a huge picture of Jesus, long hair, flowing robes, outstretched arms. The caption read: "How will you spend eternity?" Someone had spray painted a line through the word "eternity" and substituted the word "today." The graffiti artist had changed the billboard so that it featured the basic question of wisdom. It is a question Socrates asked centuries ago: "How should one live?" Wisdom, across cultures, religions, and centuries, is practical reflection on the question, "How will you spend today?"

This collection of essays is crafted around the conviction that wisdom is "a paradigmatic theme for preaching." Why? For one thing because wisdom, though a neglected biblical genre, is essential to the canon. For another thing, the wisdom question is the question people come to church to have answered. What is wisdom? Where can I get it? What difference will it make in my life? How is it better than what I'm living by now?

This essay is crafted around the conviction that we need to preach to what I'm calling the "wisdom question": How shall we live today? After a brief description of wisdom, I'm going to turn to folly, understood as the flipside of wisdom. Such a focus on the shadow may make us appreciate the light all the more. We will be equipped to invite hearers onto the path of wisdom, made even more appealing because we have shown them the dangers of the path of folly. While the focus will be primarily on folly as it is portrayed in the Book of Proverbs, along the way I'll mention how both wisdom and folly are depicted in other biblical wisdom books.

Wisdom in the Book of Proverbs is often spoken of as "The Way," suggesting that wisdom involves repeated patterns of behavior that are in keeping with the guiding presence of God.[1] Wisdom scholar Glenn Pemberton points out that "Like Wisdom, Folly is a path, or way of life, that shapes a person into a fool, not a one-time decision or failure."[2] We'll explore that process more fully later.

When we speak of biblical wisdom (Hebrew *hokmah*, Greek s*ophia*), we mean the art of discerning how best to think and act in specific situations of daily life in ways that conform to the character of God. The first chapter of the Book of Proverbs states that its sayings have been collected so that the young and gullible (the *peti*) may learn "shrewdness" and those already schooled in wise living might learn "skill" (*tahbulot*) in putting wisdom teachings into practice.

Biblical wisdom in the Old Testament is concentrated in three books that come between the end of the salvation history and the beginning of the Prophets: Proverbs, Job, and Ecclesiastes. Each of these books reached their final form during the post-exilic period. The savings acts of God (the Exodus and crossing of the Red Sea and the giving of the law at Sinai) do not appear in these books. While all three address our billboard artist's question, each provides a different answer. Their focus is looking for patterns in nature and human relationships that yield useful lessons for specific future situations, lessons often packaged in proverbs and parables.[3] In the New Testament, a practical, ethical focus, framed by an eschatological vision, characterizes the sayings and parables of the synoptic Jesus, which offer an answer to the question: "How shall we live today?" that subverts conventional wisdom.[4]

Wisdom in the Bible is not just a collection of sayings to memorize and quote. Wisdom is more like a jewel with several facets which we are to turn

in the light. Wisdom is a Teacher, a curriculum or body of teachings, and the
way of life that results from following those teachings. Not to jump the gun,
but keep in mind that folly is promoting oneself to the role of Teacher, disre-
garding the teachings of wisdom, and blundering through a path that leads
to self-destruction. Says Woman Wisdom in chapter 8, "For whoever finds me
finds life . . . but those who miss me injure themselves; all who hate me love
death" (8:25-36).

In the first place, wisdom, especially as we encounter it in the Book of
Proverbs, is an aspect of the character of God. That character is personified in the figure of Woman Wisdom who, in 1:20-33ff and 8:1-21, stands
at the crossroads calling youth onto the path of life.[5] Second, wisdom is a
body of teachings for how to live in conformity with that divine character.
Third, wisdom is the way of life that results from adhering to those teachings.
Proverbs is the only wisdom book that puts these teachings in the mouth of
Woman Wisdom, but Job and Ecclesiastes as well as Proverbs offer a picture
of what the wise life looks like. The pictures are different. In Proverbs the wise
life looks moderate and industrious. It is primarily built on the continuity
between act and consequence, assuming that wise actions lead to positive outcomes and foolish ones to negative results. It is characterized by respect for
God, parents, and others, including the poor. In Job, the wise life looks like the
courage to question traditional and simplistic notions of divine retribution.
It means living by the insight that human understanding is limited and God,
though mysterious, is present with us when we suffer unjustly. In Ecclesiastes
the wise life looks like acceptance of the harshness and seeming arbitrariness
of life. It takes the form of a life focused on the gifts of God in each precious
and precarious moment: life, health, relationships, work, food, and drink. In
the synoptic gospels, Jesus' countercultural wisdom results in a life lived by a
risky, faith-fueled reliance on God that trumps making security the project of
one's lifetime.[6]

Wisdom, then, is Teacher, curriculum, and a way of life that results from
following that curriculum. To preach in answer to the question of wisdom
("How shall we live today?") is to preach so that God's light shines through
all three facets of wisdom's biblical identity. First, it introduces listeners to
their Teacher: God, the giver of wisdom. When we do this, our sermons have
a function similar to that of Woman Wisdom herself who introduces listeners

to the character of God. Second, to preach in response to the wisdom question is to introduce people to a body of teachings for daily living. When we do this, our sermons have a function similar to that of the sages of Israel who wrote and collected the sayings and reflections that make up biblical wisdom literature. Finally, to preach to the wisdom question is to preach so listeners can envision situations in which they will apply those teachings. It takes the form of spelling out the negative results they can avoid and the positive results they can expect. When we do this, our sermons function like the proverbs themselves, offering nuggets of vivid ethical guidance, depicting scenes of blessedness and of folly that flow from human choices.[7] To preach to the question of wisdom is to make a homiletical commitment to preach to invite, instruct, engage, and equip.[8] It is to commit ourselves to preaching that is personal, practical, and preemptive.

Since the early 1990s, working on my doctoral dissertation on preaching on proverbs from Proverbs, Qohelet, and the synoptic Jesus, I have written numerous articles and books about wisdom and preaching wisdom. I've written about how wisdom came to be personified as a woman in the postexilic period when traditional male authority figures and institutions of king, court, temple, and priest were non-functioning and the role of women as teachers of wisdom in the home came to be highly, if temporarily, valued.[9] I've written about Proverbs 31:10-31, the" Ode to the Woman of Worth," pointing out that she is not the total woman none of us can be, but Woman Wisdom herself, inviting us into the well-run household of wisdom.[10] I've written about how Jesus, a student of wisdom, through his parables and subversive aphorisms, invites us into the household of God and how John's Prologue copies Woman Wisdom's job description from Proverbs 8 and pastes it into that of the Incarnate Son, the Word made flesh.[11] I've written about the difference between self-help wisdom and biblical wisdom and our need as preachers to offer biblical wisdom's vision of God's character and the good life to a world that just can't seem to help itself.[12] I've written about the four qualities of the wise life according to the wisdom of the Old and New Testaments.[13]

That's six sentences now that have started with the words "I've written." I'm either an egotist or I'm obsessed with wisdom. You can't be both. I like to think it's the latter. Why would someone spend all that ink writing about preaching and teaching wisdom? It's because I believe wisdom questions are the questions postmodern people are asking. And biblical wisdom is so much better than its secular competitors. I suspect that the time may be ripe for people to have ears to hear the biblical answers to the wisdom question. As we proceed into the second decade of the twenty-first century, many people are interested in spiritual formation and forming community, but not necessarily in institutional religion. Most learn interactively and visually and often carry with them to worship a craving for multisensory experiences. Many are biblically illiterate but hungry for wisdom. They are, at the same time, aware of their own yearning for wisdom and unaware of the resources of our biblical wisdom tradition. So they stand in the self- help section flipping through the latest book whose cover features a success guru in an expensive suit flashing a dazzling smile.

I say we preachers introduce them to biblical wisdom, a "God help us" wisdom as opposed to "self-help" wisdom. That would mean preaching sermons that offer strategies for living that come from God and lead to God, contribute to the good of our community, and do not dead end with ourselves. Biblical wisdom's practical messages and memorable forms are tailor-made for postmodern people who want answers to the question, "How shall we live today?" Postmoderns want these answers in sermons that are memorable, sensory, practical, and dialogical.

Preaching Wisdom from the Flipside

Wisdom's time has come in our pulpits. And it's time to think about wisdom from a fresh angle, time to reflect on preaching wisdom from the flipside, using folly to understand wisdom.

One of the themes of Joseph Webb's helpful book *Preaching for the Contemporary Service* is that postmodern people love to go behind the scenes. They love reality shows. Maybe in our preaching we ought to go behind the scenes of wisdom and take a look at folly. One of my students went on a home tour recently, where people with lovely homes let other people tromp through them and "ooh" and "aah" during the holidays. There is nothing wrong with that. I've been on a few myself and enjoyed them. But my student said to her spouse, "Nobody's life is this perfect." So they started looking for the overflow room, the junk room, the "let's throw everything that blows the pretence of show home in here" room. She said they always found one. It was roped off and there was a sign that said "Do not enter."

So for the rest of this essay we are going to ignore the "Do not enter" sign and go behind the scenes of wisdom to see what's in the forbidden zone. We're going to talk about folly.

When was the last time someone said to you, "Don't do that; that's folly?" Folly has become a quaint word, not to be taken seriously. During the 1700s rich people in England built little replicas of Roman Temples or Egyptian Pyramids on the grounds of their estates. They were called "follies." For a long time I assumed they were named follies for some ethical reason, because people did things in them they later realized only seemed like a good idea at the time. But no, I came to find out folly just meant lighthearted or frivolous, built primarily for decoration.

The kind of folly the biblical wisdom book of Proverbs talks about is not a reference to habits of life and thought that are lighthearted diversions. Folly in the Bible is dangerous to the point that it is life-threatening. It is the opposite of wisdom. As wisdom is synonymous with righteousness, so folly is synonymous with wickedness (Prov. 1:3; 2:20-22). I think folly is still alive and well today, even though we don't talk about it. We're afraid to name it and claim it, because we don't really know what it is. We can't define it because it's the flipside of wisdom and we really don't know what wisdom is. Well, we think we do. We're just wrong. We're often operating out of a secular definition of wisdom rather than a biblical definition. And since folly is the flipside of wisdom, when we're living by the wrong definition of wisdom, we have an inaccurate notion of what constitutes folly, foolish behavior and actions. If we understood folly more graphically, it stands to reason that we would experience wisdom more intimately.

Self-help wisdom is a billion dollar business. Some of its writings encourage a life lived for values beyond the self. It's not fair to caricature the thought of Deepak Choprah, Eckhart Tolle, Stephen Covey, Wayne Dyer, and Marianne Williamson as shallow and self serving. But much secular self-help thought assumes that the way to get wisdom is to use human will power for personal goals. It's self-motivated, self-directed, and often self-absorbed.

For secular self-help literature, wisdom is mustering the discipline, persistence, positive outlook, and strategic networking to achieve personal goals. For some new age self-help literature, wisdom is harnessing the power of the universe to fulfill my heart's desire, provided my heart's desire is moral and legal and benefits others in some way. By this definition, how do we under-stand its flipside, folly? It would be the inability to focus and persist in taking steps to meet my goals. Folly would mean allowing myself to be sidetracked from high self-esteem and high achievement by anything, even a time com-mitment or a person who does not further my agenda.[14] On the surface, there are similarities between this outlook and that of Proverbs. Only the wisdom of Proverbs is regarded as coming from and leading to God, not with the goal of personal success but of community *shalom* and peace with with justice for all members of the community.

Preaching the Identity of the Wise Person from the Flipside:
Portraits of the Fool in the Book of Proverbs

One way to preach to wisdom from the flipside would be to preach about the varieties of fool in Proverbs and to invite people to see themselves in each. Bringing in the positive wisdom alternative would be crucial for the sermon to inspire hope and change. The sages of Israel envisioned life as a path. There were two distinct groups traveling the path, the wise and the fools. The wise were righteous, while the fools were wicked, and there was really no middle ground. The fool has a very different answer to the question, "How shall we live today?"

Wisdom scholar James Crenshaw points out that there are distinctions among fools in the eyes of the sages. There are six different terms for fools in the Book of Proverbs, each with a different nuance. One can't help but call to mind the song lyrics, "What Kind of Fool Am I?"

Six Biblical Terms for the Fool

Peti—naïve, untutored individual

Kesil—innately stupid person

Ewil—person characterized by obstinacy

Ba ar—a crude individual

Nabal—a brutal, depraved person

Les—a foolish talker who values his or her own opinions overmuch[15]

The preventive medicine for all these types of folly is a healthy dose of the fear of the Lord which is the beginning of wisdom. Acknowledging God as the source of insights for daily living keeps us from gullibility, obstinacy, and loving the sound of our own voice more than the still small voice of God.

But if the fear of the Lord doesn't appeal to us, it's good to know we have options. In our contemporary consumer culture we enjoy options. It may be that, when it comes to ways of being a fool, it's not one per person. Like a greedy child with her hand in the trick-or-treat bowl, I can grab a whole handful of foolish characteristics. If folly is a lifelong path, perhaps a person can come to be characterized by almost all of these descriptors at various times and in various occasions. Looking down the list, I see a few qualities and habits I find within myself right now. I can be gullible at times. I have been known to allow a commercial to play on my insecurities and buy a product that is supposed to enhance my self-esteem or image. I can be oblivious to the feelings of someone sitting across from me at the table. I don't consider myself brutal or depraved but I'm capable of the occasional petty or envious thought, which is a step in that direction. Once I make up my mind about something, I am sometimes immune to contrary evidence. So I can be naïve, thick headed, stubborn, petty, and opinionated at times. But that doesn't mean I'm a fool, does it?

Preaching the Path of Wisdom from the Flipside:
Tracing the Career Path of the Fool

Another way to preach wisdom from the flipside would be to trace the career path of the fool. Wisdom scholar Dianne Bergant points out that the designation of wisdom in the Book of Proverbs as "the Way" calls to mind a path worn by constant use. The implication is that wisdom involves patterns of behavior, not isolated acts. The purpose of this "way" is the formation of an interior disposition. Biblical wisdom affirms that this "way" can be seen as a divine gift.[16]

Folly is a path, too. Glenn Pemberton describes it as a gradual "deformation of character." Being a fool is not something anyone decides when they're young they want to be when they grow up. It happens gradually, because folly is seductive. He marks four stages in the career of the fool. The first stage is an isolated foolish action. Most foolish actions, according to Proverbs, result from a lack of self control. Where self control is lacking, behaviors that produce strife in individual and communal life occur: drunkenness, quarreling, anger, hatred and greed. The ideal of the sages of Proverbs is one who is "cool in spirit" (17:27). "One who spares words is knowledgeable; one who is cool in spirit has understanding." "Those who are hot-tempered stir up strife, but those who are slow to anger calm contention (15:18).

An isolated foolish act doesn't make someone a fool anymore than an isolated wise act makes someone a sage. But continued foolish acts lead to the second stage of folly: when folly becomes a sport. The sages put it graphically, "Like a dog that returns to its vomit is a fool who reverts to his folly" (26:1). The fool comes to enjoy his folly even if it makes him sick. Its destructiveness has become part of its allure. It is wisdom that the fool can't stand. "A desire realized is sweet to the soul, but to turn away from evil is an abomination to fools" (13:19).[17]

The third career stage moves the fool beyond correction. "Fools despise wisdom and instruction" (1:7). They follow the path of least resistance to quick rewards, fast money (1:13), excitement (1:11-12), sexual pleasure (5:3-6), and acceptance (1:14).[18] The sages urge the young to avoid the company of third stage fools; they are corrupt beyond correction and nothing good can come of associating with them. To quote a non-biblical but time honored proverb, "You lie down with dogs; you rise up with fleas."

The final stage in the career of the fool is what Pemberton calls "collapse and rage." We all know people whose lives are littered with patterns of destructive behavior that impact others as well as themselves. They often blame everyone and everything but themselves for their ongoing predicament. They even blame God. This is the stage four fool. "Fools self-destruct and then hold God responsible for all their problems. Nothing is their fault. Family, friends, society, and God are to blame for the disarray of their lives."[19]

Such is the career of the fool, if he or she is not intercepted by the teachings of the sages. It begins with an initial foolish act born out of lack of self-control, which is common to the young. Folly proceeds to the enjoyment of repeated foolish acts. It moves on to the state of being beyond correction. Folly ends in collapse and rage. Throughout the process the fool is dangerous, not only to himself but to those whose lives he touches.

Tracing the career path of the fool in a sermon or sermon series would have rich homiletical potential. The preacher can convict listeners (as long as she is humble enough to include herself) without pointing the finger. Just holding up the picture of the fool will invite listeners to see themselves in the mirror. The unappealing image might make us take a second look at the flipside of folly, the career path of wisdom.

In my reflection on wisdom over the past several years, I have found some ways of thinking about what wisdom is and the kind of life to which it leads that are helpful for preaching. I've worked out what I see as the three pillars of wisdom in the Bible, both Old and New Testaments. I've reflected on the four virtues of the wise life according to the wisdom of the Old and the New Testaments. So let's look at them from the flipside, from the perspective of folly and see what insights we might gain for preaching to postmodern people in a way that invites, instructs, and equips them for a life shaped by the wisdom of God. What would it look like to approach wisdom from the flipside?

Preaching Wisdom's Three Pillars from the Flipside

In studying biblical wisdom, I dug up three pillars of wisdom.[20] The first is that wisdom begins with the "fear of the Lord" in Proverbs, defined, not as fear of imminent punishmen,t but radical respect for God the Creator as source of all moral guidance.[21] In the New Testament, wisdom begins with faith in Christ as the Wisdom of God.

The second truth is that wisdom leads to an order of life. While no amount of human planning can master the mystery and unpredictability of life, when we live industriously, moderately, and with respect for the poor in our midst, we enhance the harmony of the community. In our personal lives, we act as our own best friend rather than our own worst enemy.

The third pillar of the wisdom approach in the Bible is that wisdom is a gift from God. Woman Wisdom embodies this truth in Proverbs; Jesus later walks the earth, teaches, heals, is crucified and resurrected as Wisdom in Person, God's gift to humankind in the New Testament and today.

Keeping in mind the wisdom question everybody brings to church, "How shall we live today?" a three-week sermon series that began with the flipsides of these three truths could be intriguing. We could contrast folly's approach with three pillars of its own.

Week One: "Trust in myself is the beginning of folly." This is the flipside of the affirmation that "the fear of the Lord is the beginning of wisdom" (1:7). The path of folly would advise us to begin our journey by putting our complete trust in ourselves. Who wants to fear God? We know it means faith, not fear of punishment, but still. Who wants to live in accountability to God? I respect God, but does it have to go beyond that? What if I don't have the will or discipline to engage in the habits that would invite God's wisdom into my life: prayer, worship, small group study, searching the Scriptures, and acts of kindness in the community?

Bob Dylan wasn't kidding when he sang, "It may be the devil or it may be the Lord, but you're gonna have to serve somebody." This week the preacher could dig around and find out what it is that we really trust, really fear in life. What kind of fears pop up when we think we have only ourselves to rely on? God is the only thing we are told to fear in Scripture. Not being alone, illness, death, job loss, rejection, or aging. The fear of the Lord is the beginning of wisdom. That's why God and sometimes God's emissaries tell all kinds of people in the Old and New Testaments, "Don't be afraid, for I will be with you."

Week Two: Folly leads to a disordered life. The flipside of the insight that wisdom leads to an ordered life is that folly leads to a disordered life. The path of wisdom tells us that following the teachings of wisdom leads to a certain order of life: knowledge of God, harmonious relationships, a reputation for integrity in our dealings with others, and a sense of purpose in life. But what if I don't want that? What if I want disorder in my life? What if I want to get rid of boundaries? What if I want the rewards of a relationship with God without the effort of prayer, Bible study, involvement in the community of faith, and work toward social justice? Or what if I want the good things of life easily and quickly? What if I want to live just for myself? What if I don't want to have to curb any of my appetites? What if I don't see how that is anyone's business but my own? We can begin by not fearing the Lord and proceed by jettisoning self-control and accountability to anyone beyond ourselves. But eventually, somebody's going to ask us the Dr. Phil question: "How's that going for you?"

The advantage to preaching for changed lives by means of folly is that it holds up a nameless person who is at the same time none of us and all of us. It's at the same time non-threatening and convicting.

What if I want relief from the disorder of my life but I cannot achieve it myself? What if I am in bondage to an addiction or habit of life I cannot overcome on my own strength of will alone? Before self-loathing leads me onto the path of folly, I need a wisdom intervention, with insights and presence that can come only from God the giver of wisdom.

Week Three: Folly is a continual rejection of God's gift of wisdom. The flipside of the insight that wisdom is a gift from God is that folly is the continual rejection of the gift of God's wisdom. Why does God insist on offering the gift over and over again? Why won't God take no for an answer? To continue on the path of folly, the path of least resistance toward fast rewards, actually takes quite a bit of energy. We have to keep clicking on the "will not attend" box on God's e-vite. We have to keep turning down the gift of God's presence to guide us through daily life and figure out how is the best way to live today on our own. The best way to live today, for the fool, is to live it for me. If there were a box the fool could click on to convey to God "Don't show this invitation again," she would. But it keeps popping up. What a nuisance for the fool! Folly is the continual rejection of the gift of God's wisdom.

Preaching the Four Virtues of the Wise Life from the Flipside

My research into the way of life presented in the Bible's wisdom literature reveals that it depicts four wisdom virtues, each of which is necessary for the wise life.[22]

The bended knee is a metaphor for the reverence for God and the gift of wisdom that is the prerequisite for receiving and growing in wisdom. ("The fear of the Lord is the beginning of wisdom" (Prov. 1:7).

The listening heart or the discerning mind is what Solomon asked for in 1 Kings 3:9. It is the ability to be attentive to the dynamics of situations and the needs of those around us so we can be avenues of God's wisdom.

The cool spirit is the self-control necessary to curb one's appetite for folly and stay on the path of wisdom for the good of the community. "Like a city breached, without walls, is one who lacks self-control" (Prov. 25:28).

The subversive voice is the moral courage to speak up and act out when traditional religious, cultural values are at odds with the wisdom of God. We see this in Job and Ecclesiastes, who challenge the assumption that wise living automatically leads to good fortune and that suffering is therefore a sign of folly and wickedness. We hear the subversive voice in Jesus' challenge to the ritual purity and table fellowship conventions of his day.

If we want to live wisely, according to the Bible, our lives will exhibit these four virtues, habits of the heart or dispositions. But if we don't:

We will live "wise in our own eyes" (Prov. 3:7). No one, even God, can tell us anything.

We will live focused on our own agendas and needs to the exclusion of those around us, who only exist for our benefit anyway.

We will live indulging our appetites without thought for how our lack of restraint affects others. It's none of their business anyway.

We will not stick our neck out for anybody else but will only speak out when it's our rights and life that are on the line.

I moved to Texas from Pennsylvania several years ago, and so I no longer drive by the billboard I mentioned earlier. But I can still see its question in my mind's eye: "How will you live today?" Wisdom has one answer. Folly has another. In your preaching, try starting with folly's answer for a change, so that its shallow, destructive face shows up in high definition. Then offer people 3D glasses through which to view the way of wisdom: displaying its scenic beauty, using the vivid language, imagery, and themes of the sages, Jesus included. Preaching this way may make our own steps along the way more confident. And if we close our eyes and listen, we just might just hear the sound of new footsteps joining the wisdom journey.

What Kind of Fool Are You?
Options from the Book of Proverbs

Pete (simple; gullible)

1:4 to teach shrewdness to the simple

1:32 Waywardness kills the simple and the complacency of fools destroy them.

8:5 O simple ones learn prudence; acquire intelligence you who lack it.

14:15 the simple believe everything. The clever consider their steps.

Kevil (innately stupid)

> 3:35 the wise inherit honor, stubborn fools, disgrace.
>
> 10:18 lying lips conceal hatred and whoever utters slander is a fool.
>
> 14:16 the wise are cautious and turn away from evil, but the fool throws off restraint and is careless.
>
> 17:12 Better to meet a she-bear robbed of its cubs than to confront a fool immersed in folly.
>
> 18:2 A fool takes no pleasure in understanding but only in expressing personal opinion.
>
> 18:6 A fool's lips bring strife and a fool's mouth invites a flogging.
>
> 18:7 The mouths of fools are their ruin; Their lips are a snare to themselves.
>
> 26:4 Do not answer fools according to their folly or you will be a fool yourself.
>
> 26:5 Answer fools according to their folly or they will be wise in their own eyes.
>
> 26:11 Like a dog that returns to its vomit is a fool who reverts to his folly.
>
> 26:12 Do you see persons wise in their own eyes? There is more hope for fools than for them.
>
> 29:11 A fool gives full vent to anger, but the wise quietly holds it back.

Ewil (obstinate fool)

> 1:7 The fear of the Lord is the beginning of wisdom, fools despise wisdom and instruction.
>
> 10:21 The lips of the wise feed many, but fools die for lack of sense.
>
> 14:9 Fools mock at the guilt offering, but the upright enjoy God's favor.
>
> 15:5 A fool despises a parent's instruction, but the one who heeds admonition is prudent.
>
> 16:22 Wisdom is a fountain of life to one who has it, but folly is the punishment of fools.
>
> 17:28 Even fools who keep silent are considered wise; when they close their lips, they are deemed intelligent.
>
> 20:3 It is honorable to refrain from strife, but every fool is quick to quarrel.

24:7 Wisdom is too high for fools. In the gate they do not open their mouths.

Ba'ar (crude, brutish person)

12:1 Whoever loves discipline loves knowledge, but those who hate to be rebuked are stupid.

Nabal (brutal, evil person)

30:22 Under three things the earth trembles; under four it cannot bear up

A slave when he becomes king and a fool when glutted with food.

30:32 If you have been foolish, exalting yourself, or if you have been devising evil, put your hand on your mouth.

Les (scoffer)

3:34 Toward the scorners he is scornful, but to the humble he shows favor.

9:7 Whoever corrects a scoffer wins abuse; whoever rebukes the wicked gets hurt.

9:8 A scoffer who is rebuked will only hate you, the wise, when rebuked, will love you.

13:20 Whoever walks with the wise becomes wise, but the companion of fools suffers harm.

14:6 A scoffer seeks wisdom in vain, but knowledge is easy for one who understands.

14:7 Leave the presence of a fool, for there you do not find words of wisdom

15:12 Scoffers do not like to be rebuked. They will not go to the wise.

19:25 Strike a scoffer and the simple will learn prudence.

21:24 The proud, haughty person named "Scoffer" acts with arrogant pride.

22:10 Drive out a scoffer and strife goes out. Quarreling and abuse will cease.

24:9 The devising of folly is sin and the scoffer is an abomination to all.

29:8 Scoffers set a city aflame but the wise turn away wrath.

"You May Be a Fool if . . ."

Proverbs

According to the Book of Proverbs, you may be a fool if . . .

Speech:

You blurt out angry words that make bad situations worse or ruin good ones (15:1,4, 18; 16:32; 17:27; 22:24; 29:22).

> You don't know the value of judicious, pleasant speech (16:21; 23; 24).
> You slander others (10:18).
> You gossip, ruining others' reputations (11:12-13).
> You pick fights (26:21).
> You say dishonest things (12:19; 19:22).
> You blather on, saying little of importance (10:8; 12:23; 13:3; 18:2).
> You brag and boast about your accomplishments (30:2).
> You can't ignore an insult (12:16).
> You have not learned the importance of listening (18:2; 17:28).
> You are a know-it- all (12:15; 18:13).

Possessions

You think having lots of material possessions will make you happy and contented (15:16; 17:1; 16:16-19).

> You place gaining money above your integrity and relationships (14:20; 18:23; 28:11)

Appetites

You cannot control yourself in certain areas of your life. This is having a negative effect on you and others, but you are not doing anything about it (6:6; 23:30; 24:30-34; 25:28; 30:24-31).

> You lack self control (25:27-28).
> You are lazy (1:7b; 6:6; 18:9; 24:30-34; 30:24-31).

Relationships

You are unfaithful to primary relationship and betray the one closest to you (6:27-29; 15:6; 22:4).

> You keep company with people who bring out the worst in you (13:20).

You enjoy spoiling the good fortune and happiness of others through deceitful speech and actions (16:27-30; 17:19; 17:23; 18:6-8).

You meddle in other people's concerns that are none of your business (26:17).

You cannot stand to be corrected (1:7b; 25:11-12).

You disdain those who are poor(17:5).

You hold grudges (17:9).

Qohelet (Ecclesiastes)

According to Qohelet, you may be a fool if . .

You're always looking for a future lucky break rather than dealing with the unchanging realities of the present (1:4-11).

You think your hard work can bring security (2:18-22; 9:11-12).

You think wealth will bring you contentment (5:10-12).

You think your accomplishments can bring you a lasting memory (2:18-22).

You think your wise living can help you escape from death (3:16-22).

You think you can know all there is to know about life and God (5:1-7; 8:10-17).

You are impatient and try to force events to premature conclusions (3:1-8).

You live as if you will never get old (12:1-8).

You think you can live life without coming in contact with tragedy and injustice (4:1-7).

Job

According to Job, you may be a fool if . . .

You believe you are the center of the Universe

Your motive for obedience to God is personal gain

You equate the presence of suffering with the absence of God

You believe that suffering must be God's fault or the sufferer's fault

You are quick to offer unsolicited theological interpretations of other people's suffering

Jesus

According to Jesus, you may be a fool if . . .

> You think you can harbor evil, foolish thoughts, and they will stay your
> little secret (Matt. 5:21; 5:27).
>
> You think wealth can bring you lasting benefit (Matt. 6:29).
>
> You are gullible to false teachers and resistant to Jesus' message (Matt.
> 7:15-16).
>
> You think obsessive worry does any good (Matt. 6:25ff).
>
> You are preoccupied with personal security (Matt. 16:24-26).
>
> Your desire to be well thought of leads you to engage in displays of public
> religiosity (Matt. 6:2).
>
> You believe you are in a position to judge others (Matt. 7:1).
>
> You believe you are entitled to retaliate for wrongs done to you
> (Matt. 5:38).
>
> You hinder the approach of others to God (Mark 9:33-37; Matt. 18:10-14).
>
> You cannot ignore an insult (Luke 22:51; Matt. 16:1-52).
>
> You have no trouble sleeping while others suffer (Gethsemane).

LEAVES FROM THE NOTEBOOK OF A RECOVERING FOOL

Proverbs 15:1-4, 14

STEPHEN C. JOHNSON

En Route to the Sermon

A gentle answer turns away wrath,
but a harsh word stirs up anger.
The tongue of the wise commends knowledge,
but the mouth of the fool gushes folly.
The eyes of the Lord are everywhere,
keeping watch on the wicked and the good.
The tongue that brings healing is a tree of life,
but a deceitful tongue crushes the spirit.
The discerning heart seeks knowledge,
but the mouth of a fool feeds on folly. (Prov. 15:1-4, 14)

The invitation to preach a sermon that addresses folly as the flipside of wisdom did not seem appealing at first, until I began to consider the fact that I may have a certain expertise in the arena of foolishness! One of the ways I have learned to negotiate discomfort with preaching texts and themes that lean more toward judgment than grace is to do so confessionally.[1] I am a fool. At the same time, I am not left in that state. I was reminded of this by Alyce McKenzie's and Glenn Pemberton's helpful description of the *way* of wisdom. Way designates journey or progress. We are moving in the direction of wisdom, which, of course, implies that we are moving away from folly. I am a fool, but by the grace of God, a recovering fool.

The notion of a journey toward wisdom or the recovery from folly called for several homiletic choices. I chose one of the dominant expressions of folly

in Proverbs—the speech of Proverbs 15. I also chose to set the sermon metaphorically in the context of a recovery group led by a wise woman. Such a setting allowed the sermon to capture both the journey/recovery theme and the
personification of wisdom—both prominent features of the Proverbs.

Finally, as a gospel sermon, it was important that the sermon mirror the
pericope's move toward grace. In the end, the sermon must not only say that
foolish speech leads toward death, but that the tongue that brings healing is
a tree of life.

The Sermon

It's my turn and, quite simply, I don't want to admit it. I'm happy to sit among
this circle of people and listen asthey introduce themselves "My name is . . .
and I am . . . ." Next person, "My name is . . . and I am . . . ." Round the circle
we go, prompted by our facilitator—a wise sage who's been down the road a
time or two. Here's the next poor chap, "My name is . . . and I am . . . ." I offer a
friendly, understanding expression—you know, caring, sympathetic eyes with
an encouraging half-smile, but I'd rather not be the recipient of such a gaze.
I'd rather not take my turn. I'd rather not admit it.

All eyes are on me now. I exhale a deep sigh. "My name is Stephen and I
am . . . a fool." There, I said it. I've spent my whole life trying to avoid it, trying
to look and sound wise. I've become quite adept at constructing a wise-look-
ing, wise-sounding self. Let's see now, how can I preach a sermon on foolishness that sounds really wise? See how clever I am? Deep down, though, I'm
just a recovering fool. Fool-hearted. Foolish pride. Foolish ambition. Fool.

My life is marked by foolishness. When I was a boy, bored one afternoon,
I hatched a plan to climb up the tree in the front yard with the water hose.
I'd climb up high enough to be hidden in the branches behind the leaves.
And then, when cars passed by, presto! Instant rain shower! It was genius, I
thought. Hidden up in the tree, they'd never know where I was—never mind
the water hose running across the front yard and up the tree.

I put my plan into action. I climbed up the tree with the water hose, and
crouched there in the branches, waiting patiently, watching up the road.
I didn't have to wait long until up the road comes not a car but a man on
a motorcycle. Jackpot! I waited for just the right moment, the motorcycle

approaching, and then pulled the trigger. Water sprayed out from the tree, arcing into the air, raining down on the road and the motorcycle man. Perfect! The motorcycle passed through my rain shower and screeched to a halt. I let loose the trigger and sat still in the tree, trusting my cover. The motorcycle man got off his motorcycle, walked over to the tree, peered up at my position and said, "Zachaeus, come down out of that tree. I'm going to your house today." Well, those weren't his exact words, but you get the idea. Foolish.

And I remember some years later when I was a freshman in college (need I say more?). It was winter, and some friends from back home were moving to town. They needed some help unloading the moving truck, so I thought I'd help. I remember my car was out of gas so I asked the girl I was dating if I could take her car. For whatever reason, she let me take her car even though it was the middle of an icy winter storm. Yes, you guessed it. I slid that thing right into the back end of an eighteen-wheeler out on the interstate. Smashed the front end of her new car like an accordion—totaled it. Foolish. Foolish.

And it's not like I've grown out of it. This last summer I travelled with my family to Europe for a month's worth of travel about the continent. We landed in Germany and were received by friends at a church camp in Gemünden to recover from our jet lag for a day or so. It was the afternoon, and we were working hard to stay awake that first day. Some of the youth invited my daughters to go and play Capture the Flag. On their way out to play, they turned to me and invited me to come along as well. My wife's words as I took off with the kids were, "Do not get hurt." So, of course, about thirty minutes in I got all wrapped up in chasing teenagers around a field, planted to turn and just like that, felt my hamstring tear. I rolled on the ground in pain, faced with the fact that I had become the old guy that tried to do too much and hurt himself. What am I going to do, limp at a slow pace across Europe for the next four weeks? Foolish. Foolish. Foolish.

"My name is Stephen . . . and I am a fool."

The woman in our group—surprised at how I have gone on and on talking about my own foolishness—suggests that perhaps I am in the beginning stages of recovery from my foolishness. Which leaves me to ponder where all of this began, to wonder about the origins of my foolishness, of foolishness in general. It's an important question, you know, because to be a fool is not just a matter of a silly, childish prank or an occasional poor use of judgment.

To be a fool is really a matter of character formation—or rather, malformation. "What is it that forms us, shapes who we are for good or for bad?" the woman asks.

I suppose there are many ways to answer that question. I am formed by the things that surround me. You know, like certain assumptions, attitudes, and behaviors that I soak up like a sponge, that I breathe in like the air. I am shaped for good and sometimes for bad by the worldview I inherit—assumptions about life, about what holds value. You get the idea.

I realize I am beginning to ramble. The wise woman looks at me and says, "Like being saturated in a culture that frames happiness and contentment in terms of the sheer accumulation of material possessions?"

"Yea," I say. "Like that."

I add, "I always say, 'Better is a little with the fear of the Lord than great treasure and trouble with it. How much better to get wisdom than gold!'"

I continue, "But it doesn't have to be as fuzzy as all that worldview, air-that-I-breathe stuff. Very specific things, concrete events that happen in my life, also form me. Sometimes those things that malform me are related to people, relationships that go bad. Sometimes they are related to circumstances, unexpected tragic things that happen to me that are really no one's fault."

I ramble on about that for a few minutes, until the wise woman points me back on track. "But the origins," she says, "where does all of this begin?" All the people in the circle turn their heads, look at me, and lean in close.

"I don't know. I'm not sure."

There's a long, uneasy pause before the woman breaks the silence. "My research shows that above all other potential causes of a person's foolishness is words. That's right; it begins with words."

This idea that the most basic place of foolishness is located in words has my attention. I am, after all, in the business of words—words preached, words taught, words taught about preaching. I think a lot about words—what they do, how they function. I say to the woman, "You seem to know a lot about this stuff. Maybe you should write a book or something."

"As a matter of fact, I've been working on something just like that," she says and she reaches down and pulls something that looks like a journal out of her book bag. She flips through a few pages and then begins to read:

"The discerning heart seeks knowledge, but the mouth of a fool feeds on folly."

She flips through a few more pages:

"A gentle answer turns away wrath, but a harsh word stirs up anger."

"The tongue of the wise commends knowledge, but the mouth of the fool gushes folly."

"In my book," she says, "foolishness has more to do with words than anything else. Here's what I'm thinking: if the path to foolishness begins with something as seemingly small and innocent as words, then perhaps the path to recovery begins there as well." The sage looks around at all of us and then back down at his book.

"The tongue that brings healing is a tree of life."

Now, I know this "tree of life" language. The tree of life is the source of life, that from which life emanates. In the beginning, it is said, when God had finished making the heavens and the earth, he planted a garden. In the midst of the garden was the tree of life.

"The tongue that brings healing is a tree of life."

That life draws all things together, sustains all things and holds all things together. That life reflects the peace, wholeness, and togetherness of God who gave life with nothing more than words. "And God said . . . and there was . . . and it was good."

"The tongue that brings healing is a tree of life."

Words have this kind of power—power to give life and power to take it away. In his memoirs, Ellie Wiesel remembers when he was a young Jewish boy growing up in the town of Sighet the day the Nazis arrived:

> For us it was too late, in every sense. Sacrificed, abandoned, and betrayed, delivered to the invader and left to face him alone, we were ignored by everyone but the enemy. He alone paid attention to us. And when he drove us to the ghetto, we went.
>
> I see images of exodus and uprooting, reminiscent of a past buried in memory; ravaged, dazed, disoriented faces. Everything changed overnight. *A few words uttered by a man in a uniform, and the order of Creation collapsed.* Everything was dismantled; ties were severed, words were emptied of their meaning. Homes became unrecognizable . . . .[2]

Later, Weisel would wrestle with whether he could speak about what he had experienced. He would say, "Words frightened me. What exactly did it mean to speak? Was it a divine or diabolical act?"

If it is true that words have this kind of power—to create, sustain, give life, draw and hold all things together—then it is also true that words might have the power to dismantle and tear the world apart. These words, seemingly innocent things slipping off the lips so easily, are the ground zero for foolishness.

Surely, it's important to be careful what we choose to say. But "watch your tongue!" just doesn't seem adequate. The beginning place of foolishness is nothing more than the failure to realize the power of words to give life or take life away, the potency of speech to build up or tear down. You throw words around carelessly, as if they are nothing? Foolish.

If that is the case, wise speech is not just that which reveals some secret knowledge. Wise speech is that which, like the tree of life, participates in the sustaining, nurturing, reconciling words of the creator God. My own words connected to, emanating from, echoing the sound of the God who gives life by words.

"The tongue that brings healing is a tree of life."

Thanks be to God!

THE HOUSE OF MIRTH IS EMPTY

Ecclesiastes 6:12-7:10

MICKI PULLEYKING

En Route to the Sermon

"How shall we live today?" According to Alyce McKenzie, this is the wisdom question. I agree. We go to church and listen to sermons because we yearn to hear something that is real and that will make a difference in our real lives. Yet we rarely hear the wisdom of Ecclesiastes: it is not an easy book to preach. Ecclesiastes does not get much sermon time form those of us who preach from the lectionary texts.

Mckenzie concludes that the wisdom questions are the questions postmodern people are asking. If this is the case, then we need to preach Ecclesiastes for it resonates with the themes of postmodernism. In the modern era, facts were clearly observable. In the postmodern era, ambiguity is all we have, and hope lies in possibilities. Nothing is clear. Perhaps Qohelet was a postmodernist: all is vanity, a vapor, dust in the wind.

Many times during the writing of this sermon I asked myself why I had agreed to preach on this text. Then I remembered—apparently I cannot cease to wrestle with these issues! I teach a course on "Suffering and Meaning." I wrote my dissertation on death. Does that mean I have answers? No. It means the questions won't let me go. I too yearn for the wisdom that can be found in these ancient scriptures. I have been preaching every Sunday at the Billings Christian Church for nearly twenty years. I have never before preached on Ecclesiastes. Rarely am I willing to be so personal. But as McKenzie reminds us, according to Qohelet, "you may be a fool if you think you can live life without coming in contact with tragedy." So let us preach about tragedy.

I took McKenzie's advice: I tried to create a sermon that is "sensory." In this sermon, my goal is to preach like the Teacher. I do not find a systematic structure to Ecclesiastes. It has a wandering, rambling, meandering feel. Therefore we shall wander through a few verses contemplating a few ideas that perplexed the author in the ancient world and the reader in our present time.

The Sermon

Ecclesiastes is known as *wisdom* literature. Yet it is certainly a different kind of wisdom from that to which our culture is accustomed. Philosophers investigate epistemology. Ecclesiastes is a profound epistemological treatise on the origin, nature, and limits of human knowledge or human wisdom.

Like Jesus, who declared "blessed are those who mourn" and "the last shall be first," the teacher, Qoheleth, turned conventional understandings of wisdom upside down.

What are we living for? Is there a purpose in life? Why do we keep getting up in the morning? As the Teacher seeks to make sense of life, he speaks of the reality of death in almost every chapter. Death claims us all. Nothing is worse. We are all transients and we are all terminal. The uncertainty and the questions haunt us even as our shadow is passing quickly to its end: "For who knows what is good for mortals while they live the few days of their vain life, which they pass like a shadow? For who can tell them what will be after them under the sun" (Eccles. 6: 12 NRSV).

The verse that follows is not an answer, but perhaps a path to understanding: "A good name is better than precious ointment, and the day of death, better than the day of birth" (Eccles. 7:1). The day of death is "better" than the day of birth? In some languages "better" can be translated as "is of more value" or even "is more instructive." Have you been in the room, held the hand, or cradled the body of one you love as he or she passes from life to death? The lifelong impact of such a moment is really unquantifiable. I wouldn't call it "better"—but longer lasting. A good name will last a lot longer than ointment—the day of death is eternally transformative for the living and the dying.

My mother had large sun spots and freckles on her arms and hands. Her face had deep smile wrinkles and her eyes reflected many years of living. As a child, I confess with sadness, I was embarrassed by my mother. She gave birth to me when she was forty-four, which made her considerably older than most of my friend's moms. I always thought she had the most beautiful smile. But she never fit our culture's definition of a beauty queen. (It was not her goal either, I might add.) For a moment I was alone in the hospital room where my dear mother lay dying. A major stroke had taken one side of her body and she would never be able to swallow again. She was slowly starving to death. One of her hands could feel nothing. It was limp and lifeless. Her other hand could still respond—could still stroke our hair as she sought to console *us*. She could still take her one "good" hand and pat the nurses on the back, though she was unable to speak, as a way of thanking them for turning her or changing her. Death was so close. All we could do was wait. I tried to memorize her hands. As I patted and squeezed and caressed both of them, I was overwhelmed by her—beauty! I wondered what my grandmother felt when she had first held my mother's newborn hands on "the day of birth". It struck me—surely they could not have been as beautiful then. These were the hands that kneaded the hot rolls and pie crusts for us; these were the hands that had planted the roses; these were the hands that had safely guided me across many streets in life . . . what indescribable beauty I beheld: "And the day of death is better than the day of birth." One biblical scholar writes about this passage, saying ". . .human illusions burst before the harsh reality that removes all distinctions among people."

The Teacher says, "It is better to go to the house of mourning than to go to the house of feasting: for this is the end of everyone, and the living will lay it to heart" (Eccles. 7:2).

A few weeks ago four teens in our congregation were asked by their Sunday school teacher to name the person whose influence had been the greatest upon them. I would have guessed that they might have mentioned their mom, dad, or a teacher. But no, two of the four named someone who was dead. Hayden told of his grandfather who died suddenly a couple of years ago. Spenser talked of his brother, Micah, who died before he was born. Spenser told of many early memories of frequent trips to the cemetery down the street from where he lived as a little boy. When I heard who Spenser counted as his greatest influence I cried. I am his mother—the one who took him to the cemetery in his red Radio Flyer wagon to deliver a cupcake to his brother's grave after every birthday celebration. Spenser was born into "a house of mourning" and he "laid it to heart," which is a phrase found often in Ecclesiastes to describe the process of observation and reflection. As a young teenager, Hayden was thrust into the house of mourning. The Teacher would agree: anyone who would be wise must contemplate death, our common destiny.

Some are shaped by sorrow early in life, some later. But I suspect we are all "most influenced" by our sorrows and the reality of death if we are willing to realize it. Spenser told me recently over Indian food that he sort of understands the human fascination with some kind of an apocalypse. (We were talking about the latest end of the world movie—"2012"). He said, "The apocalypse really does happen to us all. We all ultimately lose *everything*, Mom!" He's right.

So how do we live with the impending apocalypse? Psalms 90:12 says, "Teach us to number our days that we may get a heart of wisdom." Face death. Don't try to eat or drink it away in the house of feasting.

The Teachers says, "Sorrow is better than laughter for by sadness of countenance the heart is made glad" (Eccles. 7:3).

This verse reminds me of Proverbs 14:13, "The heart is sad even in laughter and the end of joy is grief." The Hebrew word for laughter is the same in both texts. It means empty fun. I don't think the Teacher is opposed to a good time. So how could sorrow possibly be better than laughter? If I thought the Teacher believed that suffering and death somehow makes one happier, I would stop reading.

The word sadness is not an abstract noun but rather refers to an experience or event that causes the face (countenance) to appear sad. Even though there is not by necessity any purpose in suffering, it is possible to learn from our sorrows. A Lebanese poet wrote, "When you are joyous, look deep into your heart and you shall find it is only that which has given you sorrow that is giving you joy. The deeper sorrow carves into your being the more joy you can contain."

The Teachers says, "The heart of the wise is in the house of mourning; but the heart of fools is in the house of mirth" (Eccles. 7:4).

The house of mirth is the house of merriment. It is where fools live. It is the house built on sand. We live in a society that loves merriment. Are we a culture of fools? Certainly we are a culture that clamors for Disneyland and Prozac! We want death quarantined behind curtains in nursing homes and hospitals. I like Disneyland—for a day or two. But I couldn't live there. It isn't real, and we all know it. So we go home, to the real world and take our meds to make us merry in the house of mirth. Twenty-seven million Americans were taking antidepressants in 2005. That's about twice the number in 1996. Let me be clear, I have no doubt that many people have been helped and help is a good thing. Clearly, I am not talking about those who suffer from severe and life threatening depression, who desperately need help to make it through the day. But I am concerned about several studies which reach one of two conclusions: first, for millions of Americans studies show that placebos are just as effective as anti-depressants. Second, for millions the depression continues, even with the meds.

In Ecclesiastes, Wisdom teaches, "The heart of the wise is in the house of mourning." In the *Dhammapada*, the Buddha concludes, "Life is suffering." Mourning is reality. Are the sages suggesting that perhaps we should accept the reality of sorrow and death rather than seeking to eradicate it? In the January/February 2010 edition of *Scientific American Mind*, researchers suggested that depression is not a mental disorder, but rather like fever, it is a response to infection that performs a specific and vital function. "Depression promotes focused rumination about problems. People in this state are better at solving complex social dilemmas" (p. 58).

I am not suggesting that everyone flush their psycho meds. I am suggesting that we consider the possibility that acceptance of the reality of mourning throughout life, not just the week after a funeral, rather than the removal of sadness is a wiser path. Is it possible that wisdom is found in the house of sorrow?

The wise Teacher continues to question common conclusions. He even questions wisdom! One scholar suggests that one of the major themes of Ecclesiastes is that wisdom cannot achieve its goal. Wisdom cannot secure existence. "Surely oppression makes the wise foolish" (Eccles. 7:7). And wisdom cannot secure the future. "Consider the work of God: who can make straight what he has made crooked?" (Eccles. 7:13). The future is insecure—those words are not words of comfort. Seeking comfort does not seem to be the goal of the Teacher.

Everyone who hears these words knows they are true: the future is insecure and God is unknowable. "In the day of prosperity be joyful, and in the day of adversity consider: God has made the one as well as the other, so that mortals will not find out anything that will come after them" (Eccles. 7:14).

It is difficult for me to imagine the Teacher singing along with the Christian country singer Josh Turner, "You could say we're like two peas in a pod, me and God."

I can, however, imagine the Teacher smiling (slightly) had he heard the adage, "The Bible says that God made humans in God's own image. And humans have been returning the favor ever since." The Teacher does not offer us an anthropomorphic, manageable, or knowable deity who will protect us from suffering. As Alyce McKenzie concludes, wisdom is realizing that our human understanding is limited and God, though mysterious, is present with us in our suffering: "In Ecclesiastes the wise life looks like acceptance of the harshness and seeming arbitrariness of life. It takes the form of a life focused on the gifts of God in each precious and precarious moment."

Death is real . . . We dwell in the house of mourning . . . . We cannot know God . . . . The wise look at these realities and do not flee—but *accept* them and choose to get up in the morning anyway. Focus on something outside of yourself. Ecclesiastes reminds us not to be foolish: do not think hard work can actually bring security; do not think wealth can bring contentment; do not think your accomplishments can bring a lasting memory; do not think you can know God; do not think your wise living can help you escape from death. How shall we live today? We must make meaning in the midst of the sorrow. Accept the realities we cannot change. Be authentic and real. Live today—

Chapter
FIVE

THE CHARACTER
WISDOM SHAPES

DAVE BLAND

Some worthwhile attempts have been made to identify the value of
wisdom for character formation from the pulpit and in academia.[1] Still
there remains a tendency for a few contemporary scholars and preachers to
ignore the book of Proverbs as a viable resource in this regard. Some Old
Testament scholars believe the proverbial sayings tend toward the pedantic,
holding no redeeming value for the serious student.[2] Others maintain that one
should not consume proverbs in large doses because, like taking medicine,
a little is a good thing but one can easily overdose.[3] In addition, they leave a
bitter moralistic taste in the mouth so one should consume them with more
palatable food![4] In response, I would argue that proverbs are less like medicine
taken only when ill and more like essential daily vitamins taken to fortify the
body. They are only moralisms if one reads them out of the context of chapters 1-9[5] and the fundamental proverb, "The fear of the Lord is the beginning
of wisdom" (1:7; 9:10).

Representing the voice of many preachers and pastors, William
Willimon announces, "Generally, I dislike the book of Proverbs with its lack
of theological content, its long lists of platitudinous advice, its 'do this' and

'don't do that.' Pick up your socks. Be nice to salesclerks. It doesn't hurt to be nice. Proverbs is something like being trapped on a long road trip with your mother, or at least with William Bennett."[6]

These voices express the view that Proverbs contains little that deserves serious reflection. Such assessments, however, are premature. The book of Proverbs has much to contribute to the faith community today, especially as it relates to the strengthening of one's character. If, for instance, someone were to say, "That person is intelligent," it would reveal nothing about that individual's character. Yet if someone were to point out, "This person is wise," that would speak volumes.[7]

The Character of the Wise

Proverbs provides the basic resources for instruction in the formation of godly character. It does not accomplish this in regimented stages or in a cookie cutter, one-size-fits-all fashion. Instead, it achieves its purpose in a way that takes seriously the complexities of life. Flexibility and diversity are a part of the process.

Wisdom is primarily relational, that is, it concerns itself with how we relate to God and to others. The opening poem in Proverbs announces that the book will instruct in justice, righteousness, and equity, all character qualities of healthy relationships (1:3).[8] Proverbs makes a vital contribution to the understanding of character by directing that character to its implementation in life, the way we interact with God and our community.[9] Proverbs gives character rigor and discipline, keeping it from becoming "just a bog of blessed assurance."[10] Character formation is pushed into the streets of daily living weaving it into the very fabric of life (Prov. 1:20-21); it is even closely tied to building a secure and healthy home life (9:1; 14:1; 24:3-4).[11] Proverbs represents Scripture's effort to put character in working clothes.[12]

Proverbs approaches the task of character formation as a process. That is why, in the opening poem, the sage says that wisdom is not just for the young and naive but also for the wise (1:5-6; cf. also 9:8-9; 15:31; 19:25; 21:11, etc.). It is for *all* who seek wisdom (8:4). It is a lifelong process for all who seek wisdom. Thus even King Lemuel continues to receive instruction from his mother (31:1-9). According to Proverbs, no one is ever too old to learn.

Folly and Wisdom Embodied

The development of character in the book of Proverbs is not a neatly organized *modus operandi*; it's messy. But the process is intentional. The book is loosely organized in a movement from anti-wisdom, displayed in the deceptive rhetoric and self-centered life of the gang (1:8-19), to mature wisdom, demonstrated in the God-centered life of the woman of noble character (31:10-31).

The gang, who represents the total absence of the fear of the Lord, embodies all the qualities of those who live the life of a fool (1:8-19). These individuals personify the vices of greed and violence. What they claim to offer appears quite attractive: adventure, easy money, and camaraderie (vv. 10-14). But their appearances are deceiving and their rhetoric manipulative. They steal, abuse, and mistreat others in order to exert power and gain wealth for themselves (vv. 13-14). Ultimately, their self-centered lifestyle results in their own downfall. With no awareness of the consequences, these scoundrels fall into their own trap and commit mass suicide (v. 18, NRSV). The sage concludes with this observation, "Such is the end of all who are greedy for gain; it takes away the life of its possessors" (v. 19). Proverbs thus begins with a full-blown image of the destructive lifestyle of fools.[13] They destroy both themselves and the community.

As the son[14] listens to his father after hearing this warning, I can imagine the son replying with shock and even hurt, "Is life really this dangerous? I'm not going out and committing robbery and murder and practicing random acts of violence! Why would you even think such a gang of hoodlums would tempt me?" Even though inexperienced and naïve, this son is not rebellious. The sages indicate that the son has started down the path of wisdom (2:8, 11, 20; 6:20). Why, then, would the father warn his son about the scandalous activities of the gang? Their way of life did not develop overnight. It happened as a result of a series of poor choices, each one leading further down the path of folly until manifested in full blown gang behavior. The father may be saying to the son, "No, I know you are not tempted to such criminal activity. However, the daily decisions related to matters of honesty or dishonesty, self-control or instant gratification, patience or impatience, kind or harsh speech, generosity or greed, and humility or pride are life and death matters."

The little daily decision to practice these virtues or vices add up to create the kind of character that will either make one wise or, like this gang, foolish.[15] That's why the proverbs are so important. Gerhard Von Rad makes the assessment that in ancient Israel proverbs were more important for making daily decisions than were the Ten Commandments.[16] In the end, one discovers that these little decisions are not so little after all.[17]

From the destructive image of the gang, the book weaves its way through a series of parental instructions and a somewhat disorganized maze of proverbial sayings building to the final image in the last chapter of a woman (31:10-31). This woman represents the character wisdom shapes. One might think that Proverbs would end with the image of a king like Solomon (1:1; 10:1) or Hezekiah (25:1) or Lemuel (31:1). After all, the royal figures overshadow the book of Proverbs. They embody wisdom and model the ideal life. But no, Proverbs ends with a description of a commoner, a woman efficiently managing the family farm.[18] Here the reader receives an image of what wisdom looks like in its mature form.

Unfortunately the church has marginalized the use of this poem in its corporate life. While an appropriate memorial service poem for a loving grandmother or in some cases for a Mother's Day celebration, the Christian use of this passage is quite myopic. In contrast, the way the poem is used in Proverbs calls for its incorporation into the mainstream of everyday life.

The misunderstandings that swirl around this poem contribute to holding it hostage to limited use. Let me respond to a few. First, this is not an example of male chauvinism with the husband sitting on his backside conversing with the elders in the city gate, while the wife works her fingers to the bones. The fact that the husband is "known in the city gates . . . among the elders of the land" serves to describe a lifetime of hard work to gain the respect among the people (v. 23).

Second, this woman is not some man's "trophy wife." True, the worthy woman lives to empower her husband in the city gate. This proverb poem, however, does not say it all; it expresses only one side of the relationship. Both the wife and the husband live to empower others and not themselves.[19] Egalitarianism in the sense of "I will do my half and you do yours" is foreign to Scripture. The woman of valor lives to serve others. She serves her family, the poor, and her community. Worldly wisdom, in contrast, is all about power, position, and status. James describes such wisdom when he asks:

Who is wise and understanding among you? Show by your good life that your works are done with gentleness born of wisdom. But if you have bitter envy and selfish ambition in your hearts, do not be boastful and false to the truth. Such wisdom does not come down from above, but is earthly, unspiritual, devilish. For where there is envy and selfish ambition, there will also be disorder and wickedness of every kind. (James 3:13-16)[20]

Worldly wisdom is self-serving. It is also divisive and arrogant (1 Cor. 1:18-31; Jer. 9:23-25). In contrast, godly wisdom lives to empower others, which is what the woman of chapter 31 is all about.

Third, this is not a picture of some women's worst nightmare. After reading this passage, a few can become discouraged and exclaim, "How can I do all the things she does?" This woman, however, is not a Martha Stewart on steroids: in a twenty-four hour period you make your own clothes, churn your own butter, and plant your garden. What the woman of valor does is not all in a day's work. Rather, it is a picture of a lifetime of hard work, discipline, instruction, and fearing God. These kinds of misunderstandings result in trivializing the value of the poem in the life of the church.

There is, however, another way of understanding the passage that more appropriately fits with its purpose in the book of Proverbs and opens up its value to the contemporary faith community. The woman of noble character is wisdom incarnated, a real woman, not a personification of wisdom.[21] She works hard to provide for her family, her friends, and her community with a particular concern for the poor. She stands in contrast to the lazy farmer in 24:30-34 and to the strange woman of chapter 7 who imports *her* sheets from Egypt, "the height of ancient conspicuous consumption."[22] The woman of valor is not unlike a farm wife of a previous generation who was called on to fulfill a multitude of tasks.

This valorous woman represents the culmination of a life focused on *becoming*.[23] The poem describes an A to Z portrait of what the virtues look like when embodied in flesh. The woman practices righteousness, justice, and equity (1:3). She combines the ideal qualities of godly women exhibiting self-control, patience, care, diligence, discipline, humility, generosity, and honesty (see again James 3:13-18). She teaches. Wisdom is in her mouth; on her

tongue is "the teaching of *hesed*" (v. 26). The poem concludes with the ultimate quality she displays: she "fears the Lord" (v. 30). She is the paradigm of
wisdom in its maturity and the goal for which all must strive.[24] Ultimately she
is a non-gender-bound model.

Bob Keeshan, known to millions as Captain Kangaroo, was for decades
the beloved host of a morning television show for children. When he began his
role as the grandfatherly Captain in 1955, Keeshan was only twenty-eight years
old. So to look the part, he had to wear a great deal of make-up, fake whiskers,
and a wig. But as he played the role through the years, his hair turned white and
wrinkles appeared. Keeshan found that he needed less and less make-up. Near
the end of his career he could say: "I have grown into the part."[25]

The Rigorous Journey between the Scandalous Gang and the Valorous Woman

Proverbs begins with an image of folly presented in the portrait of the
gang (1:8-19). The book concludes with a counter image: the image of wisdom
in its maturity, embodied in the life of an ordinary woman who fears the
Lord (31:10-31). Cradled between these two images is the sages' pedagogy for
moving individuals from a lifestyle of greed (1:19) to a lifestyle of generosity
(31:20). The sages embark on this journey with the son and with *all* who desire
the character wisdom shapes (8:4). I would like to briefly show, using large
brush strokes, the path this journey takes.

In chapters 1-9 the father prepares the son for the journey. As Glenn
Pemberton points out so well in chapter two, in several of the opening instruction poems the father is primarily concerned with getting the undivided attention of the son. No multi-tasking here; complete focus is necessary because
these are life and death matters. The father takes responsibility in instructing
the son about the temptations of life, about the company he keeps, and about
the choices he must make. Instruction in these opening chapters is unidirec-
tional, from father to son. The son remains silent and attentive.

With the beginning of chapter 10, responsibility shifts from the father to
the son—and to us as the readers. Now the son must decide for himself which
path he will choose. Will he choose Woman Wisdom or will he choose Woman
Folly? Will he choose to serve the true God or will he serve false gods?[26] As the

son launches into this phase, he faces a whole plethora of proverbs somewhat randomly collected and without context. He must decide their meaning and the specific experiences they illuminate.

The sentence literature (Prov. 10-29) demands the son and the reader invest time and energy in understanding the proverbs.[27] They are riddle-like in nature as the sages state in the opening poem (1:6), that is, there is more to the proverb than meets the eye. They are polysemous, each one provoking the mind into active thought and reflection. Because of this quality, one cannot read through this material in large chunks as if keeping to some daily Bible reading schedule.

As the son steps on stage in chapter 10, he discovers the arduous journey from the gang to the woman of valor. The sages do not orchestrate the journey in a nice step-by-step sequence. Yet the son (and the reader) observes a sense of progression in form and complexity as he moves through the collection. Contrary to the arguments of some, the arrangement of poems and sentence literature in chapters 10-29 are not completely haphazard.[28] It has been fairly well established that there is a progression of movement in terms of the rhetorical form of the sentence literature, from simple antithetic proverbs that dominate chapters 10-15, to a more challenging mixture of proverbs in chapters 16:1-22:16, to the most complex assortment of instruction, analogical, antithetic, synthetic, and synonymous proverbs in chapters 25-29.[29]

Not only is this true of the rhetorical movement, it holds true for the content as well. The various themes dealt with by the sages seem to intentionally move from a simple to a more complex treatment. William Brown observes, "Generally, the greater the variety of forms in a given collection, the more encompassing and complex the overall moral setting in which the various sentences and instructions are set."[30] The first Solomonic collection (10-15) exhibits the least variety with a predilection for clearly defined categories of righteous and wicked behavior. Then Brown remarks, "Splashes of gray are in greater evidence in the moral nuances conveyed in the latter collections than in the black-and-white world of the initial antithetical section. Stereotyped polarities are tweaked and, in some cases, transformed."[31] The pedagogy of Proverbs is complex and demanding but so is the process of forming character.

Contradiction and Character Formation

While Proverbs 10-29 contains a plethora of rhetorical and pedagogical strategies as well as character strengths and virtues, I want to focus only on one of these. It is the quality of contradiction that characterizes many of the proverbs.

Rigorous and dynamic dialogue typifies the wisdom community as it moves toward maturity. It is a community open and receptive to diverse perspectives, unafraid of controversy or complexity of thought. The book of Proverbs preserves divergent points of view, maintains ambiguity, and shows life's incongruities. The proverbs in chapters 10-29 display this dynamic quality in what is referred to as "disputational" proverb pairs that marble the landscape.[32] I like to refer to them as "dueling proverbs." The classic example is found in 26:4-5:

Do not answer fools according to their folly,
  or you will be a fool yourself.

Answer fools according to their folly,
  or they will be wise in their own eyes.

How does one explain this contradiction? Do you or do you not answer a fool? Is this Aristotle's golden mean, moderation in all things? Does one find the common denominator between them and settle on it like a person with one foot on a block of ice and the other on a hot stove announcing, "On the average, I'm pretty comfortable?" No. These proverbs, intentionally placed side-by-side, communicate an important message. The wise take responsibility to negotiate the complexities of life and manage its innate contradictions and tensions.

Our contemporary proverbs demonstrate well this tension. On the one hand, someone might encourage a young man saying good-bye to his girlfriend for the summer: "Absence makes the heart grow fonder." On the other hand, someone else counters with a less than hopeful observation: "No, that's not true. It's out of sight, out of mind." Or one person claims, "He who hesitates is lost." "Not necessarily," responds another. "Haste makes waste." But you can't deny this, "Birds of a feather flock together." True, but "opposites attract." Or someone advises a young couple: "Marry in haste repent at leisure." Yet someone else advises another couple: "Happy the wooing that's not long in doing." What about, "The early bird gets the worm?" You can't argue with that, can you? Yes, I can because it's, "The second mouse that gets the cheese!"

One participant at the Conference on Preaching at Lipscomb University told us that at Thanksgiving time when his whole family came together, everyone crowded in the kitchen and busily prepared the meal bumping elbows and bodies. Suddenly his grandmother hollered out, "Too many cooks spoil the broth." Everyone scattered, leaving her to prepare the meal in a more orderly and efficient manner. Then after the Thanksgiving dinner was over, as she walked into the kitchen with a load of dirty dishes, she announced, "Many hands make light work." All came running to help clean up. Dueling proverbs!

This same tension is at work with biblical proverbs. The sage advises on one occasion, "Better is open rebuke than hidden love" (27:5). Genuine love confronts. But another sage earlier in the collection observes, "Love covers a multitude of offenses" (10:12b). True love overlooks a wrongdoing. Different contexts demand different responses and actions. So one proverb cannot say it all. That's why "a person who knows one proverb knows none." One must possess a repertoire of proverbs. Even at that, the wise are not wise because they know a multitude of proverbs. The wise are wise because they know how and when to use the right one. In the words of Roland Murphy, "every proverbial saying needs a balancing corrective."[33] Diversity of thought, which refuses systemization, is endemic to wisdom literature. Wisdom material contains ideas intended to stand in creative conflict.

This phenomenon of disputational proverbs is best summed up in the well-known sapiential observation, "Iron sharpens iron as one friend sharpens another" (27:17). The wise are open to different voices within the community, manage the tension between perspectives, make the best decision possible for the occasion, and gain wisdom as a result.

In contras,t fools, are "wise in their own eyes" (3:7), surrounding themselves with people of like mind. Fools practices groupthink. They are not open to differing viewpoints. The fool's circle of friends is small, cliquish, and exclusive (1:8-19). Fools live in a closed community.

An open community receptive to the give and take of different perspectives is fundamentally grounded in a relationship with God. This is the theological underpinning for all the proverbs in 10-29. The fear of the Lord is the beginning and the culmination of wisdom, a premise on which the book begins (1:7; 9:10) and ultimately the one on which it concludes (31:30). In Proverbs fear of the Lord is synonymous with humility (e.g., 15:33; 22:4), which necessarily involves submission to God. In short, the truly wise one is the person who lives life focused not on self but on seeking God (Prov. 3:5-7). The wise is the one able to humbly say, "I am learning to put my life in perspective. My world is not the center of my life; God is." As a result the wise, like the woman of valor, are those who disadvantage themselves for the sake of advantaging others.[34] Fools in contrast, are those who advantage themselves at the expense of disadvantaging others (again the gang is a good example of this 1:10-19). The character of wisdom, in a word, is founded on an open dialogue in the faith community that flows out of a relationship with the Lord.

Conclusion

Unlike the monotonous cross-country road trip with your mom as caricatured by Willimon, the wise in Proverbs embark on a fascinating and often unpredictable adventure. Intrigue, disappointment, joy, suffering, conflict, dialogue, and satisfaction fill the journey. It is a journey initiated within the context of the family and perpetuated by the faith community. Wisdom offers no guarantees along the way regarding rewards or financial security or physical well-being. But the journey with wisdom does guarantee the kind of character that enables individuals to live responsibly in community and that reflects the very nature of the God they serve.

The work of preaching reflects this journey week-in and week-out as preachers proclaim God's word. Such preaching centers the congregation in a relationship with God. Wisdom preaching acknowledges the complexities of life and helps the congregation negotiate those complexities. It engages the church in open dialogue with different even contradicting perspectives enabling it to gain breadth and depth to the difficult decisions congregations face. Wisdom preaching warns listeners about the consequences of foolish decisions and the satisfaction that comes with making wise choices. Over time with patience and love, preaching that embodies wisdom's values makes a substantial contribution to the shaping of a congregation's character.

CREATING CONFLICT
Proverbs 27:14-19

DAVE BLAND

En Route to the Sermon

In my essay in this chapter, I argue that one important rhetorical strategy used to train youth in character formation is what's sometimes referred to as disputational or dueling pairs of proverbs. These are the proverbs that stand in tension with one another looking at the experiences of life from different perspectives. These proverbs represent the tensions endemic to life and healthy relationships. When individuals engage in rigorous dialogue and a healthy exchange of ideas, they are like iron sharpening iron. Or as another proverb observes, "The purposes in the human mind are like deep water, but the intelligent will draw them out" (20:5).

This sermon uses as its text the cluster of proverbs in 27:14-19. One can preach from the book of Proverbs in different ways. One of the most popular ways is thematically or topically.[1] In this approach, the preacher identifies a particular theme, such as self-control, and finds all the related proverbs and writes a sermon developing that theme.[2] Another way is to select a single proverb and unpack the types of experiences that went into making up that proverb. The sermon would identify and relate those experiences as it expanded the proverb. Tom Long suggests this approach.[3] There is still another way one can preach the proverbs. Occasionally the sages will cluster proverbs together based on a key word or image or theme (e.g. 16:1-9; 26:1-12; 26:13-6, etc.). Preachers can use these clusters as sermon texts.

Proverbs 27:14-19 is one such cluster. It comes in the larger context of 25-27 where the sages have grouped the proverbs together according to the type of parallelism used. Chapters 25-27 are dominated by analogic proverbs, proverbs in which the first line contains an analogy and the second line serves as the referent. Proverbs 27:14-19 contains mostly analogic proverbs. It also sets in a chapter in which a number of the proverbs speak of the friend or neighbor (vv. 5-6, 9, 10, 14, 17, 19).

The proverbs in 27:14-19 cluster around images of intense dialogue between people in various relationships; sometimes the dialogue is constructive and sometimes it is not. The sermon that follows is a type of exposition that explores the difference between destructive and constructive conflict. It moves toward the conclusion that a healthy community invites open and respectful exchanges of ideas.[4]

The Sermon

We often enjoy the solidarity we experience from being a part of a group. It gives us a place and an identity. Sometimes, however, solidarity becomes a liability. The passion for the harmony of the group trumps all other goals. As a result dissident views are discouraged. Independent thinking is replaced by groupthink, a phenomenon a group falls prey to when it becomes so obsessed with unity that no one can afford to raise honest doubts.[5] The super glue of solidarity causes the mental processes to stick in neutral. The desire for complete agreement leads to false consensus. The group transforms into a "good ol' boy" system.

Churches sometimes fall victim to groupthink when leaders expect followers to adhere to party lines without question. If someone differs on a single issue then, like sticking a pin in a balloon, the whole system disintegrates. This unhealthy scenario is just one of many dysfunctional ways of handling conflict.

The proverbs in this text brim with tension and descriptions of spirited conversation. They speak of conflict in a variety of relationships: between friends, family, and community. These proverbs describe both unhealthy and healthy conflict. Conflict is inevitable. In and of itself, however, it is neither good nor bad. The issue is how it is handled.

Sometimes conflict is destructive. Such is the one who blesses a neighbor with a loud voice early in the morning (v. 14). There appear two reasons why the apparent "blessing" is actually a curse in disguise. For one, it's done in a loud voice (i.e. possibly for show). For another, it's early in the morning! Though such a time might be convenient for the early riser, it is an inappropriate time for the neighbor.

The early riser represents an inconsiderate person, one who enjoys the moment at the expense of another. Early risers use cheerful words to disguise an insult. They have a hidden agenda, an ulterior motive, which always results in conflict that harms.

Not only are such destructive patterns of dialogue developed among friends, they spring up in the home as well. Husbands and wives can develop patterns of communication that eventually lead to incessant quarreling. Such is the case with the contentious spouse (vv. 15-16).[6] The imagery is both colorful and sarcastic: "A continual dripping on a rainy day, and a contentious spouse are alike." This, however, is not a lighthearted picture of a dripping faucet that simply irritates and needs minor repair.[7] Rather it is a description of a leaky roof that, if not stopped, will destroy the whole house. Such quarreling not only tears the couple apart, it affects everyone else under their roof. An African proverb describes the dynamics well: "When two bulls fight, it's the grass that suffers."

Both the insensitive friend and the quarreling spouse display images of conflict gone awry. Unfortunately many people have more negative experiences with conflict than positive. It wreaks havoc on families and friends.

As a youth I loved to tease my little sister. One of the best ways of irritating her was to mimic her. If she whistled, I'd whistle in response. If she said something, I'd echo it back. If she hollered for Mom, I'd holler for Mom. If she told me, "Stop it!" I'd reply in kind. It drove her crazy, and I loved it! The game worked beautifully because she got caught in the trap of reacting to my responses. The intensity of the game accelerated the longer I played it—and I was in control of the game!

Though my teasing was relatively harmless (at least to me it was), the mimic game serves as a paradigm for dysfunctional conflict, which is played out in different scenarios and in many different contexts. Sometimes conflict is harmful because of insensitivity to others or because we lose control. Sometimes it is harmful because of the desire for revenge. Probably the most common way conflict becomes dysfunctional is when we try any way we can to avoid it.

Avoidance is a common way we deal with conflict in the church. Typically we want to soothe the troubled waters and cover over any differences for the sake of maintaining unity. Unlike my sister who would holler and scream at me, leaders often react by patting the other person on the back; they want to oil the squeaky wheel. We are conditioned to evade any semblance of confrontation or controversy. We want peace at any price.

Because of this tendency, church leaders frequently make decisions based on what will receive the least number of complaints. So they react to the complaint in a way that will not rock the boat. They focus on fixing the complaint. What happens is that after one complaint is fixed it throws other parts of the system out of sync. The attempt at fixing complaints creates more complaints. All leaders end up doing is putting out brush fires. It's like adjusting the water in the shower. When you jump in, you turn up the hot water and get scalded. So you reach for the cold only to make it colder than you wanted. The goal is to get the water comfortably warm. It's easy for churches to fall into the pattern of focusing on "adjusting the temperature of the water." Leaders become preoccupied with complaints. So they frantically adjust the hot and cold-water faucets in an attempt to hit a happy medium. Harmony and keeping everyone happy is the goal—but it won't happen.

Conflict is inevitable. But it doesn't have to be dysfunctional. Healthy confrontation between individuals and within the church can lead to growth. Rather than dividing a church, it can enable a church to mature. This is the perspective of the proverbs in this text that follow the insensitive friend and contentious spouse.

The sage observes, "Iron sharpens iron as one friend[8] sharpens another." The first line contains an old proverb: "Iron sharpens iron." The picture is of one piece of metal sharpening a knife or a sword or some farm implement. The imagery of steel rubbing against steel is applied in the second line to a relationship between friends: "so one friend sharpens another." I have five appendages on my hand. My thumb is the odd appendage and stands over against my four fingers. If someone were to ask me which appendage would I cut off if I were forced to, the last one I'd be willing to give up would be my thumb. My thumb is essential for my hand to grasp and hold objects. It stands in tension to the other fingers. Yet the thumb is critical for the hand to perform its basic function. It's the principle of iron sharpening iron.

The last proverb in this text stands in parallel thought: "As water reflects the face, so one human heart reflects another."[9] Contrary to what some might argue, the image is not of an individual privately reflecting on personal thoughts. Rather it is of two people dialoging with one another. The result: the two come to better understand themselves.

When individuals stop trying to appease one another and engage in serious and open discussion about important life issues, they grow mentally, emotionally, and spiritually. Sometimes when iron is sharpening iron sparks can fly. But when two friends in conflict have the best interest of the other in mind, such conflict produces good results.

Churches can change destructive patterns of dealing with conflict. They can shift from conflict that divides to that which strengthens the body, from a reactionary faucet-fixing posture to focusing on the purposes, goals, and mission of the church. Yet beware. The shift from ignoring conflict and trying to please everyone to focusing on the mission of the church will itself create conflict. Like the mimic game, some will initially complain even more not less, as I did when my sister ignored me.

In the church godly leaders do not ignore complaints, but complaints do not drive the decisions made that move a church to fulfilling its mission in the community. Leaders simply stop reacting to complaints by trying to fix everyone that arises and instead focus on the larger picture. A non-reactive posture doesn't mean leaders dismiss grievances; it means they stay connected, listen, and dialogue. They first seek to understand. They welcome differences of opinions and ideas and discern if the objections will contribute to the church's mission.

For a church to grow spiritually strong, tension and struggle must be a part of its life. Here is a scenario in which two different churches face difficult issues.[10] There is a conflict brewing in Northside Church. Should the church build a new community life center? Group A is for it and so is Group D. But Groups B and C are not. There is another conflict: Should the church have a contemporary worship service? Here, however, Groups A and C want it but Groups B and D do not. Still a third conflict: Should they stay in their declining and dying neighborhood or should they move out? Groups A and D say yes but Groups B, C, and an additional Group E say no. There are also other issues at stake besides these! Confusing? This church is a maze of intertwining relationships. If you were a visitor looking for a church to serve, would you choose Northside?

Before you decide, look at Southside Church. It's about the same size and demographic makeup as Northside. This congregation also disagrees over similar issues. But at Southside there are just two distinct groups. The people in A group are in general agreement on all the issues and the people in B group oppose them on those same issues.

Now if you were seeking a church in which to serve, would you be more interested in Northside or Southside? Despite the complexity of the inter-action, the Northside Church is healthier in terms of conflict management. There is more "cross-stitching" communication going on among many different people and groups. The Southside Church is less complicated in its communication. But the lines are clearly drawn: there is Group A and there is Group B. The church is polarized. Little dialogue is taking place between the two sides. At Northside some members find themselves in disagreement about some issues but in agreement on others. There is healthy interaction. The dynamic of iron sharpening iron is actively at work at Northside.

There is a principle of conflict management, which states the following paradox: "If you want to have less conflict in your relationships, try to have more."[11] This doesn't mean trying to intentionally get people angry. More pre-cisely it means, "If you want less conflict, invite disagreement." Be open to different opinions that others have on various issues and experiences. This is a sign of a healthy family and a healthy church. Listening to and dialoguing with those who hold different views is an indication that we respect each other and take others seriously. Without friction, without tension, without conflict, we cannot grow spiritually. When iron sharpens iron not only do individuals grow, but God's community, God's church, grows as well.

RISING UP AFTER THE WOMAN OF STRENGTH

Proverbs 31:10-31

JENNIFER GREEN

En Route to the Sermon

In his essay, "The Character Wisdom Shapes," Dave Bland points to the woman of Proverbs 31 as the culmination of the book's portrayal of character. She is, he argues, "the person we all strive to imitate." Yet he points out that this figure has been interpreted in ways that are not positive, whether as an impossibly high standard for virtue or a utility who exists primarily to benefit the reputation or wealth of others. This sermon seeks to address those interpretations, albeit rather implicitly, by exploring *how* the woman of Proverbs 31 works on readers. I understand her as someone who readers do imitate in some respect, but often in rather indirect ways. Becoming virtuous does not occur in a neatly organized or coherent way, as Bland notes. It is not a wholly rational or conscious process much of the time. Instead, those impulses come from deeply emotional and aesthetic responses to the world and people in our lives. I identify one specific response in this sermon as the emotion of "elevation" and try to conjure that feeling through the image of Maria Fearing.

I first learned of Maria Fearing during Black History month. A preacher from the Maria Fearing Fund, a group established to support education and award scholarships in Fearing's name, told of her legacy, leaving me with the distinct feeling that I had just glimpsed "the woman of strength" from Proverbs 31. The way that Fearing's story moved me and other listeners in the congregation that day demonstrated powerfully how the figure of a woman, even one whose slavery caused her to be viewed largely as a utility, might shape the character of all people regardless of their gender.

As discussions about "character education" have become more frequent in many circles, Proverbs reminds us of the power of stories, poems, artwork, movies, and other descriptions of people who embody the virtues displayed in the woman of Proverbs 31. It reminds us that good teaching and preaching occur not just through rational discourse or the straightforward application of principles but also through cultivating emotional and aesthetic sensibilities.[1] This involves risk, an openness to possibilities that the educator or preacher may not have imagined, but one that is well worth taking.

The Sermon

The day is almost here. The son's room is nearly empty, and the suitcases are packed and stuffed into the back of the van, ready to head to college early the next morning. The family has finished dinner, and now the father remains at the table with his son; it's just the two of them. The son senses that "the talk" is about to happen; on some evenings in the past he kind of dreaded it, but tonight he doesn't mind so much.

There have been countless conversations between them at this table. Sometimes they played a lighthearted game of dominoes as they talked about life; other times the tone was more serious. When they were younger, the conversations often happened while throwing the ball together outside. But always, the father talked and taught; he just couldn't help himself. Many times his words came out in clever sayings, often ones his own father had said to him. There was the time when the boy felt nervous about auditioning for a school play, and his father encouraged him: "Hope deferred makes the heart sick, but a desire fulfilled is a tree of life."[2] Another time the dad offered advice in dealing with a tense situation at school: "Rash words are like sword thrusts, but the tongue of the wise brings healing."[3] At times he gave direct, even urgent, warnings to stay out of trouble: stay away from people who appear fun but will certainly drag you down.[4] Always, the father has tried to get across his deepest hope for this boy he loves with all his heart: that he would live wisely and be a good person, for this is what leads to genuine happiness.

But after the long car trip tomorrow, there will not be so many chances for conversations like the ones they've had. On this last evening at home, the father hopes this final conversation will be a special one, something that will stay with his son long after he has left. And on this night, sitting at that same kitchen table where the boy once sat in a high chair, the father finds himself not giving advice, not quoting proverbs, not declaring warnings, but talking about someone who embodies all the goodness he can imagine.

In Proverbs 31, this amazing person is presented as "the woman of strength." Vivid descriptions allow us to conjure up an image of someone engaged in particular actions. She is skilled in her work, acquiring raw materials, making garments, and selling them; she manages the estate and its workers. What is more, she is remarkably virtuous: she is generous, diligent, responsible, strong, dignified, deeply mindful of others; she reveres God. She is "more precious than jewels." Here are a few lines from the poem:

> *She considers a field and buys it;*
> > *with the fruit of her hands she plants a vineyard.*
> *She girds herself with strength,*
> > *and makes her arms strong.*
> *She perceives that her merchandise is profitable.*
> > *Her lamp does not go out at night.*
> *She puts her hands to the distaff,*
> > *and her hands hold the spindle.*
> *She opens her hand to the poor,*
> > *and reaches out her hands to the needy.*[5]

For the poet describing her, it is not enough to say simply that this woman is virtuous, or even that she is hardworking and diligent; instead, the poet wants us to envision her face illuminated by a lamp as she continues to work long into the night. We do not just read that she is generous, but we can imagine her opening her hand to the poor, even stretching, reaching out her hand to the needy. There is a physical and emotional connection in those images, not just between the woman and the people she helps, but even between her and us who picture her.

There also are subtle connections in the poem, giving it movement and flow. The lines I just read repeat the image of this woman's hands, moving from an image of her hands planting a vineyard, to holding a spindle and staff, to reaching them out to the poor. In the lines after these, she clothes her children, she clothes herself, she sells clothes, and this culminates in the image of her own character's clothes: "strength and dignity are her clothing."[6] After that, there is a focus on her mouth in various ways—she is laughing at the time to come, confident in the future; she is teaching wisdom; she has kindness on her tongue; she does not eat the bread of idleness.[7] Then this moves to the praise spoken by the mouths of others when they see her.[8]

With vivid and poetic descriptions of the woman such as these, we readers also have something of an impulse to praise her as we have emotional and aesthetic reactions to her. And this, I think, is largely the upshot of this poem. It is not exactly to motivate us to copy her (which, indeed, is something of a relief!). It is not to spell out a list of behaviors and actions that need to be checked off in order to be considered a good person; it is not to induce guilt about not measuring up. Instead the beautiful, poetic display of virtue in this woman lifts us up; it elevates us. Her children *rise up* and call her happy,[9] and we do the same.

Several years ago psychologists did an experiment in which volunteers watched one of three videos.[10] In this experiment, some volunteers saw a video of an eleven-year-old boy named Trevor who took sandwiches and blankets to homeless people in Philadelphia. Other volunteers watched a nature documentary, and a third group of volunteers witnessed a comedian performing a comedy routine. Then just after the video was over, the volunteers came in contact with a person who needed help with something. People who had watched the video about eleven-year-old boy were much more likely to stop what they were doing and provide help to the person who needed it.

This and other studies led psychologists to identify a specific emotion in humans that has particular effects. This emotion is called "elevation." It is slightly different than the emotion of admiration, when we see someone who is highly skilled, like Kobe Bryant or Michael Jordan playing basketball. Admiring someone often moves us to copy them and try to improve our own skills. I remember how often I ran outside to practice free throws after watching the Arkansas Razorbacks basketball team on TV when I was a girl!

But elevation is a bit different. It happens when we see something beautiful and virtuous, like a father pushing his son in a wheel chair to the finish line of a triathlon they have endured together, or a woman who has organized the construction of a recreation center for urban kids. Psychologists have documented specific physical reactions in people when they see something like this: often there is a lifting of the chest, a feeling of warmth, a sense of calm. And they've noted that people respond outwardly in specific ways too: they experience a kind of opening of themselves, a receptiveness to other people, and a desire to engage them and the world, and they take direct action: volunteering to help someone in need, donating money to a cause, even confessing that they've done something wrong and making it right. This feeling of elevation moves people to be virtuous themselves.

And I think this is much of what that father wants his son to experience when telling him about the "woman of strength," who seems to possess the totality of virtue, from A to Z.[11] It is not so much a desire to copy her specific actions as it is to be inspired by her. Perhaps there is a deep, even subconscious sense of wanting to do good in order to experience life as richly as she obviously does. Elevation brings a desire, as one psychologist put it, to become the best versions of ourselves that we can be.

In Proverbs, the woman of strength is never identified with a particular person. Scholars understand her as a composite figure made up from many women who lived during the Persian period—we have records of actual women from that time engaged in economic and professional activity like this woman, and being very successful at it.[12] Although this poem gives the woman a strong persona, it never names her or fully develops her as a character. And this gives an openness to her identity, which seems to invite us to find embodiments of this woman in other people too. The father speaking to his son may have described an important teacher in his life or a beloved grandmother. He may have spoken of a figure from literature or the Bible, someone like Esther who showed incredible courage or even Woman Wisdom. Or he may have described someone from history, someone like Maria Fearing.

Maria Fearing was a little girl when she first heard stories about missionaries going to Africa. Maria was a slave, whose mother took care of the house and children of the Winston family on their plantation in Alabama, and Maria was often allowed to sit with the children to listen to stories that her mistress Mrs. Winston told. Sometimes these were Bible stories; other times they were stories about Africa, and these stories left a deep impression on Maria. After growing up in slavery, Maria was emancipated at age thirty-three and used her domestic skills to get a job to pay for her education; she'd never been taught to read or write. She enrolled in the Freedman's Bureau

School and started first grade as the school's oldest student. A quick and diligent learner, she worked through the ninth grade in five years, graduated, and became a teacher. Before long she purchased her own home and was a successful professional woman for fifteen years.

Then in 1891, Maria heard a speech by William Sheppard, a missionary to the Congo, the first African-American missionary supported by the Presbyterian Church. In that speech, he asked for helpers to return to the Congo with him, and Maria, feeling a stirring in her heart, hoped to go with him. At age fifty-six, she applied to the church for support but was turned down due to her age and gender. But she reapplied at age fifty-eight, and this time the church would allow her to serve as a missionary, but only if she would pay her own way. So she sold her home, received $100 from the women of her church, and paid for the ship voyage to the Congo.

While in the Congo, Maria showed real competence in linguistics, so that she was largely responsible for translating the Bible into the local languages. But her greatest work was founding the Pantops Home for Girls; it was for girls who had been orphaned or had run away from slavery in the Congo. Maria also brought in girls whose freedom she secured by paying money to slavemasters or bartering trinkets, tools, and even salt to gain their freedom. Once at the Pantops Home, the girls received academic education as well as life skills such as housekeeping, gardening, and trading. Even more, the girls were nurtured by Maria, so that even when she moved back to the United States years later, the girls lovingly called her *Mama wa Mputu*, "Mother from far away." For more than twenty years, Maria worked among the people of the Congo until she was seventy-eight years old. She returned to the U.S. and spent many more of her years teaching at a church school; she died at age ninety-nine.[13]

Maria Fearing was certainly a "woman of strength" whose story may burn within the hearts of kids at our kitchen table, the kids in our classes, and indeed the hearts of each of us in ways we may not even understand, just as the stories Maria heard as a little girl stayed in her heart and moved her in ways she never would have thought possible. As teachers, as parents, as learners ourselves, may we tell and ponder such stories often, and may we be open to where they may lead us and to the people they shape us to be.

THE UNSETTLING POWER OF MERCY

James 3:13-18

SALLY A. BROWN

En Route to the Sermon

This sermon was preached during the season of Lent in Miller Chapel at Princeton Seminary on February 25, 2010. I wanted to engage this text, which contrasts the earthly wisdom of selfish ambition with the powerful wisdom of gentleness and mercy, amid the anxiety and implicitly competitive atmosphere of the spring job-search season.

The town of Princeton, New Jersey, where Princeton Seminary is located, exudes prosperous charm. The dignified grace of the university buildings form the backdrop to well-maintained downtown shops selling high-end merchandise and art, as well as inviting restaurants and coffee shops interspersed with several churches. Yet those who live in the town also speak, at least confidentially, of a pervasive atmosphere of intense, if mostly polite, social and intellectual competition. Princeton University prides itself on admitting only the best and the most competitive undergraduates. In the tradition of Albert Einstein, only world-class scholars in math, the sciences, and the humanities gain a place at Princeton's Institute for Advanced Study. In the Princeton public schools, high school students push themselves hard to make it into advanced math and science classes and cram their discretionary time with extra-curricular activities. They know intellectual achievement alone will not be enough to make them competitive at the best colleges. They must build a "portfolio"; and failure is just not acceptable.

Princeton seminarians in their senior year, or in the final years of their doctoral programs, find themselves competing against one another for positions in church or academy. The atmosphere for junior and middler students is a bit less fraught, although they, too, must compete for spots in Clinical

Pastoral Education programs or scarce summer internships. And of course, day-in, day-out classroom competition is an ever-present fact.

James counsels eschewing habits of rivalry and ambition in favor of a "heavenly wisdom" characterized by mercy and gentleness. But even the most casual reading of a handful of church job descriptions makes quite clear that mercy and gentleness are not high on the list of most sought-after traits in a pastor. In the twentieth century as in the first, James's vision of Christian leadership is radically counter-intuitive and counter-cultural.

My goal in this sermon is to help listeners recognize the contrast between power driven by selfish ambition, on one hand, and the transformative power of mercy that can restore lives, homes, and communities. In what one writer has described as a "merciless culture," do we dare to take James seriously?

The Sermon

Why is the book of James in the Bible? Impertinent as the question sounds, Martin Luther raised it in all seriousness a bit over five centuries ago. There are only two allusions to Jesus; and still worse, for Luther, no hint of a doctrine of justification by grace alone through faith alone. Luther eventually granted that certain passages in James can be read with profit by Christians, but his endorsement was hardly enthusiastic.

Do you remember that little book that came out in the 1990s called *Life's Little Instruction Book?* It was subtitled, *511 Suggestions, Observations and Reminders on How to Live a Happy and Rewarding Life.* The book delivers what it promises. "Say 'thank you' a lot." "Be forgiving of yourself and others." "Live beneath your means." "Sing in the shower."[1] If 511 ideas isn't enough for you, you can buy the latest update, *The Complete Life's Little Instruction Book*, with 1560 suggestions, observations, and reminders.[2]

To be honest, the book of James sounds remarkably similar: "Faith without works is dead." "Don't speak evil of a brother or sister." "Don't harbor selfish ambition." Jewish in flavor, James belongs to the wisdom genre, with its closest match probably Proverbs.

Despite its critics, the book of James has claimed and retained its place in the Christian canon; and I want to explore precisely that fact—its canonical location despite all it seems *not* to be saying with reference to Christian doctrine, as a clue to interpreting James' message. In other words, what if we read this book in a *deliberately intertextual* way, that is, in close relation to the overarching back-story of the New Testament?

What is that New Testament back-story? At the heart of it is an ugly scene of death by crucifixion. A bloody, broken, exposed human being is bleeding his life out on the crossbars of a Roman cross. Astoundingly, the New Testament witness insists that the one hanging there, Jesus, is the very Son of God. Push it a step further: the one hanging there is *the very presence and power of God* inscribed in flesh that tears and bone that breaks is on that cross, transforming all things even as he dies.

How does the story say he got to be there? The New Testament makes clear that Jesus pursued a ministry of radical mercy—mercy that expressed itself in healing for the untouchable, inclusion for the excluded, the forgiveness of sins. Jesus brought mercy-filled good news to the economically, religiously, and politically poor. And the powers of his day didn't like it at all.

The religious authorities didn't like it. It was *their* prerogative, no one else's, to maintain the boundaries of the sacred, to decide who was included and who was not, whom God approved and whom God did not approve. And it was no one's prerogative but God's to say whose sins were forgiven. Yet Jesus went about Galilee and Judea, even into the outer darkness of Samaria and finally, fatefully, into Jerusalem itself, insisting that no leper was untouchable, no sinner unwelcome at God's banquet, no day too holy for the work of healing and forgiving. Jesus was on a mission of mercy, and he didn't ask permission.

Furthermore, Jesus alienated the Roman occupiers. He claimed to be accountable not to Rome but to a higher power to which Rome itself must give account. In an Empire where everything and everyone is Caesar's because Caesar speaks for the gods, because Caesar *is* a god, Jesus was a capital offender. So they nailed him to a cross and put him up on a hill where everyone would see him and fear.

The New Testament story doesn't end there, of course, because if it had, today we would likely have no more than a couple of ancient fragments telling yet another ancient tale of heroic resistance—but we wouldn't have the Christian Scriptures. The New Testament declares that God raised Jesus from the dead.

Jesus' resurrection was the surest validation of his mission, the divine affirmation that God's power is utterly unlike the powers of this world. The "Amen!" of heaven that God's power pours itself out in mercy, it does not dominate and subjugate.

Reading James against that back-story makes all the difference in the way we understand the wisdom it urges upon us. Keep in mind that the events we've just reviewed were undoubtedly familiar to the Jewish Christian communities around Jerusalem who likely first received the teachings of this Christian wisdom book. Perhaps a few eyewitnesses still survived, or those who had heard their testimony.

Second, and more strikingly, it becomes immediately clear that James echoes from beginning to end what the back-story declares: that Jesus represented a radically different, mercy infused form of power that stands in contrast to power as this world understands it. James presses this theme from start to finish, and particularly in the text from chapter 3 we read today. Tthere are two kinds of power that bid for our allegiance as the church, and especially as leaders of the church: the worldly power that is all about self-preservation and the heavenly power that expresses itself as mercy, lives by mercy, and transforms the world by mercy. The crucial question in chapter 3 is whether or not we will choose rightly: "Who is wise and understanding among you? . . . If you live by selfish ambition and are driven by envy, don't boast. That is false wisdom, of this world and not of God. The wisdom from heaven is pure, peaceable, full of mercy . . . ."

It was true in James' day and it's true in ours: the church will be tempted every step of the way to abandon the power of mercy that is its lifeblood and instead cut a deal with the kind of power that makes self-preservation paramount, that subordinates mercy to self-interest.

We don't need to look much further than today's news to see how easily the protective, creative power of mercy can be suppressed by power driven by self-interest. The Toyota automobile company is currently under close scrutiny, and one question everyone is asking is whether company management was willing to risk putting drivers in unsafe cars to preserve the company's bottom line. A business analyst observed, "The marketplace is merciless to the merciful."[3]

Congregations typically don't so much deny that mercy is their primary mission, as defer it. Consider the congregation that pours its resources into an elaborate new building complete with amenities that mimic the mall. The reasoning for such innovations can go something like this: "Sure, it's expensive, but we have to survive to do Christ's work! We need to appeal to the world on its own terms. Seriously, in times like these, how do you expect to attract the kind of people who can pay the bills without a cappuccino bar and fitness center?" Are they entirely wrong? That's a hard question. But I can imagine where the James writer would stand.

James insists that power expressed as mercy, not self-interest, must be what distinguishes the church in every age. I have seen congregations that spend themselves for mercy. And I can tell you, mercy speaks a compelling message.

I went to preach at one of those pretty typical middle-class suburban churches. Before the service the lay liturgist who was assisting me felt she should give me a heads-up about one of the ushers for that day's service. "She's unusual," said the liturgist. "She's not too clean and she's missing a few teeth and her fashion sense kind of runs to cotton housedresses and scuff slippers. We've tried to offer her money to get her teeth fixed, but she just smiles and says, 'No, thanks.' A few folks here don't think she should usher, but she's one of us, after all."

Little did the church realize what a testimony that woman was, the glad way she marched up the aisle in her pink scuffs with the offering plate, a glittery plastic child's barrette perched in her gray hair, her eyes lit with holy joy! She knew she was welcome in this place; she mattered here, to people and to God. She was not invisible here.

And there is the congregation whose silver communion set was stolen by local small-time thieves. The perpetrators were caught and tried, but at sentencing, congregation members stood before the judge and asked that the convicted be allowed to fulfill their sentence by feeding the homeless in their soup kitchen, serving shoulder to shoulder with the very church members they robbed. That's creative, empowering mercy.

South African bishop and world spokesperson for nonviolent change, Desmond Tutu was, as you know, one of the architects of the Truth and Reconciliation process that did much to heal the ravaged soul and society of South Africa. Looking back on the Truth and Reconciliation years, Tutu writes, "The power of God's reign of righteousness is the power of mercy."[4]

The book of James is no tame *Life's Little Instruction Book for Christians*. It is the revolutionary handbook of a community dedicated in the name of its Lord to choosing the power of mercy over the power of self-preservation.

Mercy is dangerous stuff. It questions sacred boundaries in the name of a God who includes and heals. Mercy does not strategize for advantage in a field of winners and losers; it cuts across the grain of winning and losing. It doesn't so much make outsiders insiders, as negate the category "insider" altogether, sweeping us all into unmeritable grace. Mercy destabilizes empire.

What would it look like to so construct our communities that they welcome the economically vulnerable, the socially inconvenient, the not-so-successful? To place these persons at the center, with visibility, space, voice, agency, significance? What would empowering mercy look like in the youth group you lead, the domestic shelter where you work, the congregation where you worship, the school where you teach? I don't know.

But I'm betting that you do.

Chapter
SIX

JAMES' SECRET
Wisdom in James in the Mode of Receptive Reverence

SCOT MCKNIGHT

The traditional way to write a New Testament paper on wisdom is to get knee-deep into genre. Show what "wisdom"—as a genre—means, using the confident wisdom of Solomon's voice in Proverbs or the gnawing unwisdom of Qohelet's voice in Ecclesiastes or the silence of Job's voice in Job or the sophisticated wisdom of Ben Sirach, and once you've got the genre figured out, you can go to James and say, "See, here is *this genre* of wisdom!" Then you can announce that "This changes everything, and I'm about to show you how!" and be done with it.[1] There is a place and a time for getting knee- or even nose-deep in wisdom genre thinking. But the preacher wants, if he or she is wise, more than the knowledge—*gnosis* or *da'at*—that comes from knowing the various genres of wisdom, to do more than show that the letter of James is wisdom. Most preachers don't want to know that James is a very special form of wisdom, the kind one finds in some obscure text he or she heard about in seminary but hasn't seen since the hectic life of pastoring began.

No, the wise preacher joins with Cambridge University professor David Ford who observed that at the fountain of wisdom is the *cry for wisdom* out of a multitude of contexts and conditions.[2] The wise preacher wants to dwell in wisdom and wants to incite his or her congregants to thirst for it, to drink from it, and to slake the thirsts of the next generation with that same water drawn from the same well called wisdom. The wise preacher, if he or she has things squared away, wants to *be wise* and wants to move from *scientia* to *sapientia*. But that sort of paper about wisdom in James is harder because it means saying *wise things about wisdom*.[3] Wisdom, to adapt a saying of C. S. Lewis, is a wonderful idea until you are asked to *say something wise* or, even more, summoned by God to given an account of whether or not you *were wise*.

Ellen Davis, Old Testament professor and eloquent commentator, has said it well: there's such a difference between being smart and being wise.[4] Wisdom doesn't come quickly; knowledge can be acquired in a quick manner by finding what you want in a book or in Wikipedia. But wisdom and grey hairs (or baldness) are friends; youth and foolishness are another set of friends. Time, in other words, creates the path to wisdom.

Defining Wisdom

It would then be wise to begin with definitions of wisdom (*hokma* and *sophia*) because definitions seek to get to the bottom of ideas and terms. Which is what preachers have to do every Sunday. So I wondered how preachers define wisdom, and I landed first upon megachurch pastor, Andy Stanley, who asked me this summer about pressing topics to write books on and I suggested "wisdom." His response was, "I did that." His insightful book is called *The Best Question Ever*, which explores this question: "What is the wise thing for me to do at this moment in my life?" Rowan Williams, the Archbishop of the Anglican Communion, offers this definition, "Wisdom, instead of being dispassionate and distant, is God's own urgent longing, God's longing for human beings to live a vision of an orderly creation in the reality of an orderly moral life."[5] Pope Benedict XVI, who like Rowan Williams is a serious theologian, anchors wisdom in the incarnational work of God as he draws from the apocryphal Wisdom of Solomon (7:25-27): "God's Wisdom is manifest in the cosmos in the variety and beauty of its elements, but his masterpieces, where his beauty and his greatness truly appear much more, are the saints."[6] The preacher who studies deeply, though, relies on more than what other preachers say. Good preachers have the habit of reading intelligent writers, and I wish to mention a few now.

So what does "wisdom" mean to the scholars?[7] Here are a few definitions. James Crenshaw made it his career topic, so I begin with his veteran statement, which ties wisdom to the universal human quest to explain the realities of life: "The reasoned search for specific ways to ensure personal well-being in everyday life, to make sense of extreme adversity and vexing anomalies, and to transmit this hard-earned knowledge so that successive generations will embody it—wisdom—is universal." He adds its *telos*: "The goal of all wisdom was the formation of character."[8] But he observes that no one definition suffices because the evidence is too vast and the points of view too numerous. Still, Crenshaw's own quest for definition lands on tellingly important observations: first, wisdom finds its way into specific forms, like proverbs and instructions and debate and intellectual reflection; second, its substance concerns "self-evident intuitions" about "order"[9] and, third, it comes to expression with an almost humanistic propriety and pragmatism—the right idea or right word at the right time and doing the right thing at that moment,[10] what Tremper Longman calls "timing" in his chapter in this volume.

Ellen Davis, says wisdom is "living in the world in such a way that God, and God's intentions for the world, are acknowledged in all that we do." This, as she wisely points out, is for all: "The fruit of wisdom, a well-ordered life and a peaceful mind, results not from a high IQ but from a disposition of the heart that the sages (wisdom teachers) of Israel most often called 'fear of the LORD.'"[11] One of my favorite lines of hers, a wise one indeed, is this: "the sages of Israel teach that those who would be wise must aim, not at power, but at goodness."[12]

We turn next to another veteran wisdom scholar, Leo Perdue, who emphasizes wisdom as human construction. Perdue lands upon three elements to wisdom:[13]

> First, wisdom is a body of knowledge, a tradition that sets forth an understanding of God, the world and nature, humanity, and human society.

Second, wisdom is understood as discipline [*musar*], that is, both a curriculum of study and a structured form of behavior designed to lead to the formation of character.

Third, wisdom was moral discourse and behavior that constructed and legitimated a cosmology in which righteousness, both correct and just behavior as well as proper decorum, ordered the world, society, and individual existence.

All scholars also observe the richly seductive metaphor, Woman Wisdom, the personification of wisdom in Proverbs 8:1—9:6, and most make observations that those who don't live according to wisdom experience retribution. It is usually sufficient in the proverbial tradition to say such a person is a "fool."

Before we move on beyond these definitions, one more observation: most scholars of wisdom quickly point out that Old Testament theologies—and Walter Brueggemann and John Goldingay are exceptions here[14]—and those who trace the Story of the Bible more often than not ignore the wisdom tradition because it doesn't seem to fit the Torah-shaped or Story-shaped or Salvation-history-shaped framing of the message of the Bible, which tells us something about how unwise our hermeneutics, not to mention our systematic theologies, have become.

Proverbs 1:1-7

Every discussion about wisdom eventually must pass the test of Proverbs 1:1-7:

The proverbs of Solomon son of David, king of Israel:
For learning about wisdom and instruction,
    for understanding words of insight,
for gaining instruction in wise dealing,
    righteousness, justice, and equity;
to teach shrewdness to the simple,
    knowledge and prudence to the young—
Let the wise also hear and gain in learning,
    and the discerning acquire skill,
to understand a proverb and a figure,
    the words of the wise and their riddles.

The fear of the LORD is the beginning of knowledge;
   fools despise wisdom and instruction.

As is the case in most places in the Bible, we don't get a *definition* of wisdom so much as a *description* of it and a *declaration* of its value. As we get ready to discuss wisdom in James, I want simply to sketch four themes from these verses and then draw our attention to one of these themes for understanding James. First, a wise person, Proverbs informs us, "gains" instruction or correction in wise dealing (1:3a). Second, the wise person has the attributes of righteousness, justice, and equity (*tsedeq, mishpat, mesharim*; 1:3b), which is about what James says in 3:13-18. Third, the wise person is prudent and has discretion (*orma, mezimma*; Prov. 1:4; cf. 8:12). Fourth, the wise person possesses skill to know and practice these various attributes (1:5b).[15] No one could reasonably dispute that James draws on each of these, even if those themes do not morph a letter into a genre of wisdom.

Somewhere I either borrowed this expression or landed on it myself: Wisdom is characterized by "receptive reverence." Glenn Pemberton, in his chapter in this volume, emphasizes the bland word "listen" as fundamental for wisdom and our point supports his observations. "Receptive reverence" has become my summary translation of the Hebrew *laqachat musar hashekel* in Proverbs 1:3a: "to take, or receive, or absorb [qal infinitive; from *laqach*] the instruction/correction of insight [or "discipline"]."[16] The Hebrew verb *laqach* is a simple one and it is used for such things as to take in hand, or to take and carry along, to take for oneself in the sense of procuring, as well as getting and acquiring and gaining.[17] However, the hunt for the precise meaning of "wisdom" and its socio-cultural connections to Greek and Ancient Near Eastern parallels is sometimes not accompanied by a similar focus on the necessity and importance of this gaining, that is, on the *posture* of *receptivity by the young man or young woman in absorbing the wisdom of the wise.*[18]

More directly, we put it like this: *a wise person is receptive, malleable, and submissive in a reverent and respectful manner of the wisdom of one's teachers.* Just pondering this expression stops us all in our tracks, unless we were exceedingly rare as young adults. Reverent receptivity begins with the "fear of YHWH" and those who don't have either that fear or reverent receptivity are the proverbial "fools" (1:7; 'evilim). Receptive reverence, and here I

draw from Tremper Longman's commentary on Proverbs, involves observations of nature and the power of learning from experience (6:6-8); it involves
learning, memorizing, absorbing, and living out the tradition in which one is
nurtured (4:1-4; 22:17-21); it includes learning from one's mistakes and correction (10:17); but finally, receptive reverence knows it needs to respond
to God's Word as revelation—and that is why it all begins with the fear of
YHWH (1:7).[19]

This theme of receptive reverence charts the path I'd like to walk in the
letter of James, looking at James' wisdom as the wisdom of the one who had
acquired receptive reverence. In other words, James's heart and mind and
soul and body *absorbed* the wisdom of Jesus[20] and the wise persons of his day,
and it was his intent to *incarnate* that wisdom as he addressed the messianic
community. In making this claim, I am simultaneously making the claim that
James did not (simply) treat the words of Jesus as *halakhah* but as *hokma*, not
simply as "law and ruling" but as "wisdom."[21] Yes, in considering wisdom in
James, I could have stopped for a long draught at James 3:13-18, where James
explores the wise life of teachers, and that can and should be done.[22] But I
want to focus on just one idea because I think it sheds light on the whole of
James and, on top of that, both gives us a glimpse of how to acquire wisdom
and provides for us a template for preaching wisdom.

James, Wisdom, and Receptive Reverence

The letter of James has been subjected to much scrutiny over its relationship, not only to Jewish sources and to Greek sources alongside the historic
issue of his relationship to Paul (cf. James 2:14-26), but especially to Jesus.
Was James rooted in the Sermon on the Mount? Was James a reader of Q?
Was James a follower of Matthew? Or was James just connected, somehow
but with less clarity, to the Synoptic tradition?[23] We discover this: in James
*there is an overwhelming flavor of "this is like Jesus" but an underwhelming presence
of empirical evidence that he quotes Jesus.* Other than James 5:12, which quotes
Matthew 5:34-37, there is no unambiguous evidence that James explicitly
quotes the Jesus he calls Messiah and Lord. Yet, (almost) everyone acknowledges a connection.[24] It is almost like James is a little boy straining to keep his
secret at Christmas time but who finally can't contain himself any longer, so
at 5:12 he just openly quotes from Jesus.

There is a bit of a scholarly context here. In the days when scholars were wearing button up shoes and pulling down from their shelves first editions of Mark Twain's books, Louis Massebieau and Friedrich Spitta argued that James 1:1 and 2:1 were textual emendations that took a thoroughly Jewish document and made it superficially Christian.[25] However, as Patrick Hartin has stated so boldly, "The strongest argument against such a view comes from the pulsating spirit of the entire document, which breathes the very spirit of Jesus and contains numerous echoes throughout of the very sayings of Jesus."[26] Or, as the encyclopedic Richard Bauckham puts it, "More than any other New Testament writer, James is a teacher in the style of Jesus, a creative exponent of the wisdom of Jesus, a disciple who, 'having been fully trained' in his teacher's wisdom, has become himself a teacher of wisdom 'like his teacher' (Luke 6:40)."[27] It is this overwhelming flavor of Jesus that I wish to explore under the category of receptive reverence.

But, first, the evidence or what Mark Twain called the "facts," about which Twain once said, "Get your facts first, and then you can distort them as much as you please."[28] I am presently doing research and writing on the nature of the "gospel" in the earliest churches. I am convinced now that the "gospel" is the declaration of the narrative of the life, death, and resurrection of Jesus, including his sending of the Holy Spirit, as the recapitulation of Israel's Story, and as a Story that generates the need to repent and be baptized for the forgiveness of sins. James' "overwhelming flavor of Jesus" seemingly totally ignores these crucial elements of the gospel.[29] If James is rooted in the Synoptics, he's only rooted in the sayings and teachings of Jesus.[30]

Scholars have produced and reproduced many times lists that show James' connection to Matthew's gospel. Still, the following parallels deserve consideration[31]:

- The theme of joy in trial/testing is found in **James 1:2** and Matthew 5:10-12 par. Luke 6:22-23.
- The word "perfection" in **1:4** finds an important parallel in Matthew 5:48 (contrast Luke 6:36) and 19:21 (contrast Luke 18:21).
- The generosity of God for those in need is found in **1:5** and Matthew 7:7-9 par. Luke 11:9-11.
- The call to suspend anger in **1:20** connects to Matthew 5:22.

- The important theme of being a doer of the word, not just hearing the word, as seen in **1:22-25** reminds one of Matthew 7:24-27 par. Luke 6:47-49.

- The demand to do all the Law in **2:10** is matched in part by a similar demand in Matthew 5:19.

- The paramount significance of mercy in **2:13** finds something similar in Matthew 5:7.

- The call to peace in **3:18** is also matched by a Beatitude in Matthew 5:9.

- James' concern with the either-or of love/friendship with God or the world in **4:4** finds something similar in Matthew 6:24 par. Luke 16:13.

- The connection of humility and eschatological exaltation in **4:4** finds a substantive connection with yet another Beatitude in Matthew 5:5.

- The theme of not judging in **4:11-12**, which in many ways brings to completion what has been said in 3:1—4:10, not to mention other subtle connections in other parts of James, is also important to the Jesus traditions, as seen in Matthew 7:1-5 par. Luke 6:37-38, 41-42.

- The hostile reaction to rich oppressors in **5:2-6** finds close associations with Matthew 6:24, 25-34 par. Luke 16:13; 12:22-31.

- The patience of the prophets in **5:10** matches Matthew 5:12 par. Luke 6:23.

- Most notably, the statement about oaths in **5:12** must be connected to Matthew 5:33-37 as a nearly explicit quotation of a Jesus saying.[32]

A scholarly issue lies behind what we will see in James: how James treated his sources. The debate over the precise form of the Jesus traditions to which James is connected does not erase the reality of that connection, for the above references are remarkable. Some scholars are totally convinced that James used Matthew or Q. I shall follow the wisdom of Mark Twain, who said, "When in doubt, tell the truth."[33] The truth is that we don't know; the truth is *the ambiguity of that connection.* Explicit citation by James is rare and we stand on sure footings when we conclude that James acts like others in the wisdom tradition because he has made Jesus' teachings his own. It is entirely appropriate to observe that James is "emulating" Jesus' words.[34] The ambiguity is an indicator of "receptive reverence." It shows, again to mention Glenn Pemberton's study, that James listened.

This point being made about ambiguity needs to be underlined. The more common form of connection between most early Christian texts and their predecessors, and this has been frequently observed for the early church until the middle or late second century, is one of *allusion* (or even "emulation") rather than *explicit citation*.[35] One of the notable features of the earliest Christians was not only their use of traditions before them but that the mode of use was to recapture, allude to, and carry on what had been said before them.[36] This mode chafes against the all-too-common drive by contemporary historians and tradition critics to search exclusively for explicit quotations as a sign of dependence. Perhaps the analogy of "wiki" in current open source media will enable us to re-appreciate this mode: that is, as modern online encyclopedia recapture and carry on, with new additions, subtractions, and modifications, sometimes with little or no trace of citation, so James may be said to have given his own "wiki" version of various sayings of Jesus. This is not plagiarism for there was no such thing as word property; it was instead the ultimate complement and a way of carrying on the sacredness of the earlier tradition.[37]

Perhaps this can be seen more clearly if we point to the differences between various genre in the Bible. Law is about God's commands for his people, while prophecy is a message from God through a prophet to the people of God. History renders events into a meaningful narrative that drives the people of God to what God is doing in this world, while apocalyptic divulges the secrets of heaven to God's people. The Gospels and Acts of the Apostles draw us into the narrative world of Jesus and the early Christians to learn what happened, while the Epistles provide for us one end of a phone call from an early Christian leader to a church, or churches to another leader. But wisdom is a sage's experience-derived truths of the way the world works when God's people live before God. Law must be memorized and interpreted; prophecy must be heeded and directions changed; history needs to be heard and entered into; apocalyptic asks its hearers to take due warning; the Epistles guide us in similar circumstances and give us major ideas for theology, while wisdom petitions its listeners to absorb, pass on, and re-formulate. If we have to choose one of these genre to describe James, wisdom works best.[38] A fundamental characteristic of wisdom is to listen to, absorb, and re-articulate what you have learned. The entire letter is soaked in receptive reverence of what Jesus taught.

How, one might ask, is *reverence* found when explicit citation is not present? I believe Peter Davids covered this well in one of his ground-breaking studies on James when he concluded that *allusion* is James' mode of citation. That is, an allusion is "a paraphrastic use of phrases or ideas from a logion, with the probable intent of reminding the reader of it."[39] His oblique re-use of the Jesus traditions—at which point, without mentioning so, the author intends to remind readers of a common authoritative tradition or teaching— is an act of reverence. The *receptiveness* comes from the admission that James is not on his own: he is bringing to new life an old saying of Jesus by finding a way to bring the substance of what Jesus said into a new context. He does so without quoting Jesus but once. Perhaps this silence, James' secret, is a sign of wisdom. We want now to provide two examples of James' receptive reverence.

James and the Jesus Creed

James 2 forms the bedrock of all the debates about James, but what set off James' comments and those debates was a visible act of partiality toward the rich and against the poor (2:2-4).

> For if a person with gold rings and in fine clothes comes into your assembly, and if a poor person in dirty clothes also comes in, and if you take notice of the one wearing the fine clothes and say, "Have a seat here, please," while to the one who is poor you say, "Stand there," or, "Sit at my feet," have you not made distinctions among yourselves, and become judges with evil thoughts?

James says this is "partiality" or "favoritism," and completely inconsistent with believing in Jesus Christ, the Glorious One, as Lord. One can assume that James is here recalling the poverty and hardship of Jesus, and that following such a Jesus would entail a natural empathy for the poor instead of antipathy toward the poor. James is relentless in his critique of what is occurring.[40] He begins with this: that same Jesus blessed the poor and was more than a little harsh on the power-mongers of Jerusalem, especially the oppressive rich (cf. Luke 6:20-26). Adding to this, God's pattern of working with the poor makes their behavior even more inconsistent: "Has not God chosen the poor in the world to be rich in faith and to be heirs of the kingdom that he has promised to those who love him?" (James 2:5).[41] On top of this, common sense about their civil life should guide them: "Is it not the rich who oppress you? Is it not they who drag you into court? Is it not they who blaspheme the excellent name that was invoked over you?" (2:6-7).[42] The wise build inductive cases from the realities of this world and discern the ways of God, which is precisely what James is doing here. No quotations; just wisdom in the mode of receptive reverence.

At this point we find a special indication of receptive reverence. I have written about this in both popular and academic contexts,[43] and I have attempted to make the argument that it was Jesus who first combined the historic *Shema* of Deuteronomy 6:4-5 with Leviticus 19:18.[44] I have called this newly-formed, double-sided moral lens the "Jesus Creed." What is often not observed is that no one "quotes" Leviticus 19:18 (as explicitly as does Jesus) from the time of Moses (or the priestly tradition, depending on how you like to say things in your context) to the time of Jesus. The explicit combination of Deuteronomy 6:4-5 and Leviticus 19:18 is distinctive to Jesus. Furthermore, there is evidence the earliest followers of Jesus repeated this twice daily, and some of that evidence includes Galatians 5:14 and Romans 13:8-10, not to ignore the pervasive sense of love in 1 Corinthians 13, 1 John, and John 13:34-35 (cf. also Didache 1:2).[45] I take as my starting point, then, that Jesus both combined Deuteronomy 6:4-5 and Leviticus 19:18, and that he did so to show that the Torah was to be interpreted through the two-fold law of loving God and loving others. On top of this, I believe this two-fold understanding of the *mitzvoth* gave to the earliest Jewish Christians a distinctive way of learning how to live. The wisdom of James, because he is receptively reverent in appropriating Jesus, leads to what animated Jesus' ethic: love.[46]

Another point often not made: this Jesus Creed is found in its entirety in James. We hear one of James' "receptive reverence" echoes in 1:12, where he says that the crown of life is promised to "those who love him," and we find the same expression in 2:5, where those who "love him" are promised the kingdom. While loving God is not found *only* in the *Shema*, the constant recitation of the *Shema* by observant Jews leads me to think that these two passages indicate an echo of the *Shema*. But there's more. In James 2:8-10, in order to make his point that favoritism is contrary to everything Jesus taught and lived, James explicitly quotes the second half of the Jesus Creed, which is drawn from Leviticus 19:18, and I quote now only James 2:8: "You do well if you really fulfill the royal law according to the scripture, 'You shall love your neighbor as yourself.'" A sensitive reader of James knows that the "royal law" of 2:8 evokes the "perfect law, the law of liberty" in 1:25, and ties these two together—royal and liberty—to the second half of the Jesus Creed. In context, the "neighbor" has just become the "poor" of James 2:1-7.[47] For James, the Jesus Creed provided a lens through which the Torah was to be read.

But we are still not done. In James 2:18-19, that most difficult of texts to comprehend, James taunts his interlocutor with these words: "You believe that God is one? You do well!" There it is: no one can say "God is one" and not think of the Hebrew word *echad*, which forms the foundation of the *Shema*: "Hear, O Israel! The Lord is our God, the Lord *alone*." (Or, as I say it daily, "The Lord our God, the Lord is *one*.")

It was Jewish Torah to recite the *Shema* daily. It was also Jewish *Hokma* to recite it and live it. But to live the *Shema* according to Jesus was to recite and practice a *Shema* that was expanded by Jesus to include not only loving God but also loving others. It is my contention that James indicates receptive reverence in being someone who did what his older brother did—recite the Jesus Creed—and then worked it out in new situations for his messianic communities—as his brother did. Yes, he quotes Jesus who also quoted Leviticus 19:18, but he does so without attribution. This word is so vital to him and so well-known to his readers that he can assume when he quotes Leviticus 19:18 his readers will recognize this as central to Jesus. They recognized his secret.

James, Jesus, and the Poor

Most Protestants can safely ignore Mary, mother of Jesus, and treat her like someone's exotic aunt. Many former Catholics who have converted into the various forms of Protestantism snarl when a Protestant even mentions Mary. "From now on," we seem to translate, "all generations (except Protestants) will call me blessed." But Mary, or at least the Magnificat of Luke 1:46-55, undergirds a theme in Jesus and in James that indicates yet another example as we consider James through the lens of receptive reverence. Mary's Magnificat has influenced James but that influence was mediated through Jesus. The distinguishing feature of the Magnificat of Mary is the theme of

what is often called "reversal" but what might better be called "inversion."
Life's conditions aren't just turned around; they are turned upside down
because they are turned inside out.

> His mercy is for those who fear him
>> from generation to generation.
> He has shown strength with his arm;
>> he has scattered the proud in the thoughts of their hearts.
> He has brought down the powerful from their thrones,
>> and lifted up the lowly;
> he has filled the hungry with good things,
>> and sent the rich away empty. (1:51-53)

There is nothing here that can't be found in Isaiah and the Psalms and the
Wisdom tradition, but locating the originating source is hardly the point.
At least it indicates social condition: most scholars think this poetic song is
characteristic of the *Anawim* tradition, those pious poor who lived near the
Temple, longed for justice, and awaited that consolation in the Messiah.[48]
Jesus, too, taught the themes of the Magnificat. In fact, the Lukan beatitudes
are set up in such a way that a narrative reader of Luke wonders if Jesus' isn't
re-using his mother's theme of inversion (6:20-26). I happen to think he is.

> "Blessed are you who are poor,
>> for yours is the kingdom of God.
> "Blessed are you who are hungry now,
>> for you will be filled.
>> "Blessed are you who weep now,
>>> for you will laugh.
> "Blessed are you when people hate you, and when they exclude you,
>> revile you, and defame you on account of the Son of Man."

Nothing surprising here. But what makes the Lukan beatitudes distinct is the
powerful inversion theme of the "Woes" that follow, and it is here that we
start to gain as we approach James:

> "But woe to you who are rich,
>> for you have received your consolation.

"Woe to you who are full now,
for you will be hungry.
"Woe to you who are laughing now,
for you will mourn and weep.
"Woe to you when all speak well of you, for that is what their ancestors
did to the false prophets."

What is noticeable here, as is the case with the Magnificat, is the theme of
inversion: the rich come down, the poor go up; the fattened go without food,
the hungry are filled with food. In short, power is inverted.

James is riveted together with this theme, and he never once quotes
Jesus—but if you know the Magnificat and if you know the Beatitudes, not
to mention other sayings of Jesus (cf. Matt. 20:16; 23:12; Luke 13:30; 14:11;
16:19-31; 18:14), and if you know something about the *Anawim* tradition,
when you hear James say what he says, you will say James is exhibiting *receptive reverence* of Jesus' teaching in a different context. In the boldest and blunt-
est of terms, like a preacher who needs a bold image to make his point, James
equates the word "poor" with the word "good" and the word "rich" with the
word "bad."

The passages are clean and clear and disturbing:

Let the believer who is lowly boast in being raised up, and the rich
in being brought low, because the rich will disappear like a flower
in the field. For the sun rises with its scorching heat and withers the
field; its flower falls, and its beauty perishes. It is the same way with
the rich; in the midst of a busy life, they will wither away. (1:9-11)

For if a person with gold rings and in fine clothes comes into
your assembly, and if a poor person in dirty clothes also comes in,
and if you take notice of the one wearing the fine clothes and say,
"Have a seat here, please," while to the one who is poor you say,
"Stand there," or, "Sit at my feet," have you not made distinctions
among yourselves, and become judges with evil thoughts? Listen,
my beloved brothers and sisters. Has not God chosen the poor in
the world to be rich in faith and to be heirs of the kingdom that he
has promised to those who love him? But you have dishonored the
poor. Is it not the rich who oppress you? Is it not they who drag you

into court? Is it not they who blaspheme the excellent name that was invoked over you? (2:2-7)

Come now, you rich people, weep and wail for the miseries that are coming to you. Your riches have rotted, and your clothes are moth-eaten. Your gold and silver have rusted, and their rust will be evidence against you, and it will eat your flesh like fire. You have laid up treasure for the last days. Listen! The wages of the laborers who mowed your fields, which you kept back by fraud, cry out, and the cries of the harvesters have reached the ears of the Lord of hosts. You have lived on the earth in luxury and in pleasure; you have fattened your hearts in a day of slaughter. You have condemned and murdered the righteous one, who does not resist you. (5:1-6)

Some have taken James' words as needlessly harsh. In fact, Ronald Sider tells the story that Upton Sinclair read James 5:1-6 to a group of ministers and then attributed the words to the rebel, Emma Goldman, and the ministers said, "This woman ought to be deported at once!"[49] To be sure, Sinclair had socialist and Goldman anarchist leanings, but what I've not been able to comprehend is how a group of ministers wouldn't have recognized the text as the words of James! I've also heard that the Magnificat has been banned from daily recitations, which Catholic have practiced for centuries, by tyrants who know the potency of her words. What I'm saying is that Mary's words are indeed harsh; and so are Jesus'; and so are James'. It is the harshness of James' words, connected as they are to the theme of inversion, that makes me think that James has absorbed the wisdom of his mother and his brother, and his *receptive reverence* has kicked in for him to re-use the theme of inversion in his context. One more famous line from Mark Twain: "It ain't those parts of the Bible that I can't understand that bother me, it is the parts I do understand." (It is apt that I finish with that quotation, because, like James, I can't find the original source in Twain's writing.) Wherever James got his idea of inversion, his theme is clear.

In this context of inversion we are to read one of James' potent aphorisms, an aphorism I believe directed at teachers and preachers: "And a harvest of righteousness is sown in peace for those who make peace" (James 3:18). If the way of the powerful (and the world) is the way of zeal and selfish ambition (cf. 3:14-16; cf. 4:1-10),[50] the way of wisdom is the way of humility and good works (3:13). What comes out on top for how teachers are to live is purity and peaceableness and gentleness and willingness to yield to others and mercy and good old-fashioned good works—and all done simply and genuinely. Those who pursue God's will by sowing peace are the ones who will harvest what is right (3:13-18). This sounds like Jesus, with echoes perhaps of Mark 7 and the Beatitudes and the end of the Sermon on the Mount. James never mentions the cross, and Jesus saw the cross as the paradigm of service for others (Mark 8:34—9:1; 10:35-45). But the same self-sacrificing lifestyle that Jesus advocated, which was perceived then as radical, shows up in James often enough that one has to return again and again to the category of receptive reverence.

Conclusion

It is not possible, of course, to do a full sketch of how often James echoes the teachings of Jesus, but Patrick Hartin and Peter Davids are accurate: Jesus presence is omnipresent in James, and a good preacher draws the congregation back to Jesus in nearly every passage. Jesus is on every page and in every paragraph of this short letter, the way a parent is in a child and the way a profound mentor is in her student every moment of every day. We have been concerned in this essay to approach James' wisdom through the lens of Proverbs 1:3a, through what we have called *receptive reverence*, the willingness to listen, to surrender, absorb, and to let that wisdom shape every word and every step. James, Richard Bauckham says, "is a wisdom teacher who has made the wisdom of Jesus his own, and who seeks to appropriate and to develop the resources of the Jewish wisdom tradition in a way that is guided and controlled by the teaching of Jesus."[51]

I don't know if it is accurate to call James a genre of wisdom, but I do know this: James was a wise man, wise because he was *receptively reverent* of the wisdom he had learned from his mother and brother. May we be as wise, and may we, in our preaching, exhort others to become wise.

⸱CHRISTIAN CIVILITY?⸱
James 1:19-21

JIM KITCHENS

In his essay Scot McKnight describes the "fundamental character-istic" of wisdom to be "to listen, to absorb, and to re-articulate what you have learned" from your teachers. It is on this basis that he deems the book of James to be wisdom literature: James has thoroughly absorbed the wisdom of Jesus and is re-articulating that wisdom to his readers in order to show them, in turn, how to live.

James is, therefore, more interested in telling his readers how to live *like* Jesus than in peppering the book with quotes *from* Jesus. James wants us to understand that it's far more important to walk the walk of Jesus than it is to talk the talk.

McKnight claims, "A wise person is receptive, malleable, and submissive in a reverent and respectful manner of the wisdom of one's teachers." This is the kind of embodied wisdom James has in mind when he encourages his readers to "be quick to listen, slow to speak, (and) slow to anger" (1:19) and to "welcome with meekness the implanted word" (1:20).

My sermon, delivered to the congregation at Second Presbyterian Church in Nashville, Tennessee, seeks to re-articulate that same pattern of wisdom by exploring what form a specifically Christian understanding of civility might take in the public arena. It was written in the week following (and in response to) an un-holy trinity: Rep. Joe Wilson of South Carolina outburst during the State of the Union address, rapper Kanye West's charge onto the stage during the MTV music awards ceremony, and tennis star Serena Williams' expletive loaded verbal assault on a line judge at the U.S. Open.

Against this backdrop of brash invective, I sought to help the congre-gation think through James 1:19-21 and to hear how it is an example of the "receptive reverence" McKnight says is the key to our incarnating the gospel in daily living.

The sermon was a "mob sourced" sermon. By this, I mean that I invited a wider community to reflect with me on the word God wanted to speak to the congregation out of this text that week. I posted a series of questions asking whether there might be a specifically Christian form of civility and what particular form that civility might take on both my personal Facebook page and a Facebook group page we have set up for our congregation. Given postmoderns' mistrust of authority figures (and especially younger Christians' mistrust of a "talking head" preacher who speaks for twenty to thirty minutes about the meaning of a biblical text with no opportunity for any other voices to be heard), a more communal approach to discerning God's word in sermons will be an increasingly important issue for preachers in the future.

The Sermon

"You lie!"

"Taylor, I'm really happy for you . . . but Beyoncé had one of the best videos of all time!"

(Holding up a tennis ball) No, I'm not even going to go there.

U.S. Representative Joe Wilson, the singer Kanye West, and tennis player Serena Williams generated a national conversation about the lack of civility in American public life earlier this year. Even though we should have become impervious to the issue because of the media's regular reporting of boorish behavior and personal political attacks, there was something about the vehemence and the close proximity in time of these three remarks that finally broke the camel's back of public tolerance for such behavior.

A lot of people have responded by saying, "Oh, but this is nothing new," and, of course, they're right. Any study, for example, of nineteenth-century American presidential politics will show far worse treatment of public figures by their opponents than anything we've experienced recently. And yet there is something particularly galling about the cry, "You lie," shouted in the context of a joint session of Congress and directed not only at the person Barak Obama but also at the office of the American presidency.

As we reflect on what we think about such behavior, we also have to be honest and say that it is just as likely to happen in church life as it is in politics, sports, and popular culture. Any neutral observer who read the kind of invective directed at various opponents in our denomination's ongoing debate over any number of issues—abortion, GLBT ordination, or support of our nation's wars, to name a few—would surely say that the American church has no reason to claim the high ground in this matter.

But I haven't found myself thinking about whether we've gotten worse recently or whether some institutions are better than others when it comes to civility. That's not where my mind and heart have gone in the aftermath of the recent un-holy trinity of outbursts. Instead, I've found myself wondering if there is a particularly *Christian* form of civility that we in the church ought to exhibit as a form of Christian witness to the wider culture.

Those of you who are my Facebook friends know that I posed that question early in the week. I've been gratified not only by the number of you who responded but by your thoughtfulness. I wasn't surprised, though, because I know this is a community of thoughtful people. Let me share with the rest of you some of the insights I carried away from that on-line discussion.

I think all of us were agreed that civility is not a solely Christian virtue. For example, one post read:

> Civility and respect should be human virtues that we are able to extend to one another regardless of our faith. My wife's wise thought on the matter is that everyone, regardless of their faith, should be encouraged to find the threads of mercy, grace, and kindness in their faith tradition and utilize those in daily social interaction.

After all, there is a history of reflection on the nature of civility in Greek philosophy that predates the birth of Jesus by hundreds of years, not to mention the similarly ancient strands in Buddhist, Confucian, and Hindu religious traditions.

If civility is not only a Christian virtue, then might there be pointers in Scripture and tradition toward what a specifically Christian *form* of that common human virtue might look like?

One of you wrote a helpful post in which she wondered if the real issue isn't so much a lack of civility as the "growing selfishness and self-centeredness in our society." She goes on to note that, "Selfishness is the opposite of altruism, and altruism is truly a Christian value."

I think we're beginning to zero in on something here.

People added another perspective to the discussion by saying that civility does not require that one be impassive about the issue under discussion.

A friend on the West Coast wondered if "a clearer understanding of the notion of discernment as to what is 'righteous indignation' and what isn't is in order?" She and others reminded me of the passion with which Jesus sometimes addressed his adversaries and his not-so-calm demeanor during that awkward "money changers in the temple" episode. Another Facebook friend further refined this point: "Civility doesn't have to mean the absence of passion. But I think that a standard of civility demands that we treat God's children respectfully, even if they aren't doing the same."

My thinking was honed even more sharply when—perhaps reflecting on this summer's town hall meetings on health care reform—a member posted the following:

"The people who yell, scream, interrupt, threaten, demonize, curse and so on are operating out of fear and ignorance. I'm not sure ignorance is addressed in the Bible, but fear certainly is. I believe there is a clear connection between fear and the lack of civility." After all, "There is no fear in love, but perfect love casts out fear" (1 John 4:18).

Which brings me, finally, to my best thought on the matter, at least thus far. I don't offer this as the *definitive* insight into how Christians ought to practice civility, but as yet one more contribution to what I hope will be an ongoing conversation.

I wonder if a particularly Christian form of civility wouldn't center around a deep understanding that the person with whom I disagree, the person with whom I am in debate, the person whom I think is deeply mistaken about the matter at hand is, nonetheless, a child of God, a person whom I am commanded to honor and to love. I can well imagine the author of the book of James counseling us to "be quick to listen, slow to speak, slow to anger" (1:19) as we regard that person sitting across the table, across the sanctuary, or across the presbytery meeting from us. S/he, too, is someone God knows by name and considers precious.

I don't believe Rep. Wilson was seeing President Obama as a fellow child of God when he shouted at him. I don't believe Kanye West was thinking of Taylor Swift as being equally beloved of God when he stormed the stage at the MTV awards. And I don't sense "child of God" was anywhere among the jumbled thoughts swirling about in Serena Williams' head as she stormed toward that line judge.

I also wonder if James' wise counsel that "your anger does not produce God's righteousness" wouldn't help us practice the discipline of taking a much-needed pause for reflection before we speak or act. Our mother's admonition to us to "count to ten" before speaking in anger, after all, has deep roots in the biblical tradition. A colleague in ministry sent a post in which she said:

> I think part of the foundational brokenness of our culture right now is how distracted and diverted we have become. . . . Wordsworth said that poetry is emotions/feeling 'recollected in tranquility.' Since we have lost a place for tranquility, we lose that sacred space and time we need to translate our initial feelings into a meaningful contribution to dialogue. . . . The church needs to be the first place to teach people the spiritual discipline of silent reflection.

James must have had something similar in mind when he wrote in chapter 3: "(T)he wisdom from above is first pure, then peaceable, gentle, willing to yield, full of mercy and good fruits, without a trace of partiality or hypocrisy" (3:17). Perhaps weaving more times for silence into our word-stuffed worship services might help us learn corporately the discipline of allowing the Spirit to show us a deeper wisdom in the face of the temptation to lash out immediately against those who oppose us.

I want to draw our communal reflection to a close by telling you about a couple of people I have met who have taught me something about how a specifically Christian civility might look.

The first is John Moore, who—by the time I met him—was a retired United Methodist pastor in northern California. John had served as a campus minister at UC-Davis during the tumultuous 60s. He and his wife had lost a daughter in the mass suicide at Jim Jones' Peoples Temple settlement in the jungles of Guyana. He had the reputation of being the "old liberal lion" of the Northern California/Nevada Annual Conference. John served as my mentor from time to time while I was a pastor in the Central Valley of California.

One day we were talking about some contentious debate in the presbytery in which I was attempting to provide a bit of leadership, and I asked John how he engaged in such debates. His reply still shapes my own response in church politics. He said, "I long ago gave up on trying to convince anyone of anything, or thinking that it was my job to convert them. I came to the conclusion that my only call was to give witness to my own beliefs, to what God had given me light to understand. Convincing my opponents is work I leave to the Holy Spirit."

I seek to honor how much John's words have shaped me by what I have written in the "about me" box on my Facebook page. It reads, "Giving witness to the truth I have discerned by the light God has given me thus far in my life . . . and open to the possibility of further insight and correction." John's humility has provided a continuing witness to me as I have sought to say carefully what the Spirit has shown me but also to hear a word of correction from the Spirit in the voice of my opponent.

The second person who has shaped my understanding of a specifically Christian civility—and in particular my response to Joe, Kanye, and Serena—is a member of our congregation who is a music producer and songwriter here in Nashville. I saw him a couple of days after the MTV awards and asked him what his associates in the music industry were saying about Kanye. He said he had talked just the day before with the students in the songwriting class he teaches at Belmont University about Kanye's behavior. They all agreed that Kanye had acted horribly.

It was what he said next that was a witness of the Spirit to me.

He told his students that he knew a lot of people like Kanye in the music industry and that he even knew something about Kanye's own past, especially his childhood. He explained to them that Kanye had had a lot of pain in his past and that his music was, in part, an attempt to deal with the demons that raged inside his soul.

"But he couldn't get them all out in his music," he continued. "He couldn't get them all out. What you saw that night was evidence that he hasn't been able to deal with all of them."

Then he did what he described as a "typically Southern thing."

"I suggested that maybe what we all ought to do is to pray for Kanye."

Praying for Kanye, praying that his inner demons might be exorcised, and praying that he might know the "peace which passes all understanding" that comes from a deep relationship with God in Christ was the best way he could think to promote civility in American culture and peace in the human heart.

Praying for Kanye and for all who struggle with inner demons can help us begin to embody that particular version of civility most clearly incarnated in Jesus. But before we pray for them, we first must pray for ourselves. By engaging our own inner demons and our own narcissism, we enter a discipline that can enable us, by God's grace, to become the kind of disciples Jesus calls us to be. By dealing with the ways in which we ourselves daily disregard people, we not only help to build a more civil society but also to transform that society into something that more nearly resembles the Realm of God.

DOING GOSPEL
James 2:1-19

Jonathan Storment

En Route to the Sermon

Almost a decade ago I had a Bible study with a young man who was very interested in the story of Jesus. We went through the gospel of Mark together, and at the end of our time together I asked him what he thought about the story of Jesus. His response baffled me. He said that he was glad this was true for me, but it wasn't true for him. Since then I've heard this answer many times, but I had never heard it before then. It caught me off guard. After thinking about this a while, I think I know what he was saying in the best way he knew how. He was saying he didn't want to be like me. If this is where this truth has led me, he didn't want to follow it.

This sermon is for him.

In a world of spin-doctors and language deconstruction, I believe wisdom has a unique appeal for a post-modern world. They've heard the debates over absolute truths and they've also seen planes flown into buildings and television preachers have moral failings. We've seen people speak about truth as if was something that could be put into a test tube. But wisdom is more than abstract attempts at truth. This is because wisdom is not something that is only spoken. It's a way of life, something that must be embodied. James' particular application of the wisdom tradition to a new Christian movement is a powerful reminder for any overly cognitive heritage that what we believe is best seen by how we live.

I'm in debt to Scot McKnight for his serious work in showing the importance of an embodied gospel. I especially appreciate his insight on the Shema as one of the central themes of James' second chapter (not to mention the rest of the New Testament), and particularly how James' message fits so closely with the teachings of his brother's. It's been said that Scripture is like a diamond that can turn a thousand different ways, each reflecting a different angle. I am grateful for McKnight's ability to turn the gem in a direction I would have missed without him.

The following sermon was delivered to the Richland Hills Church of Christ in November 2009. Approaching this sermon, I tried to start with the story of Scripture as the deepest reality and help the congregation to view life through it. The goal was for the community to hear the story of Scripture as their story and then live it out. My hope was to convey the story James was telling as compelling and ongoing, a story that must be entered into. And like James, I wanted to end this sermon by giving examples of people from our context who have embodied truth. We have a history of working toward social justice, and actively doing good in the community around us. We also have a rich tradition of preaching the grace of God. My goal was to help them realize these two things must go together.[1]

The Sermon

When I was a junior in college I went to Greece for a semester abroad. I grew up on a farm, so it wasn't just my first time out of the country, it was just about my first time out of the state of Arkansas, and it showed. The first week in Athens, I was walking alone down a busy downtown street when a nice European man approached me and asked, "Are you an American?" Surprised by his intuition, I told him that I did in fact hail from America, and he offered to show me around.

I told my new friend that I would like to buy flowers for my girlfriend, and he, out of the goodness of his heart, offered to take me to a flower shop. After following my impromptu tour guide for a few blocks, he took me to this seedy looking building in a back alley, then down some stairs to a platform where people were dancing and smoke hung in the air.

My tour guide took me over to a bar to "introduce" me to someone, a girl named Anna. While Anna was busy asking me my name and making small talk, I happened to notice the scandalous pictures all over the wall. And when Anna asked me to buy her a drink, I had a profound realization.

This wasn't a flower shop after all.

My experience reminded me of one of the metaphors used in the opening chapters of Proverbs—a woman named Folly looking for a young man to seduce into mischief. Lady Folly stands for more than just a poor decision; she's the way that leads to death. But she isn't alone. Her counterpart is a much more noble, Lady Wisdom. The picture Proverbs paints is clear and succinct. Here is a man facing a choice, with two women calling out to him. And the text leaves us with a question: Which one will he choose?

But there are deeper questions to ask. Why does Scripture want to personify wisdom in the first place? Maybe it's because Wisdom is the very rhythm that the cosmos bends and sways with. Or perhaps it is because wisdom was never intended to be something theoretical, but something lived out. In other words, wisdom is not just a body of knowledge but knowledge looking for a body.

Ellen Davis calls wisdom "The sweet fruit of intimacy with God." It is a natural by-product from walking with the Lord. It's not abstract, but a way of life, the kind lived alongside the One who made life.

James is commonly held to be one of the only New Testament wisdom books. But we mustn't let our misguided conceptions of wisdom literature fool us into thinking that James is just a collection of good ideas. He's got a bigger target in mind than clever aphorisms or fortune cookie advice. His goal is for the wisdom of God to form the lives of his people.

So for a moment today, I want you to think about being James. You're one of the main leaders of this new Christian movement, and you're trying to shape a community of faith to carry on what Jesus started.

Jesus, your brother, the one many now trust in as the Messiah, was also someone you played with as a child. You had watched him interact with people. You had seen how well he treated everyone, from those on the margins of society to those who stood at the epicenters of power. And then you're called to help form a community that bears his name.

Now you're in the shoes of James.

Historically, Christians have gotten tied up in James' seeming contradiction with Paul. But that is to miss the point. James is trying to develop a community around the radical new ethic of Jesus. He is not arguing with Paul, or Martin Luther, for that matter. He is helping his community see what it means to do gospel living.

And James is standing in a tradition as old as Israel herself.

When YHWH had first brought Israel out of captivity, he began to give them instructions on how to best live as this new people of God. In response the Israelites said, "We will do and we will hear." Which sounds backward. Normally you hear and then do. But these recently freed slaves knew something that our Western world forgets all too easily. True faith starts with action. What you do is what you really believe.

The most poignant scene in Scripture is also one of its most tragic. Jesus is standing in one of the corridors of power, in front of a man named Pilate who's asking what Truth is. And despite the fact that a well-argued response might save his life, Jesus says nothing. John has crafted this story brilliantly. Pilate asks for Truth, and Truth is staring him in the face. John is letting us know that Truth is not something that is first spoken, but embodied. This is the very heart of wisdom. It's when Truth puts on skin and walks around.

To know the way of Jesus without embodying it is like holding the sheet music to Beethoven's Fifth Symphony without playing it. It is incomplete.

Truth needs a body.

The primary movement of Scripture has always been from Word to Flesh. And James is making sure we connect the dots. Some of his best-known words come from his opening chapter: "True religion is to care for widows and orphans. Keeping ourselves unspotted from the world." For James this was more than just a good idea. In that culture, you were considered an orphan if you had only one parent. And most scholars think that James' dad Joseph died when he was a child.

So James' knew what it was like to be dependent on others for basic needs like food and shelter. His words are wisdom from life experience. He had watched as a child as believers put skin on God's preferential treatment for the least of these. James knows the benefit of wisdom, of God's way of life, and so he says this:

> What good is it, my brothers, if a man claims to have faith but has no deeds? Can such faith save him? Suppose a brother or sister is without clothes and daily food. If one of you says to him, "Go, I wish you well; keep warm and well fed," but does nothing about his physical needs, what good is it? In the same way, faith by itself, if it is not accompanied by action, is dead. But someone will say, "You have faith; I have deeds." Show me your faith without deeds, and I will show you my faith by what I do.

The point James is making here is both huge and personal. I imagine that
he'd seen dead faith before. He had seen it in the footsteps of people who went
to the Temple but walked past his family, in the faces of those who knew the
correct language about God, without the orthodox behavior of neighborly
love.

And he refuses to let that happen within this new movement that bears
his brother's name. "You believe that there is one God. Good! Even the demons
believe that—and shudder."

James is citing the Shema, The ancient Jewish prayer, one that had defined
orthodoxy for generations. If that's where your faith stops, James' says, then
it's demonic. Because if God really is one, then we don't have two different
ways of treating people based on their roles in society.

Because what you believe about God is seen by what you do.

James knows human nature. He knows it's easy to belong to a God that is
analyzed, but not obeyed. But this is not the God revealed in Jesus. James had
seen in Jesus the unexpected movement of God. Here was a man who put flesh
on what Torah had been saying for centuries. Jesus was God's surprising way
of showing his people that wisdom needs a body.

Growing up, my parents were never the ones to teach Sunday school class
or preach about the nuances of the faith. If you were to ask them if they were
wise, they'd probably say no. But, they were foster parents to dozens of kids
from broken or non-existent homes. They sacrificially gave of themselves to
those who could not give back. They showed their faith by what they did.

Because the wisdom of God forms the lives of God's people.

I know a man. He's not a scholar, and he's not rich. But he has a passion
for the world to be what God intended it to be. A few years ago when the tsunami ravaged Southeast Asia, he watched the news unfold with everyone else.
Except this man didn't just watch. By the end of the day he had booked a flight
to Sri Lanka to leave within the week. He asked a team of Philippine doctors
to accompany him and gave months of his life, away from his business and
family. He rallied hundreds of volunteers to help rebuild an entire village. All
to help repair an area of the world that was broken.

The wisdom of God forms the lives of God's people.

A few weeks ago, right before I preached, I had a new Christian come
up to me. She wanted to tell me that her good friend was coming to church

that day, so not to blow it. Her friend hadn't been to a church in two decades. Which is quite a streak. Her friend was the Cal Ripken Jr. of not coming to church. And then this woman told me something interesting. She said her friend was attending church that day because she had noticed a transformation in the way this new Christian treated her.

Because the wisdom of God forms the lives of God's people.

This is not about earning grace, this is about doing gospel.

It's embodying the belief that in the Kingdom of God everybody is a somebody, because Jesus is Lord.

Albert Schweitzer, a noted New Testament scholar and medical doctor, was asked by a reporter late in his life why he decided to uproot his privileged life in Germany to slave in the jungles of the Belgian Congo. He told the reporter, "I have decided to make my life my argument."

And this too is wisdom.

WHAT'S YOUR PROBLEM?
James 4:1-10

CHRIS SMITH

En Route to the Sermon

In his essay, Scot McKnight declares that "Jesus is on every page and in every paragraph of this short letter, the way a parent is in a child and the way a profound mentor is in her student every moment of every day." While James only quotes Jesus one time, it is obvious that the wisdom of Jesus was never far from him, with allusion to the Master on every page. It is as if "James's heart and mind and soul and body absorbed the wisdom of Jesus," according to McKnight.

Following along this line, I compare the tone of James with Jesus in the following sermon. It is tempting to think that James is "needlessly harsh." (Over the years students in my Bible classes have frequently told me James is their favorite book in the New Testament. My unspoken response is, "You're kidding!") James is uncompromising, bleak, black and white, and in your face. A quick perusal of the Sermon on the Mount, however, reminds us that James is not the first preacher to pound away in such an unrelenting fashion.

When James confronts the Christian community concerning their conflicts and disputes, he uses words like "murder" and "adultery" and proposes the combatants are enemies of God. As much as we may wince and want to draw back, we must admit that James did not make this message up. He got it from Jesus.

At this point the sermon has not been delivered. It will be interesting to see if the Fred Craddock-like ending endures on delivery or if I will be tempted to add to the conclusion.

The Sermon

The preacher James reminds me of a youngster I saw once in a speech contest years ago. My fourth grade daughter and her speech—"Abraham Lincoln was

born in a log cabin near Hodgensville, Kentucky"—did not win but neither
did she lose to the precocious boy with jet black hair and horn rimmed classes.
His speaking style was modeled after the oratory of a century ago. This junior
Williams Jennings Bryan had the total package—sweeping hand motions,
pitch that varied from a whisper to a shout, pregnant pauses, dramatic flour-
ishes. It was quite a show.

One wonders if James is using a similar over-the-top oratory in James
4:1-10 because he sounds awfully worked up in this passage. According to
him conflicts and disputes are not inevitable outcomes that must be managed but sin that originates from cravings that war within us (v. 1). He uses
the standard Greek word for war, conjuring images of phalanxes and shields
and bloodshed. Then in the next verse, he laments that coveting leads to disputes and conflicts and we certainly know that is true. Church fights are as old
as the Gentile/Jewish wrangling in Jerusalem as well as Euodia and Syntyche
in Philippi. One old preacher told his students, "There are three kinds of
churches: the church that just had trouble, the church that is having trouble,
and the church that is about to have trouble."

James says the problem is an internal one. These conflicts come from cravings that are within us. We know the preacher is not exaggerating at this point.
Any congregational leader who has endured worship wars knows the issues
are often no deeper than personal preference and "what I want." Theological
language may be used to criticize the shallowness of a praise chorus or the
archaic language of a snappy Stamps Baxter song, but ultimately it is all about
who is going to win. (One day when I have a keen sense of job security I will
tell the complainer who did not like the songs, "That's okay. We weren't singing to you.")

We are in full agreement that disputes and conflicts are not good, but
why does James have to add, "You want something and do not have it; so
you commit murder." Really? I've been in some testy business meetings, but
murder! Come on, James, you don't really mean that do you?

The preacher continues to overplay his hand with the harsh words of
verse 4. "Adulterers! Do you not know that friendship with the world is hatred
with God? Therefore whoever wishes to be a friend of the world becomes an
enemy of God." Does James really mean this? We are an enemy of God just
because we don't always get along with folks down at church?

And while we may wonder what scripture James quotes in verse 5 since we can find no match in the Old Testament, we understand the tone of "God yearns jealously for the spirit that he has made to dwell in us." We know plenty of stories about a jealous God. They are not the kind of stories that receive top billing in children's Bible hour. They are the stories we try to explain away because they worry us. Frankly, these stories of punishment scare us. A loving God—that will preach. We will even take the generous God that James mentions in chapter 1. But a jealous God! Who wants to hear that, even if it is in the Ten Commandments?

James sounds like he woke up on the wrong side of the bed. Why is he so angry, we wonder. If he were one of our preaching peers we might suggest a visit to a counselor to discuss these anger issues. We would tell him it might make you feel better to rant and rave like some Old Testament prophet, but it is no way to build up a church or have an effective long-term ministry. Preachers who deliver jeremiads like this make frequent visits to the post office to get change of address forms and have U-Haul on speed dial.

Perhaps James is simply trying to create a certain effect. I remember my first gospel meeting years ago. The second night I did my best to encourage the brethren but also to impress them at the same time. "You have taught Sunday school for years and you often wonder if it is worth the effort," I said. "You go home on Wednesday night and think you are just going to quit." I then paused for dramatic effect, took a step or two toward the congregation and said, "Listen. You are serving God." The only problem was I did not say the line. I screamed. My intention was to be forceful and loud, but I miscalculated. The reason I know it was a scream is because every time I visited my preacher friend in the future we pulled out the sermon tape and listened to it. Inevitably we would wind up on the floor laughing.

Is this what James is doing, shouting for emphasis? If he is we want to tell him to take it down a notch. Unlike the apocryphal preacher story of the minister who had in the margins of his sermon notes, "Point weak, yell here," James doesn't need to raise his voice. He has our undivided attention as he turns from diagnosing the problem to his proposed solution. After quoting the Proverb, "God opposes the proud, but gives grace to the humble" (v. 6), James rattles off an impressive list of imperatives. "Submit yourselves therefore to God. Resist the devil, and he will flee from you. Draw near to God, and he will draw near to you. Cleanse your hands, you sinners, and purify your hearts, you double-minded. Lament and mourn and and weep. Let your laughter be turned into mourning and your joy into dejection. Humble yourselves before the Lord, and he will exalt you" (4:7-10). James is as subtle as a jackhammer and as soft as. . .well he is not soft at all. In the words of the ball diamond, he is throwing high heat.

James strikes us as so in your face and so over the top. He holds out an olive branch of grace and hope with the line, "Draw near to God and he will draw near to you," but it doesn't seem like much in the barrage of "do this" and "don't do that." We would like to tone him and his message down by using words like hyperbole and overstatement. Certainly hyperbole is used in this text, just as we do when we use the phrase, "Let somebody get away with murder" to delineate any number of infractions. And the use of the word adultery to describe a wayward people has a rich history in Scripture. But there is more going on here than expansive language. Before writing James off as overwrought or too intense, we would do well to reread the Sermon on the Mount. Jesus is just as direct and uncompromising.

> You are the salt of the earth; but if salt has lost its taste, how can its saltiness be restored? (Matt. 5:13)
>
> But I say to you that if you are angry with a brother or sister, you will be liable to judgment. (5:22)
>
> But I say to you that everyone who looks at a woman with lust has already committed adultery with her in his heart. (5:28)
>
> But I say to you, do not resist an evildoer. But if anyone strikes you on the right cheek, turn the other also. (5:39)
>
> But I say to you, Love your enemies and pray for those who persecute you. (5:44)
>
> Be perfect, therefore, as your heavenly Father is perfect. (5:48)
>
> No one can serve two masters; for a slave will either hate the one or love the other, or be devoted to the one and despise the other. You cannot serve God and wealth. (6:24)
>
> Enter through the narrow gate; for the gate is wide and the road is easy that leads to destruction, and there are many who take it. (7:13)

> Not everyone who says to me, "Lord, Lord," will enter the king-
> dom of heaven, but only the one who does the will of my Father in
> heaven. (7:21)

Reading the Sermon on the Mount and James does not leave one feeling comforted—bruised and battered, but not comforted. Both texts drive us back to
the first beatitude: "Blessed are the poor in spirit, for theirs is the kingdom of
heaven" (Matt. 5:3). Surely James was thinking of this beatitude when he concluded this section with "Humble yourselves before the Lord, and he will exalt
you" (James 4:10). For James, personal comfort follows repentance.

Maybe church squabbles bother James more than they do us. As George
Stulac writes, "James simply writes with a stronger conviction of the seriousness of sin than most of us are willing to hold."[1] Is it really this simple? James
thinks sin, particularly the sin of congregational in-fighting, is a bigger deal
than we do. Do we think so little of sin because we have confused being non-
judgmental with moral lethargy? (Any observant student of our culture would
admit that the ultimate sin, and maybe the only sin today, is to be judgmental.)
In our efforts to be accepting and accommodating to the community, have we
so lowered the bar of expectation that anything goes? In our fear of being
labeled self-righteous have we forgotten how to stand up for what is right? At
what point does a spirit of acceptance become "friendship with the world"?

If we are honest as we read this text, we really want to take James aside
and say, "Listen, I know you mean well, but people don't respond to this kind
of preaching anymore. Our motto around here is 'we are a hospital for sinners, not a temple for the saints.' You've got to chill out. You can't bludgeon
people with the truth." We may not come right out and say it, but a question
does come to mind as we read not only this section but the entire sermon
James preaches. We want to ask our uncompromising, flinty friend, "What's
your problem?"

"What's your problem?" This is an interesting use of words for church
leaders who tolerate misbehavior in the pew and write it off as inevitable.
Using the language of business instead of the Bible, we talk about managing
conflict rather than rooting out evil. We cluck our tongues and smirk when we
hear of a church split. Instead of weeping for the troubled church we calculate
how many members we may pick up in the process.

Marriages crumble around us and other than suggesting counseling we do nothing. No wait, that is not exactly true. We pray for the troubled couple. We utter the words, "God help Bill and Susie," but we do not visit them, plead with them, or cry over them. In our litigious society we have given up discipline of the wayward for fear that someone will sue us. It is a convenient excuse for inaction.

We court the rich to support our building programs and sit on our boards. We don't necessarily fawn over the wealthy but we go out of our way not to antagonize them. Our brothers and sisters drive to the church building in luxury vehicles, send their children to private schools, vacation in Vail and give away less than 2% of their income. Do we follow James and call on them to "weep and wail for the miseries that are coming to you" (James 5:1)? Not likely.

We allow people to bite and devour one another while we stand aside and watch. We refuse to confront the divisive or call the hardhearted to repentance. We pride ourselves on being patient and kind when actually it just looks like we are blind.

Perhaps James is right. Maybe we are the ones with the problem.

NOTES

INTRODUCTION

1. Commemorating the tenth anniversary of this tragedy see, *The Sunday Oregonian*, May 12, 1996, "Mount Hood's Deadly Deceit: A Remembrance," by Tom Hallman Jr.
2. Michael V. Fox, *Proverbs 1-9*, Anchor Bible, Vol 18a (New York: Doubleday, 2000), 32.
3. Stuart Weeks defines wisdom as "the knowledge of how to stay on the path which leads to life, because it is approved by God." See "Wisdom in the Old Testament," in *Where Shall Wisdom Be Found?* (Edinburgh: T & T Clark, 1999), 26.
4. William Brown, *Character in Crisis: A Fresh Approach to the Wisdom Literature of the Old Testament* (Grand Rapids: Eerdmans, 1996), viii. James Crenshaw affirms the same goal: "The goal of all wisdom was the formation of character" (p. 3). *Old Testament Wisdom: An Introduction*, revised and enlarged (Louisville: Westminster John Knox, 1998).
5. Fox, *Proverbs* 1-9, 29.
6. Ibid., 348.
7. Proverbs 2 alone contains twelve references to path(s) or way(s): 2:8[2X], 9, 12, 13[2X], 15[2X], 18, 19, 20[2X].
8. N.T. Wright, lecture delivered at a Doctor of Ministry seminar at Fuller Theological Seminary, spring 2009. In this present volume, Scot McKnight and Tremper Longman address the theological context of wisdom's imperatives. Sally Brown's sermon on "The Unsettling Power of Mercy" in Chapter Five also does a fine job of putting the sayings of James in the larger canonical context of the New Testament.
9. James Davison Hunter, *The Death of Character* (New York: Basic Books, 2000), 227.
10. Chapter Four is an exception with only two sermons.

CHAPTER ONE—Wisdom as Paradigmatic in Scripture

1. Though *hokma* is the main word for wisdom in the Hebrew Bible, there are a number of associated terms. See Tremper Longman, *How to Read Proverbs* ((Downers Grove, Ill.: InterVarsity Press, 2002), 16-17. Technical discussions of these terms are found in Michael V. Fox, *Proverbs 1-9*, Anchor Yale Bible Commentary (New Haven: Yale University Press, 2000).
2. Translations from Proverbs come from Tremper Longman, *Proverbs*, BCOTWP (Grand Rapids: Baker, 2006).
3. D. Goleman, *Emotional Intelligence* (Bantam Books, 1995).
4. Of course, some people with a high IQ are also emotionally intelligent.
5. While Proverbs 1:7 is the best known statement of this principle, it is found throughout Proverbs and elsewhere in biblical wisdom literature (see Prov. 1:29; 2:5; 3:7; 8:13; 9:10; 10:27; 14:2, 26, 27; 15:16, 33; 16:6; 19:23; 22:4; 23:7; 24:21; 28:14; 29:25; 31:30 and Job 28:28).
6. See Tremper Longman, "Proverbs," in *Zondervan Illustrated Bible Backgrounds Commentary*, vol. 5, edited by J. Walton (Grand Rapids: Zondervan, 2009), 464-505.

7. See Proverbs 26:7 and 9 which state that a fool who knows a proverb without knowing when to apply it is useless (like a "paralyzed leg") or even dangerous (like a "fool brandishing a thorny branch").

8. Translations from Ecclesiastes come from Tremper Longman, *Ecclesiastes*, NICOT (Grand Rapids: Eerdmans, 1998).

9. For a full description and defense of the Song as an anthology of love poems, see Tremper Longman, *Song of Songs*, NICOT (Grand Rapids: Eerdmans, 1998).

10. See B. S. Childs, *Introduction to the Old Testament as Scripture* (Philadelphia: Fortress, 1979), 573-75; F. Landy, *Paradoxes of Paradise: Identity and Difference in the Song of Songs* (Sheffield: Almond, 1983), 33; M. Sadgrove, "The Song of Songs as Wisdom Literature," in *Studia Biblica* 1978 (Sheffield: JSOT Press, 1978), 245-48.

11. See the argument of J. Munro, *Spikenard and Saffron: A Study in the Poetic Language of the Song of Songs* (Sheffield: Sheffield Academic Press, 1995), 104.

12. The matter is debated, as can be observed by comparing J. L. Crenshaw, "Method in Determining Wisdom Influence upon 'Historical' Literature," JBL 88 (1969), 129-42, and M. V. Fox, "Wisdom in the Joseph Story," VT 51 (2001), 26-41.

13. For more on the connection between wisdom and the Daniel and Joseph stories, see T. Longman, *How to Read Proverbs* (Downers Grove, Ill.: InterVarsity, 2002), 92-100.

14. Most famously, W. Eichrodt, *Theology of the Old Testament*, 2 vols. (SCM Press, 1967), but many others as well especially in the Reformed and Presbyterian camp.

15. But still, it is not a major theme of wisdom. See Leo Perdue, *Wisdom and Cult: A Critical Analysis of the Views of Cult in the Wisdom Literature of Israel and the Ancient Near East*, SBLDS 30 (Missoula, Mont.: Scholars Press, 1977).

16. Meredith Kline, *The Structure of Biblical Authority* (Eugene, Ore.:Wipf and Stock, 1997).

17. For the form of the covenant/treaty, see Meredith Kline, *Treaty of the Great King* (Grand Rapids: Eerdmans, 1963).

18. See Proverbs 1:8; 2:1; 3:1; 4:4; 6:20, 23; 7:1-2.

19. As pointed out by R. van Leeuwen, "Wealth and Poverty: System and Contradiction in Proverbs," *Hebrew Studies* 33 (1992), 25-36.

20. B. S. Childs, *Biblical Theology of the Old and New Testaments: Theological Reflection on the Christian Bible* (Minneapolis: Fortress, 1993), 76.

21. Walter Brueggemann, *Theology of the Old Testament: Testimony, Dispute, Advocacy* (Minneapolis: Fortress, 1997), 107.

22. See Longman, *Proverbs*, 64-69; idem., *Ecclesiastes*, 39-40; and for Job, T. Longman and R. Dillard, *Introduction to the Old Testament*, 2nd edition (Grand Rapids: Zondervan, 2006), xx-xx.

23. In the Greek Old Testament, the word proverb (*mashal*) was often rendered by the Greek parable (*parabole*).

24. A false god or idol. See D. Allender and T. Longman, *Breaking the Idols of Your Heart: How to Navigate the Temptations of Life* (Downers Grove, Ill.: InterVarsity Press, 2007).

The Good Life

1. The translation is my own.

2. The thoroughgoing and sensitive treatment of this psalm by F. W. Dobbs-Allsopp is very helpful on this point. See F. W. Dobbs-Allsopp, "Psalm 133: A Reading," *Journal of Hebrew Scriptures* 8 (2008), 2-30.

3. See the work of D. Schloen, *The House of the Father as Fact and Symbol: Patrimonialism in Ugarit and the Ancient Near East* (Winona Lake, Ind.: Eisenbrauns, 2001).

4. Dobbs-Allsopp, "Psalm 133," 9.

5. Dobbs-Allsopp points to Esarhaddon's description of his welcome to his guests on the occasion of the dedication of a new palace. He boasts: "I drenched their heads with finest oil and perfumes." Dobbs-Allsopp, "Psalm 133," 10. He cites *CAD* R, 431b.

6. See R. Arav, "Hermon, Mount," in *ABD* 3:158-160.

The LORD Set His Heart on You

1. Paul Ricoeur, "The Nuptial Metaphor," in A. La Cocque and P. Ricoeur, *Thinking Biblically: Exegetical and Hermeneutical Studies*, trans. D. Pellauer (Chicago: University of Chicago Press, 1998), 266-303.

2. Mishnah, 782; m. Yadayim 3.5.

3. Bernard, Sermon 52, quoted in Ann W. Astell, *The Song of Songs in the Middle Ages* (Ithaca and London: Cornell University Press, 1995), 98.

4. Duane Garrett, *Proverbs, Ecclesiastes, and Song of Songs* (Nashville: Holman Reference, 1993).

5. Renita J. Weems, *What Matters Most: Ten Lessons in Living Passionately from the Song of Solomon* (West Bloomfield, Mich.: Walk Worthy Press, 2004).

6. Michael Perry, *Truck: A Love Story* (New York: Harper Collins, 2006), 236.

7. Richard S. Hess, *Song of Songs* (Grand Rapids: Baker Academic, 2005), 242.

8. Thanks to my teacher Wolfgang Roth for this, one of many valuable insights.

9. Malcolm Muggeridge, *Chronicles of Wasted Time I: The Green Stick* (New York: W. Morrow and Co., 1973), 269.

10. Ricoeur, "The Nuptial Metaphor."

11. Robert W. Jenson, *Song of Songs* (Louisville: John Knox Press, 2005), 93.

Astonished and Silent

1. See Thomas G. Long's essay in this volume's third chapter.

2. Frederick Buechner, *Telling the Truth: The Gospel as Tragedy, Comedy, and Fairy Tale* (New York: Harper Collins, 1977), 22-23.

3. Karl Barth, *The Word of God and the Word of Man* (New York: Harper, 1957), 107.

4. Terry Waite on the BBC program "Listener's Tales," found at http://www.bbc.co.uk/worldservice/specials/1339_listener/page12.shtml.

5. Paul Tillich, *The Shaking of the Foundations* (New York: Scribner's, 1948), 10.

CHAPTER TWO—Proverbs, Persuasion, and Preaching

1. Compare to compositional statements in John 20:30-31 or 1 John 1:4, 2:1,12-14; 5:13.

2. See 1:8, 3:1, 4:1,10,20, 5:1.

3. See 1:8-19, 2:1-22, 4:1-9, 4:10-19.

4. See 5:12-14 and the first speech of Woman Wisdom in 1:24-33.

5. We may read the dangerous women individually or as a single composite of Woman Folly.
6. In the Song of Songs the man refers to his beloved as "my sister, my bride" (Song 4:9, 10, 12, 5:1).
7. The translation "I was brought forth" (NRSV, NASV, KJV) is vague to me. The NIV translates the term "The Lord possessed me" in verse 22 and then "I was given birth" in verse 24.
8. Along these same lines my colleague and editor, Dave Bland, points out that while the saying "A rolling stone gathers no moss" is taken as a positive thing in American culture (one should stay busy!), it receives a negative response in England. A moss-covered rock in a brook is a beautiful image. But if it is always rolling it will never acquire such beauty.

The Beginning of Wisdom

1. "Notes and Comments," *The New Yorker*, August 27, 1984, 25.
2. Christine Roy Yoder, *Proverbs* (Nashville: Abingdon Press, 2009), 2.
3. An adaptation of Desiderius Erasmus, "Preparing for Death," in John W. O'Malley, ed., *Spiritualia and Pastoralia*, vol. 70 of *Collected Works of Erasmus* (Toronto: University of Toronto Press, 1998), 400.
4. Richard Lischer, *Open Secrets* (New York: Doubleday, 2001), 81.
5. See Elam Duffy, *The Voices of Morebath: Reformation and Rebellion in an English Village* (New Haven: Yale University Press, 2003).
6. Saul Bellow, *Mr Sammler's Planet* (New York: Penguin, 2004), 260.

Caution: Contents May Be Hot

1. Tremper Longman, *How to Read Proverbs* (Downers Grove, Ill.: InterVarsity Press, 2002), 14-15.
2. Walter Brueggemann, "Passion and Perspective: Two Dimensions of Education in the Bible," *Christian Perspectives on Faith Development*, ed. Jeff Astley and Leslie Francis (Grand Rapids: Eerdmans, 1992), 74.

The Proverbial Dead End Street

1. Author's translation
2. From the English Standard Version, 2001.

CHAPTER THREE—Vanity of Vanities

1. Annotation on Matthew 5:3 in *The Discipleship Study Bible* (Louisville: Westminster John Knox Press, 2008), 1705.
2. I have described the move away from narrative preaching in more detail in *Preaching from Memory to Hope* (Louisville: Westminster John Knox Press, 2009), especially 1-26.
3. Tremper Longman, *The Book of Ecclesiastes* (Grand Rapids: Eerdmans, 1998).
4. Ibid, 36.
5. Ibid., 38.

6.   William P. Brown, *Ecclesiastes* (Louisville: John Knox Press, 2000), 122.
7.   Ibid., 136.

Where Is Our *Position* on Disaster?

1.   Adapted from the New American Standard Version.
2.   Nicholas D. Kristof, "Our Basic Human Pleasures: Food, Sex and Giving," *New York Times*, January 16, 2010, page WK 10, New York edition.
3.   See: "The Poor Will Always Be with Us—Just Not on the TV News," in FAIR Study, Neil deMause and Steve Rendall, 2007, (http://www.fair.org/index.php?page=3172). "Poverty and inequality receive astonishingly little coverage on nightly network newscasts. An exhaustive search of weeknight news broadcasts on CBS, NBC and ABC found that with rare exceptions, such as the aftermath of Katrina, poverty and the poor seldom even appear on the evening news—and when they do, they are relegated mostly to merely speaking in platitudes about their hardships."

Qoheleth's Question

1.   Frederick Buechner, *Peculiar Treasures* (San Francisco: Harper & Row, 1979), 87.
2.   David Kinnaman and Gabe Lyons, *unChristian: What a New Generation Really Thinks about Christianity . . . . and Why It Matters* (Grand Rapids, Mich.: Baker Books, 2007), 27-28.
3.   Jedediah Purdy, *For Common Things: Irony, Trust and Commitment in America Today* (New York: Vintage, 2000), 9-20.
4.   Wallace's oral remarks at Kenyon College have been published in edited form in David Foster Wallace, *This Is Water: Some Thoughts, Delivered on a Significant Occasion, about Living a Compassionate Life* (New York: Little, Brown and Company, 2009), 95-110.
5.   D. A. Hubbard, "The Wisdom Movement and Israel's Covenant Faith," *Tyndale Bulletin* 17 (1966), 30.

CHAPTER FOUR—Preaching Wisdom from the Flipside

1.   See Proverbs 2:1f,10; 3:1,3,5; 4:4,21,23; 6:21; 7:3.
2.   Glenn D. Pemberton, "It's a Fool's Life: The Deformation of Character in Proverbs," *Restoration Quarterly*, Volume 50 Number 4 (2008), 217.
3.   Because the wisdom literature does not mention salvation history and teaches principles, in many cases, also found in the wisdom writings of other Ancient Near Eastern cultures, it has had a hard time gaining respect among scholars. Biblical scholars have, for the past 25 years or so, come to pay wisdom more respect, realizing that it was a crucial means of maintaining the nation's identity is a time of turmoil when traditional authorities and institutions like temple and court had been destroyed. See Dave Bland's helpful article "The Formation of Character in the Book of Proverbs,"*Restoration Quarterly*, Volume 40 Number 4 (1998), 221-237.
4.   The theme of wisdom, careful observation of life to discern practical ways to live in keeping with God's character, is by no means limited to Proverbs. Wisdom themes appear in the Song of Solomon, Deuteronomy, the Joseph story, the Succession

Narrative (2 Samuel 9-20; 1 Kings 1-2), and several psalms (1, 32 ,34, 37, 49, 112, 128). Two apocryphal books, The Wisdom of Solomon and The Wisdom of Sirach (or Ecclesiasticus) also belong to the wisdom genre. See Roland E. Murphy, *The Tree of Life: An Exploration of Biblical Wisdom Literature*. The Anchor Bible Reference Library (New York: Doubleday, 1990), Chapter 7, "Wisdom' Echoes," 97-110.

In the New Testament, wisdom themes occur in 1 Corinthians in Paul's reflections on the wisdom of this world versus the folly of God, as well as in the Book of James. The Prologue to the Gospel of John describes the Logos, the Word made flesh in terms borrowed from Proverb 8's description of Woman Wisdom.

5.   By no coincidence, folly in chapter 7 is also personified as a woman; she represents forces that tempt the young to self destructive behavior.

6.   At the end of this article, I include a whimsical outline called "You may be a fool if" that offers a view of the flipside of wisdom, folly, in these wisdom books.

7.   Dave Bland in his article "The Formation of Character in the Book of Proverbs," 234, points out how the sages of Proverbs exposed youth to pictures of the negative experiences to which folly leads as well as the positive experiences to which wisdom leads.

8.   Thomas G. Long, in his article "Out of the Loop," in *What's the Shape of Narrative Preaching?*, edited by Mike Graves and David J. Schlafer, points out that many people today do not perceive of their life project as creating a coherent narrative out of the disparate events of their lives. Rather, they are what some are calling, "episodics," multi tasking, live in the moment, people who have either lost interest in or lost the ability to engage in story spinning. He suggests that proverbial or wisdom preaching may be an effective way to engage their interest and eventually reconnect them with the story of salvation.

9.   Claudia V. Camp, *Wisdom and the Feminine in the Book of Proverbs*, Bible and Literature Series, 11 (Sheffield: Almond Press, 1985), 107.

10. Thomas P. McCreesh, O.P., "Wisdom as Wife: Proverbs 31:10-31," *Revue Biblique* (1985), 25-46. See my article "The Appeal of Wisdom, Proverbs 31:10-31" *Quarterly Review* (Summer 2000).

11. See my *Preaching Biblical Wisdom in a Self Help Society* (Nashville: Abingdon Press, 2002), Chapter Nine, "The Wisdom Gospel: John." See also Martin Scott's article entitled "Sophia and the Johannine Jesus," *Journal for the Study of the New Testament Supplement Series* 71 (Sheffield, England: Sheffield Academic Press, 1992).

12. McKenzie, *Preaching Biblical Wisdom*.

13. Alyce M. McKenzie, *Hear and Be Wise: Becoming a Teacher and Preacher of Wisdom* (Nashville: Abingdon, 2004).

14. See Stephen Covey's *The 7 Habits of Highly Effective People: Restoring the Character Ethic* (New York: Simon and Schuster, 1989), 18-19 for an account of the history of what he calls "American success literature."

15. James L. Crenshaw, *The Old Testament: An Introduction* (Louisville, Ky.: Westminster John Knox Press, 1998), 67-68. There are two other terms describing fools in Old Testament wisdom writings, *sakal* and *holel*. *Sakal* describes one who persists in folly, and *holel* describes one who is irrational. *Sakal* occurs five times in Ecclesiastes (see 1:7) and *holel* occurs four times (see Eccles. 2:12).At the end of this essay I've included a list of passages that refer to these types of fools in Proverbs.

16. Dianne Bergant, *Israel's Wisdom Literature: A Liberation Critical Reading* (Philadelphia: Fortress Press, 1997), 81-82.
17. Pemberton, "The Deformation of Character in the Book of Proverbs," 220-221.
18. Ibid, 221.
19. Ibid, 223.
20. See my *Preaching Proverbs: Wisdom for the Pulpit* (Louisville, Ky.: Westminster John Knox Press, 1996), 36-38.
21. Injunctions to fear the Lord punctuate Proverbs: 1:7; 9:10; 15:33; 31:30.
22. See my *Hear and Be Wise: Becoming a Teacher and Preacher of Wisdom* (Nashville: Abingdon Press, 2004).

Leaves from the Notebook of a Recovering Fool

1. One should be aware of both the advantages and disadvantages of preaching in the first-person and that self reference in preaching should be done sparingly. See William Brosend, "Enough About Me: There's No 'I' in Preaching," *The Christian Century* 127:4 (February 23, 2010).
2. Ellie Wiesel, *All Rivers Run to the Sea: Memoirs* (New York: Schocken Books, 1996),64.

CHAPTER FIVE—The Character Wisdom Shapes

1. For example, see Alyce Mckenzie's works: *Preaching Proverbs: Wisdom for the Pulpit* (Louisville: Westminster John Knox Press, 1996); *Preaching Biblical Wisdom in a Self-Help Society* (Nashville: Abingdon, 2002); *Hear and Be Wise: Becoming a Teacher and Preacher of Wisdom* (Nashville: Abingdon Press, 2004). See also William Brown, *Character in Crisis: A Fresh Approach to the Wisdom Literature of the Old Testament* (Grand Rapids: Eerdmans, 1996).
2. James Crenshaw, *Education in Ancient Israel: Across the Deadening Silence*, ABRL (New York: Doubleday, 1998), 232.
3. So believes the literary critic Robert Alter according to a lecture by Phil Long, "Ancient Wisdom for Contemporary Life: Studies in Proverbs," CD Regent College, 2003.
4. Children's author Katherine Paterson refers to them as the "sour pills of morality," "From Story to Stories," Academy of Homiletics keynote speech, December 1, 1995.
5. See Tremper Longman's essay in Chapter One of this volume.
6. William Willimon, *Pastor* (Nashville: Abingdon Press, 2002), 255-256. Also quoted in *Proclamation and Theology* (Nashville: Abingdon Press, 2005), 28.
7. Diogenes Allen, "Wisdom of the World and God's," *The Princeton Seminary Bulletin* 23, no 2 (2002), 198.
8. Qualities that Glenn Pemberton rightly argues at the beginning of his essay in Chapter Two that connect the sages with the prophets.
9. Dave Bland, *The College Press NIV Commentary: Proverbs, Ecclesiastes, & Song of Songs* (Joplin, Mo.: College Press, 2002), 13; Dave Bland, "Formation of Character in the Book of Proverbs," *Restoration Quarterly* 40 no 4 (1998), 221-237.
10. A phrase used by Fred Craddock. See "The New Homiletic for Latecomers: Suggestions for Preaching from Mark," eds. David Fleer and Dave Bland, *Preaching Mark's Unsettling Messiah* (St. Louis: Chalice Press, 2006).

11. Richard Clifford, "Reading Proverbs 10-22," *Interpretation*, 63, no. 3 (July, 2009), 244.
12. Derek Kidner, *The Proverbs*, Tyndale Old Testament Commentaries (Downers Grove, Ill.: Tyndale, 1964), 35.
13. For further exploration of the lifestyle of the fool, see Alyce McKenzie's chapter in this volume on "Preaching Wisdom from the Flipside."
14. Why are only sons addressed in Proverbs and not daughters? Clearly, Israel's culture was patriarchal. In addition, Bruce Waltke suggests that daughters were not as likely to rebel as were sons. The "son is singled out because by nature he is most tempted to stray from the inherited tradition. . . . Furthermore, the son will inherit the primary responsibility for his own household's spiritual identity (cf. Num 30; Prov 4:3-4). The daughter was expected to follow her husband's lead." Waltke, "Proverbs, Theology of," *New International Dictionary of Old Testament Theology & Exegesis* (Grand Rapids: Zondervan, 1997) , 4:1085. See also Waltke's commentary, *The Book of Proverbs: Chapters 1-15* (2004), 116-117. In addition, the fact that mothers served as teachers indicates that daughters were involved in the process of instruction somewhere along the line.

However one perceives the omission of daughters, the interpretive flexibility and mindset of wisdom calls on later generations that read the material to apply the instruction of Proverbs equally to both genders. The reader must also remember that all books of the Bible are occasional. They are addressed to specific audiences and situations. For example, Philippians was written to the church at Philippi, Titus was addressed to Titus. The reader takes responsibility for appropriately interpreting these letters for the church today. One approaches Proverbs in the same way.

Tremper Longman makes an astute observation, "Isolated from the rest of Scripture, Proverbs addresses young men. Once it is included within the broader sweep of Scripture, a fuller application may be sought. After all, though individual biblical books are addressed to specific audiences at the time of their writing, the canon of Scripture is directed to all God's people." Longman, *How To Read Proverbs* (Downers Grove, Ill.: InterVarsity Press, 2002), 133.
15. It is the principle behind the contemporary proverb, "mind your p's and q's." One must attend to the little acts of behavior in which we engage. This contemporary proverb comes from a teacher's "warning to keep handwriting legible by distinguishing between the lower-case letters p and q." E. D. Hirsch, Jr et.al. eds. *The Dictionary of Cultural Literacy* (Boston: Houghton Mifflin, 1988), 52.
16. Gerhard von Rad, *Wisdom in Israel* (Nashville: Abingdon, 1972), 26.
17. A poem-like proverb expresses the process well:
Sow a thought, reap an act
Sow an act, reap a habit
Sow a habit, reap a character
Sow a character, reap a destiny
18. Ellen F. Davis, *Scripture, Culture, and Agriculture: An Agrarian Reading of the Bible* (New York: Cambridge University Press, 2009), 147-154.
19. The husband serves and empowers the wife (24:27; read Psalm 112 from the NIV).
20. See Sally Brown's sermon on this text that follows in this chapter entitled, "The Unsettling Power of Mercy."

21. For an argument that the woman of valor is wisdom personified, see Christine Roy Yoder, *Proverbs*, Abingdon Old Testament Commentaries (Nashville: Abingdon, 2009), 290.

22. Ellen Davis, "Preserving Virtues: Renewing the Traditions of the Sages," in William Brown, *Character & Scripture: Moral Formation, Community, and Biblical Interpretation* (Grand Rapids: Eerdmans, 2002), 196.

23. Proverbs is less a "how to" book and more a "how to be" book. See Bruce K. Waltke, *The Book of Proverbs: Chapters 1-15*, New International Commentary on the Old Testament (Grand Rapids: Eerdmans, 2004), 104.

24. If someone insists that this is about the kind of woman a man should marry, then what kind of man do you think she would she marry!?

25. See Darryl Tippens, *Pilgrim Heart: The Way of Jesus in Everyday Life* (Abilene, Tex.: Leafwood Publishers, 2006), 203.

26. See Chapter One and Tremper Longman's insightful perspective on this.

27. Christine Roy Yoder, "Forming 'Fearers of Yahweh': Repetition and Contradiction as Pedagogy in Proverbs," *Seeking Out the Wisdom of the Ancients: Essays Offered to Honor Michael V. Fox on the Occasion of His Sixty-fifth Birthday*, eds. Ronald L. Troxel, Kelvin G Friebel, and Dennis R. Magary (Winona Lake, Ind.: Eisenbrauns, 2005), 168.

28. James Crenshaw argues that the collection of proverbs is random. See *Education in Ancient Israel: Across the Deadening Silence* (New York: Doubleday, 1998), 230. Tremper Longman also argues against seeing an intentional organization to the sentence literature. Longman maintains that the sentence literature is more or less random with a few isolated collections here and there. There is, in his opinion, no overarching systematic structure to the book. He observes, ". . . a systematic collection of proverbs may give the wrong impression . . . that life is systematic and that Proverbs was a 'how-to' fix-it book" (p. 40). The lack of structure is intentional and "reflects the messiness of life" (p. 40). He believes the trend to see structure and clusters is imposed rather than discovered. See Tremper Longman III, *Proverbs*. Baker Commentary on the Old Testament Wisdom and Psalms (Grand Rapids: Baker Academics, 2006).

29. Raymond C. Van Leeuwen, "Proverbs," in *The New Interpreter's Bible* (Nashville: Abingdon, 1997), 105. William Brown, "The Pedagogy of Proverbs 10:1-31:9," in *Character & Scripture: Moral Formation, Community, and Biblical Interpretation*, ed. William Brown (Grand Rapids: Eerdmans, 2002).

30. Brown "The Pedagogy of Proverbs 10:1-31:9," 180.

31. Ibid.

32. Harold C. Washington, *Wealth and Poverty in the Instruction of Amenemope and the Hebrew Proverbs* (Atlanta: Scholars Press, 1994), 193.

33. James Crenshaw, "Murphy's Axiom: Every Gnomic Saying Needs a Balancing Corrective," *The Listening Heart: Essays in Wisdom and the Psalms in Honor of Roland E. Murphy, O. Carm*, eds., Kenneth G. Hoglund, Elizabeth F. Huwiler, Jonathan T. Glass, and Roger W. Lee (Sheffield: JSOT Press, 1987) , 1-17.

34. Waltke, *The Book of Proverbs: Chapters 1-15*, pp. 109-110.

Creating Conflict

1. Several approach Proverbs topically or thematically, including the following: Elizabeth Achtemeier, *Preaching From the Old Testament* (Louisville: Westminster John Knox, 1989), 170-172; Kenneth Aitkin, *Proverbs* (Philadelphia: Westminster Press, 1986); John Miller, *Proverbs*, Believers Church Bible Commentary Series (Scottdale, Penn.: Herald Press, 2004). Thematic preaching from the sentence literature is what Tremper Longman recommends as well in the opening chapter in this volume.

2. Bruce Waltke identifies this as a viable approach to Proverbs: "In topical preaching the preacher designs his own message, consistent with the book's teachings, by selecting wisdom sayings from various groupings to support his message and then arranging them according to his own logic." See "Fundamentals for Preaching the Book of Proverbs, Part 1," *Bibliotheca Sacra*, 165 (January-March, 2008), 4.

3. Thomas G. Long, "Preaching on Proverbs," chapter four in *Preaching the Literary Forms of the Bible* (Philadelphia: Fortress, 1989), 53-65. Walter Brueggeman does this as well. See, "What You Eat Is What You Get: Proverbs 15:17," in *The Threat of Life*, ed. Charles L. Campbell (Minneapolis: Fortress Press, 1996), 116-121.

4. This sermon is a major revision of an earlier one published in the journal *Leaven*, "Iron Sharpens Iron: From Exposition to Sermon (Prov. 27:14–19)," 8 no 1 (April, 2000), 70-74.

5. Irving Janis, *Victims of Groupthink* (Boston: Houghton Mifflin, 1972).

6. It must be noted that in Proverbs not only can women be censorious, but men can be just as scathing. Read the description of a contentious man in Proverbs 26:20–23 (NIV). The focus on the male, however, is lost in the inclusive language of the NRSV. I find it appropriate here, however, to interpret 27:15-16 in gender-neutral terms.

7. This is the way Eugene Peterson translates it. See Eugene Peterson, *The Message: Proverbs* (Colorado Springs: NavPress, 1995). "A nagging spouse is like the drip, drip, drip of a leaky faucet; you can't turn it off, and you can't get away from it."

8. The Hebrew term can be translated either "neighbor" or "friend."

9. This proverb is cryptic in nature and literally reads as follows: "As water the face unto the face, so the heart of man to man." The interpretive question is: Is this one person engaging in introspection or are there two individuals interacting with one another? Because of the number of proverbs in this chapter dealing with the friend, I follow the NRSV in interpreting the proverb as displaying interaction between two people.

10. This scenario is paraphrased from a video entitled *Conflict in the Church: Division or Diversity?* (Akron, Penn.: Mennonite Central Committee, 1988).

11. From *Conflict in the Church: Division or Diversity?*

Rising Up After the Woman of Strength

1. On the role of emotions in Proverbs, see Christine R. Yoder, "The Objects of Our Affections: Emotions and the Moral Life in Proverbs 1-9," in *Shaking Heaven and Earth: Essays in Honor of Walter Brueggemann and Charles B. Cousar*, eds. Christine R. Yoder, Kathleen M. O'Connor, E. Elizabeth Johnson, and Stanley P. Saunders (Louisville: Westminster John Knox, 2005), 73-88.

2. Proverbs 13:2, all translations from NRSV.

3.   Proverbs 12:18

4.   Proverbs 1:8-19

5.   Proverbs 31:16-20

6.   Proverbs 31:25

7.   Proverbs 31:25-27

8.   Proverbs 31:28-29

9.   Proverbs 31:28

10. Sara B. Algoe and Jonathan Haidt, "Witnessing excellence in action: the 'other-prais-ing' emotions of elevation, gratitude, and admiration," *Journal of Positive Psychology* 4 (2009), 105-27.

11. Each line of the poem begins with a letter of the Hebrew alphabet, moving alphabetically from the first to the last letter.

12. Christine R. Yoder, *Wisdom as a Woman of Substance: A Socioeconomic Reading of Proverbs 1-9 and 31:10-31* (New York: Walter de Gruyter, 2001).

13. Sylvia Jacobs, "Their 'Special Mission': Afro-American Women as Missionaries to the Congo, 1894-1937," in *Black Americans and the Missionary Movement in Africa*, ed. Sylvia Jacobs (Westport, Conn.: Greenwood Press, 1982), 155-76.

The Unsettling Power of Mercy

1.   H. Jackson Brown. *Life's Little Instruction Book: 511 Suggestions, Observations, and Reminders on How to Live a Happy and Rewarding Life* (Nashville: Rutledge Hill Press, rev. ed., 2000), maxims 8, 11, 17, and 20.

2.   H. Jackson Brown, *The Complete Life's Little Instruction Book* (Nashville: Rutledge Hill Press, rev. ed., 2007).

3.   Guan, Tan Sin. "Practicing Mercy in a Merciless Culture," http://mccc.org.my/Articles/FaithatWork/Practicing%20mercy.htm (1).

4.   Desmond Tutu. *God Has a Dream: A Vision of Hope for Our Time* (New York: Doubleday, 2005), 121.

CHAPTER SIX—James' Secret: Wisdom in James

1.   A bit of this can be seen in Ben Witherington's *Jesus the Sage: The Pilgrimage of Wisdom* (Minneapolis: Fortress, 1994), 236-247, where he discusses the conventional vs. non-conventional, or order vs. counter-order, wisdom traditions, and concludes that James belongs to the former while Jesus belongs to the latter.

2.   David F. Ford, *Christian Wisdom: Desiring God and Learning in Love* (Cambridge: Cambridge University Press, 2007), esp. 14-51.

3.   See L. T. Johnson, "Reading James Wisely," *Louvain Studies* 28 (2003), 99-112.

4.   Ellen F. Davis, *Proverbs, Ecclesiastes, and the Song of Songs* (Louisville: Westminster John Knox, 2000), 1.

5.   "Doth not Wisdom cry? And understanding put forth her voice?" Sermon at the Temple Church. Source: http://www.archbishopofcanterbury.org/1184 (accessed 9.30.2009).

6.   "Pope Benedict's Homily at the Canonization Mass, June 3, 2007." Source: http://www.assumptionsisters.org/mother/070603Pope.html (accessed 9.30.2009).

7. For sketches of recent studies in J. Crenshaw, *Old Testament Wisdom: An Introduction*, rev. ed. (Louisville: Westminster John Knox, 1998), 1-19; B. K. Waltke, D. Diewert, "Wisdom Literature," in D. W. Baker, B. T. Arnold, *The Face of Old Testament Studies: A Survey of Contemporary Approaches* (Grand Rapids: Baker, 1999), 295-328. I heartily recommend the *Dictionary of the Old Testament: Wisdom, Poetry, and Writings*, ed. T. Longman III, P. Enns (Downers Grove, Ill.: InterVarsity Press, 2008), as a tool of much use for the preacher.

8. Crenshaw, *Old Testament Wisdom*, 3.

9. See here R. E. Murphy, *The Tree of Life: An Exploration of Biblical Wisdom Literature*, 3rd ed. (Grand Rapids: Eerdmans, 2002), 115-118.

10. Crenshaw, *Old Testament Wisdom*, 11. The most potent modern example of wisdom I have seen is that of Rabbi Menachem Mendel Schneerson, and a lively account of him and the Lubavitcher movement around him can be found in Sue Fishkoff, *The Rebbe's Army: Inside the World of Chabad-Lubavitch* (New York: Schocken, 2005).

11. Davis, *Proverbs*, 1.

12. Ibid., 27.

13. Perdue, *Wisdom Literature: A Theological History* (Louisville: Westminster John Knox, 2007), 29-30. See also D. F. Estes, "Wisdom and Biblical Theology," *IVP Dictionary of the Old Testament*, 854. A good exposition of this inductive approach has been outlined by Walter Brueggemann, *Theology of the Old Testament* (Minneapolis: Fortress, 1997), 680-682.

14. Brueggemann, *Theology of the Old Testament*, 680-694; John Goldingay, *Old Testament Theology, 2: Israel's Faith* (Downers Grove, Ill.: InterVarsity, 2006), 576-631.

15. A good summary can be found at Proverbs 9:7-12.

16. On "discipline" (*musar*), see also 1:8; 4:13; 8:10; 23:23 24:32.

17. See *Brown-Driver-Briggs Hebrew and English Lexicon of the Old Testament* (Peabody, Mass.: Hendrickson Publishers, 1966), 542-544.

18. See J. Blenkinsopp, *Sage, Priest, and Prophet* (Louisville: Westminster John Knox, 1995), 9-65; Perdue, *Wisdom Literature*, 1-36.

19. See Longman, *Proverbs* (Grand Rapids: Baker, 2006), 74-79.

20. I don't mean to argue here that James primarily understands Jesus through the lens of a sage or that his primary christology is sapiential. In fact, I don't believe that; what we know from James is that Jesus is the Messiah (1:1) and the Glorious Lord (2:1). Anyone who is Messiah and Glorious Lord is surely a sage, but the issue here is one of priority: Messiah and Lord are prior to sage. I like what Bauckham does with this; cf. *James*, 97-108, where he surfaces the central elements of Jesus' teachings (like radicality) and then compares those to James and concludes that James operates as did Jesus.

21. I would not classify the genre of James as a halakhic use of Jesus, even if Peter Davids preferred that term (but only "loosely") in his important article on this theme. See P. Davids, "James and Jesus," in *The Jesus Tradition Outside the Gospels*, Gospel Perspectives 5; ed. D. Wenham (Sheffield: JSOT, 1984), 63-84, here p. 74. Wesley Hiram Wachob, *The Voice of Jesus in the Social Rhetoric of James*, SNTSMS 106 (Cambridge: Cambridge University Press, 2000), explores the Greco-Roman rhetorical context to find a similar conclusion for James.

22. Another approach is to examine the themes of James in light of wisdom; this has been done well by R. F. Chaffin, Jr., "The Theme of Wisdom in the Epistle of James," *Ashland Theological Journal* 29 (1997), 23-49; see also the thematic sketch in J. B. Adamson, *James: The Man and His Message* (Grand Rapids: Eerdmans, 1989), 363-391.

23. An excellent sketch can be found in L. T. Johnson, *The Letter of James*, AB 37A (New York: Doubleday, 1995), 26-80; for his relationship to the Synoptics, see pp. 55-57. Another good sketch by a specialist in this question is P. J. Hartin, *James*, Sacra Pagina 14 (Collegeville, Minn.: Liturgical Press, 2003), 81-88.

24. Perhaps the most complete commentary on James is the German study of W. Popkes, *Der Brief des Jakobus*, THKNT 14 (Leipzig: Evangelische Verlagsanstalt, 2001); he contends for the connection at the level of a general early Christian atmosphere (pp. 32-35).

25. L. Massebieau, "L'Épitre de Jacques, est-elle l'Ouevre d'un Chrétien?," RHR 32 (1895), 249-283; F. Spitta, "Der Brief des Jakobus," in his *Zur Geschichte und Litteratur des Urchristentums*, 4 vols. (Göttingen: Vandenhoeck & Ruprecht, 1893-1907), 2.1-239. Pheme Perkins, in her article, "James 3:16—4:3," *Interpretation* 36 (1982), 283-287, justified James' wisdom teaching as an expression of the Jewish world but, in so doing, she minimized the influence of Jesus on the text. Furthermore, her approach neglects the profound observations of J. A. Kirk, "The Meaning of Wisdom in James: Examination of a Hypothesis," *New Testament Studies* 15 (1970), 24-38, which shows how closely connected "wisdom" in James is to "Spirit" elsewhere, as well as the careful connections to be found in W. H. Wachob, *The Voice of Jesus in the Social Rhetoric of James*.

26. P. J. Hartin, *James*, 81; see his sketch on pp. 81-88. On this topic, see also the learned small volume of R. Bauckham, *James: Wisdom of James, Disciple of Jesus the Sage*, New Testament Readings (London/New York: Routledge, 1999), esp. 29-111.

27. Bauckham, *James*, 30.

28. I found this oft-quoted remark in *The Wit and Wisdom of Mark Twain*, ed. A. Ayres (New York: Penguin, 1987), 73.

29. But see the insightful observations of Rob Wall in his excellent commentary on James: *Community of the Wise: The Letter of James* (Valley Forge, Penn.: Trinity Press International, 1997), 27-34.

30. One can infer plenty from James 1:1 ("Jesus" and especially "Christ"), from 2:1 ("our glorious Lord Jesus Christ" which might imply ascension, which would imply resurrection and death and life), and from 5:15 (with "raise them up" and "be forgiven"), but one will eventually have to admit that what one finds remains inference. James keeps his secrets.

31. This section is taken from my forthcoming commentary on James (S. McKnight, *James*, NICNT (Grand Rapids: Eerdmans, 2010). See J. B. Adamson, *James: The Man and His Message*, 169-194; J. S. Kloppenborg, "The Reception of the Jesus Tradition in James," in *The Catholic Epistles and the Tradition*, ed. J. Schlosser; BETL 176 (Leuven: Peeters, 2004), 91-139, and "The Emulation of the Jesus Tradition in the Letter of James," in R. Webb, J. S. Kloppenborg, *Reading James with New Eyes: Methodological Reassessments of the Letter of James*, LNTS 342 (London: T & T Clark, 2007), 121-150; P. J. Hartin, *James the 'Q' Sayings of Jesus*; "James and the Q Sermon on the Mount/

Plain," in *Society of Biblical Literature* 1989 Seminar Papers, ed. D. J. Lull (Atlanta: Scholars Press, 1989), 440-457; J. S. Kloppenborg, "The Reception of the Jesus Traditions in James," in *The Catholic Epistles and the Tradition*, ed. J. Schlosser; BETL CLXXVI (Leuven: Leuven University Press, 2004), 93-141.

32. There are other possible parallels but at least these can also be mentioned: James 1:6 (Mark 11:22; Matt 21:21); James 2:8 (Mark 12:31; Matt 22:39; Luke 10:27); James 3:1 (Matt 23:8-12); James 3:2-3 (Matt 12:36-37); James 5:9 (Mark 13:29; Matt 24:33; Luke 21:31). See V. V. Porter, Jr., "The Sermon the Mount in the Book of James," *BSac* 162 (2005), 344-360, 470-482; M. Shepherd, "The Epistle of James and the Gospel of Matthew," *JBL* 75 (1956), 40-51, who famously argued that James was pervaded by Matthean parallels.

33. Mark Twain, *Following the Equator* (New York: Dover, 1989), 35.

34. Bauckham, *James*, 35-56, sketches formal parallels in aphorisms (beatitudes, "whoever" and "the one who is" sayings, conditional sayings, synonymous couplets, antitheses and paradoxes, wisdom admonitions with motive clause, aphoristic sentences, statements of reciprocity, and debate sayings) and similitudes/parables (nine different forms). On James' reformulation of wisdom sayings, see 83-93; for the shaping of Jesus on James, 97-108. See also J. S. Kloppenborg, "Reception" and his "The Emulation of the Jesus Tradition," in Webb, Kloppenborg, *Reading James*, 133-142. James' use of the "Old Testament" is similar in the style of emulation and intertexture; see R. Bauckham, "James, 1 and 2 Peter, Jude," in *It Is Written: Scripture Citing Scripture. Essays in Honour of Barnabas Lindars, SSF*, ed. D.A. Carson, H. G. M. Williamson (Cambridge: Cambridge University Press, 1988), 306-309; W. Popkes, "James and Scripture: An Exercise in Intertexuality," *New Testament Studies* 45 (1999), 213-229; W. H. Wachob, "The Epistle of James and the Book of Psalms: A Socio-Rhetorical Perspective of Intertexture, Culture, and Ideology in Religious Discourse," in *Fabrics of Discourse: Essays in Honor of Vernon K. Robbins*, ed. D. B. Gowler, L. G. Bloomquist, D. F. Watson) Harrisburg, Penn.: Trinity Press International, 2003), 264-280.

35. An excellent discussion of this can be found in L. T. Johnson, *James*, 48-80; Bauckham, *James*, 29-60.

36. Many words are used by scholars, including "intertexture" and "intertexuality" and the German *Vergegenwärtigung*.

37. On this in general, see R. D. Hays, *The Conversion of Imagination* (Grand Rapids: Eerdmans, 2005).

38. This paragraph was generated by comments by Bauckham, *James*, 31, 74-83.

39. P. Davids, "James and Jesus," 68.

40. A clear exegetical analysis, one beneficial for preachers, can be found in C. L. Blomberg, M. Kamell, *James*, Exegetical Commentary on the New Testament (Grand Rapids: Zondervan, 2008), 111-120.

41. Much is made of James 2:5 in W. H. Wachob, *The Voice of Jesus in the Social Rhetoric of James*, 114-153.

42. In a private conversation with Thomas Long at the Conference, Tom suggested to me that he sees what many scholars have seen in this text: an inconsistent life for those who have been baptized. Many have seen baptism in "the excellent name that was *invoked* over you."

43. See my *The Jesus Creed: Loving God, Loving Others* (Brewster, Mass.: Paraclete, 2004); also a piece for a forthcoming festschrift for N. T. Wright with T & T Clark, edited by R. L. Webb.
44. An important article by L. T. Johnson explores, more or less successfully, the allusions to Leviticus 19 in *James: Brother of Jesus, Friend of God*, 123-135.
45. See also Galatians 5:22-26; 1 Corinthians 8:4-6; Romans 12:19-20. One can find numerous parallels in Jewish literature to the importance of loving God or loving others (*T. Sim* 4:7; *T Iss* 5:2; *T Dan* 5:4; Philo, *Spec Laws* 1.299-300, 324), or to the importance of love (*Odes Sol* 41:1-6), but something about Jesus and his followers remains distinct: the connection of Leviticus 19:18 to Deuteronomy 6:4-5. The daily recitation of *Shema* as followed by Leviticus 19:18 forms that distinction. Further, early Christian texts that touch on the use of *Shema* include 2 Clement 3; Ignatius, *Ephesians* 14; *Smyrnaeans* 6; Justin, *Apology* 16; *Dial. Trypho* 93; Irenaeus, *Ag. Heresies* 4.2.2; 4.11.2; 5.22.1; Tertullian, *Answer to the Jews* 2; *Against Marcion* 2.13; 4:25; 5.8. See D. C. Allison Jr., "Matthew and Its History of Interpretation," *Expository Times* 120 (2008) 1-7, here p. 5, where Allison points to the interpretive power of this combination; E. P. Sanders, "Jesus and the First Table of the Jewish Law," in *Jews and Christians Speak of Jesus*, ed. A.E. Zannoni (Minneapolis: Fortress, 1994), 55-73; L. T. Johnson (with W. Wachob) speaks of the "abundance of Jewish and Christian sources that corroborate the use of Lev 19:18 as a summary of the whole law" but cites much later rabbinic texts, New Testament and early Christian texts (*Brother of Jesus, Friend of God* [Grand Rapids: Eerdmans, 2004], 151). The appeal to later rabbinic texts does not count for an "abundance" of texts for determining whether or not Jesus' use of Leviticus 19:18 was simply part of his Jewish context. Methodologically, concluding that Jesus was evidently the one who raised Leviticus 19:18 to a central location does not make him either non-Jewish nor the other groups of Judaism less Jewish or less loving. We return to the main point: it is connecting Leviticus 19:18 to the Shema that marks Jesus' distinctive use of Leviticus 19:18, and inasmuch as the Shema was a foundational sacred rhythm in Israel's praxis, the addition to the Shema makes for a foundational shift in emphasis by Jesus.
46. Such is the thesis of E. Borghi, "La sagesse de la vie selon l'épitre de Jacques: Lignes de Lecture," *New Testament Studies* 42 (2006), 123-141.
47. E.g., F. Mussner, *Der Jakobusbrief*, HTKNT 13/1 (Freiburg: Herder, 1987), 123-124.
48. A good sketch can be found in R. E. Brown, *The Birth of the Messiah*, updated edition; ABRL (New York: Doubleday, 1993), 350-355.
49. Ronald Sider, *Rich Christians in an Age of Hunger*, 5th ed. (Nashville: W Publishing, 1997), 133.
50. See L. T. Johnson, *James*, throughout pp. 267-290.
51. Bauckham, *James*, 30.

Doing Gospel

1. This sermon was also influenced by Ellen Davis' *Getting Involved with God* (Cowley, 2001), Edgar McKnight & Christopher Church's excellent commentary on *Hebrews-James* (Smyth & Helwys, 2004), and Ralph Martin's work in the James' Word

commentary (Word Books, 1988). All Scripture citations come from the NIV (Zondervan, 1973).

What's Your Problem?

1.　George Stulac, *James* (Downers Grove, Ill: Intervarsity Press, 1993), 145.

LaVergne, TN USA
15 September 2010
197134LV00003B/2/P